Balance of Power:
THE NEGRO VOTE

Balance of Power:

THE NEGRO VOTE

by Henry Lee Moon

DOUBLEDAY & COMPANY, INC.

GARDEN CITY, NEW YORK, 1949

The lines from *Race, Class, and Party,* by
Paul Lewinson, are copyrighted, 1932, by
Oxford University Press, New York, Inc.

PRINTED IN THE UNITED STATES AT
THE COUNTRY LIFE PRESS, GARDEN CITY, N. Y.

TO MOLLIE

Acknowledgments

To all those who in one way or another have aided in the production of this book, my thanks. Especially am I indebted to my colleagues of the Political Action Committee of the Congress of Industrial Organizations—Jack Kroll, Director; Frederick Palmer Weber, Director of Research; and Charles C. Webber, Director of the Virginia State CIO-PAC; to Frank S. Horne for permission to make use of certain parts of a manuscript on which we collaborated in 1940; to Martha Rockwell for valuable research assistance; to Loren Miller, Ted Poston, Vernon C. Riddick, and Roy Wilkins for reading and offering helpful criticisms and suggestions on certain chapters; and to Bucklin Moon for painstaking editorial guidance and assistance.

Preface

INTENT UPON ATTAINING FULL EQUALITY OF CITIZENSHIP in his native land, the Negro American today sees in the ballot his most effective instrument in the long and hazardous struggle toward this goal. From such equality, he realizes, flow all the good things of life in a democratic society—the freedoms and enjoyments long denied him. His recent experiences have convinced him that his greatest hope for continued and accelerated progress lies in independent political action subject to the domination and control of no political party. He has arrived at this conviction through a circuitous route; indeed, after traversing a complete cycle: political action, the acquisition of property, the pursuit of learning, and now, again, political action. These were the converging roads he trod in search of freedom.

With the ratification of the Fifteenth Amendment in 1870, the nation belatedly acknowledged the Negro's hard-earned right to citizenship and the franchise. The hopeful ex-slave believed, when first he came into possession of the highly prized ballot, that his prayers had been realized and that he was on his way to the promised new freedom. This was to be his great opportunity to assume new responsibilities and to enjoy new privileges. The ballot was to be the key to a future of progress. That he used his franchise for socially useful purposes is indicated by his role in the establishment of public school systems, the abolition of property qualifications for voting, and the introduction of other long-overdue reforms in the South. His participation in Reconstruction, commonly discredited by historians, was bitterly opposed by the defeated and demoralized planter class and finally betrayed by northern politicians and industrialists. In 1877 this experiment in democracy was

7

abandoned and the elements which had lately been in rebellion against the sovereign authority of the United States Government were restored to power with the shamefaced connivance and support of the North.

Denied political expression, yet determined to achieve recognition of their freedom, the Negro masses in the South turned to other instruments to gain this end. Land was what they needed. Yes, land and property, for was not ownership the earmark of respectability and citizenship in our society? Was this not what distinguished the lordly planters? But the ephemeral expectation of "forty acres and a mule" for every freed family vanished even as a dream. Despite low prices in a land ruined and depressed by war, the acquisition of property on any significant scale was all but impossible without federal aid. Only a fortunate few were prepared to become landowners without such aid.

Even as the beginnings in the acquisition of property were being made, new obstacles confronted the freedmen. Property, yes. But property alone would not be enough. Education was the *real* need. This became the magic key to citizenship. Democracy is unsafe in the hands of an untrained electorate, the Negro's pseudo friends told him. Democracy is for the intelligent elite. There could be no intelligent electorate without education. The freedman was not prepared for freedom, they said.

This doctrine of unpreparedness which made even sympathetic whites question the wisdom of enfranchising the Negro stemmed directly from the harsh character of slavery under Anglo-Saxon domination. Slavery in the United States, unlike that in Latin America, had evolved a rationale which stripped the slave not only of legal rights but also of moral personality. Having denied the Negro every opportunity to develop, the southern oligarchy decried his unfitness for freedom and incorporation into the body politic on equal terms.

The freedmen themselves were, in a measure, sold on the plausibility of this doctrine of unfitness for citizenship. While not entirely abandoning the demand for suffrage, the Negro masses under the guidance of the young Booker T. Washington, then emerging as the new Negro leader, directed their energies and talents to preparing themselves for citizenship through the raising of their economic level and the education of their youth for work and life. But the educated soon found themselves equally disfranchised with the uneducated.

Today the southern Negro is demanding an end to this dilatory probation imposed upon him. He has demonstrated that he can stand the test. He has moved steadily forward in education and in the acquisition of worldly goods. He knows that he is now prepared to assume the responsibility of unrestricted citizenship. Culturally and economically he today surpasses the masses of the Rumanians, Bulgars, and Poles for whom, ironically, former Secretary of State James F. Byrnes of South Carolina demanded "free and unfettered elections" at a time when this right was being denied to millions of Americans. To this end Negro Americans are mobilizing their resources as never before. And in this decisive struggle they have, today, wider support in the South than any time since they were disfranchised by terms of the compromise of 1877.

The ballot, while no longer conceived of as a magic key, is recognized as the indispensable weapon in a persistent fight for full citizenship, equal economic opportunity, unrestricted enjoyment of civil rights, freedom of residence, access to equal and unsegregated educational, health, and recreational facilities. In short, a tool to be used in the ultimate demolition of the whole outmoded structure of Jim Crow.

Already recognized as an important and sometimes decisive factor in a dozen northern states and in at least seventy-five non-southern congressional districts, the Negro is beginning to exert increasing political influence in the nation, although still not accorded the recognition his voting strength warrants. Meanwhile, he is again emerging as a positive political factor in the South, where for nearly two generations his suffrage rights have for all practical purposes been nullified.

The area of his political activities and influence, once confined largely to the great industrial cities in the East and North, has been expanded and extended by wartime migration into the Pacific coast states and into many of the smaller midwest and northeastern cities. The war stimulus, too, has generated a resurgence of political activity in the South following the invalidation of the "white primary" by the Supreme Court decision of April 3, 1944.

The maximum Negro voting strength is about seven and a quarter millions, which represents the total number of colored citizens over twenty-one years of age, according to the 1940 census. For the nation as a whole there are 91,600,000 citizens of voting age. These figures are, of course, far in excess of the total vote which under present conditions can be turned out. In 1940, the year of the greatest vote, there was a total turnout of only 49,815,000. In 1942, an off year, this figure dropped to 29,441,000, rising in 1944 to 48,025,000, and dropping again in 1946 to 35,000,000.

Two thirds of these potential Negro voters still reside in the South. Most of these, living as they do in inaccessible rural areas and small towns, probably will not become politically activized for a number of years, despite the truly significant increase in Negro voting strength in many southern cities.

By the end of 1946 there were 750,000 qualified Negro voters in the southern states, a significant increase over the 250,000 Ralph Bunche estimated in 1940.[1] Meanwhile, this number has steadily increased despite efforts of some southern legislatures to circumvent the Constitution and Supreme Court decisions. Despite, also, intimidation and fraud. By November 1948, more than a million southern Negroes may well be qualified to vote. A total of 3,500,000 Negro voters in the 1948 elections is not only possible but likely.

Politicians of both major parties have long been aware of the strength of the Negro vote in the cities of such states as New York, Pennsylvania, New Jersey, Ohio, Indiana, Michigan, Illinois, and Missouri. And no one today seriously contemplates launching a third party without considering this vital vote along with other potentialities necessary for the success of such an undertaking. Southern and western politicians have now joined their eastern and northern colleagues in bidding for this vote.

The size, strategic distribution, and flexibility of the Negro vote lend it an importance which can no longer be overlooked. As significant as was this vote in the 1944 elections—and without it Franklin D. Roosevelt could hardly have been re-elected—it can, with wise and independent leadership, be even more important in the 1948 elections.

The importance of this vote is now generally conceded. What is not usually recognized, and even less acknowledged, is that this vote is more decisive in presidential elections than that of the Solid South. In sixteen states with a total of 278 votes in the electoral college, the Negro, in a close election, may hold the balance of power; that is, in an election in which the non-Negro vote is about evenly divided. The eleven states of the old Confederacy comprising the Solid South have a total of 127 votes in the electoral college. And these votes, except on rare occasions, are pre-committed to

[1]Ralph J. Bunche, *The Political Status of the Negro*. Unpublished MSS. quoted by Gunnar Myrdal, *An American Dilemma* (New York: Harper Bros., 1944), pp. 487–88.

any candidate the Democratic party may nominate on whatever platform. Unlike the southern vote, the Negro vote today is tied to no political party. It cannot be counted in advance.

This development is of prime importance not only to the political future of the Negro, but also to that of the South and the nation. If the white politicians are unwilling to face the full implications of this historic shift of political power, the Negro leaders are fully aware of its significance and are prepared to press for fuller recognition of the race's just demands for first-class citizenship.

An alert, independent, and aggressive Negro electorate in collaboration with organized labor and other progressive forces may be an important factor in determining the political complexion of Congress. The growing Negro vote in the South, allied with white progressives, can bring about changes of far-reaching importance in that region. Indeed, the resurgence of Negro voting in Dixie presages the return of the two-party system. The passing of the "white primary," the imminent demise of the poll tax in the seven states which still retain it, the progressive militancy of Negro citizens, all tend toward broadening the base of suffrage in the South among both blacks and whites. This new electorate of both races threatens the continued domination of the courthouse gangs which have been the controlling factors in the Democratic party in the southern states. The success of such a coalition is limited only by the degree to which the white working class in the South can be liberated from the specious doctrine of "white supremacy" as preached by the Bilbos, the Rankins, and the Talmadges.

The Negro's political potential is not merely positive through the exercise of the franchise. The negative aspect of his political existence has permeated the political thinking of this nation from colonial times down to the present. Indeed, the struggle to negate the positive political influence of the Negro remains the dominant factor in southern politics to which all other considerations have been ruinously subordinated. A great body of crippling, discriminatory legislation in the South attests the negative influence of the Negro citizenry. As a result of this preoccupation with the political status of the Negro, the South remains, culturally and economically, the most backward region in the nation.

All our noble expressions of political idealism, from the Declaration of Independence down to the enunciation of the Truman Doctrine, have been confronted with the grim specter of the disfranchised Negro mocking our democratic pretensions. Our national schizophrenia has not only retarded the development of democracy at home but has also been a continuing source of embarrassment in our international relations. It has earned for us the scorn of Communist and Fascist alike, of colonial and imperialist, as well as of true democrats everywhere. It effectively thwarted Secretary Byrnes in his demand for democratic elections in the Balkans. Again and again it has exposed our vulnerability. Even the passionate and all-inclusive humanitarianism of Franklin D. Roosevelt was unable to surmount completely this needless handicap.

The campaign of 1948 promises to be one of the most vitriolic in the history of the nation. The Democratic coalition which has been in power since 1933 has been split into at least three well-defined groups: the left-wing followers of Henry A. Wallace who have launched a new party; the center which continues to follow the leadership of the party's chief, Harry S. Truman; and the political zombies who comprise the anachronistic right wing. Within the ranks of the major divisions there is further fragmentation. What with Universal Military Training and the Marshall plan dividing their ranks, the Republicans have little enough to crow about on the score of party unity. In this fluid and confused political milieu it would take a rash prophet to say in March for whom the Negro voters will cast their ballots in November. This much it is safe to predict: they will not vote for any candidate satisfactory to the political zombies who infest the sub-Potomac region.

H. L. M.

March 8, 1948

Contents

	PREFACE	7
I	F.D.R., THE NEGRO AND THE SOUTH	17
II	VOTES FOR SALE	39
III	EXPERIMENT IN DEMOCRACY	54
IV	THE GREAT BLACKOUT	68
V	REFUGE IN THE NORTH	83
VI	THE COUNTERATTACK	98
VII	GREENER PASTURES?	119
VIII	LABOR AS AN ALLY	132
IX	GRASS-ROOTS POLITICAL ACTION	146
X	DIXIE IN TRANSITION	174
XI	THE NEGRO VOTE IN 1948	197
XII	THE ULTIMATE OBJECTIVE	215
	APPENDICES	221
	INDEX	249

Balance of Power:
THE NEGRO VOTE

CHAPTER I

F.D.R., the Negro and the South

NOTHING IN THE PUBLIC CAREER OF FRANKLIN D. ROOSEVELT prior to his election to the presidency had given any convincing indication of a sympathetic understanding of the problems of the Negro in America. As governor of New York he had paid but slight attention to the colored population of the state. What casual contacts he had were chiefly through James A. Farley, who, as Democratic leader, overlooked no potential voter. He made no outstanding appointments of Negro Democrats. He initiated no legislation which was of intimate concern to this minority. Indeed, the Negroes of New York received little recognition from Governor Roosevelt either by way of appointments or legislative program. Although hailed as a progressive, he seemed blithely unconcerned about the darker segments of humanity. It was then that Norman Thomas said of him that no man ever won the accolade of "liberal" more cheaply.

Even though disillusioned by President Hoover's cold indifference and reeling under the impact of the depression, which hit them hard and early, Negro voters were in 1932 deeply skeptical of the Roosevelt candidacy. On the basis of the record they had good cause for apprehension. Roosevelt had been a member of the unlamented Wilson administration. He had served as Assistant Secretary of the Navy under Josephus Daniels, who had played a leading role in the disfranchisement of Negroes in North Carolina. As far as is known he never questioned the unconcealed anti-Negro bias of that administration. Moreover, he had chosen as his "second home" Warm Springs, Georgia. He had wooed and won the support of the southern Democrats, and finally his vice-presidential candidate was John Nance Garner of Texas. He had, however, the Roosevelt name, and there were Negroes who remembered Theodore Roosevelt reverently despite the evasive maneuverings that attended the birth of his Progressive party.

Robert L. Vann, the able and canny publisher of the Pittsburgh *Courier,* repudiated Hoover Republicanism in 1932 and boarded the Roosevelt band wagon. The *Courier,* one of the most widely read and influential of Negro publications, carried the campaign for Roosevelt into every Negro community in the country. There was also, as had become customary, a Negro division in the Democratic campaign headquarters, the work of which was handicapped by the silence of the party platform on Negro rights and the void in the candidate's record. But this drive was not enough. In the main, the Negro vote remained safely Republican. Tammany Hall, through its well-organized district clubs, was able to deliver the Negro vote in New York, as was the Pendergast machine in Kansas City, Missouri. The depressed and disillusioned Negro workers in Pittsburgh, and Detroit also went for Roosevelt. Elsewhere the Negro clung in desperation to the sinking Republican ship—in Chicago, Philadelphia, Cleveland, Cincinnati, Baltimore and Columbus. In the Negro wards of Chicago, Roosevelt received only about 23 per cent of the total vote. Hoover carried the districts by about the same margin as in 1928. In Cleveland, four predominantly Negro wards, which in 1928 had given Alfred E. Smith 7456 votes or 30 per cent of all ballots cast in those districts, returned only 7153 for F.D.R. in 1932, which accounted for 24 per cent of the total. The Hoover rating among colored voters in Cleveland climbed to 72 per cent! In voting for Hoover in 1932, Negro citizens trailed well behind the national trend, for the man who in 1928 had been swept into the presidency by winning 58 per cent of the nation's popular vote received slightly less than 40 per cent of the total four years later.

By 1936, after four years of the New Deal, colored voters in the urban centers of the North and East had caught up with the procession. The mass migration out of the Republican camp was in response to the Roosevelt program which, they were convinced, recognized and made an effort to meet some of their more urgent needs. In 1934, Chicago sent to Washington Arthur W. Mitchell, the first Negro Democrat to be elected to Congress. Mitchell's victory was not the result of a solid Negro vote. Indeed, he was aided by a traditionally Democratic white minority in his district which exercised a balance of power when the New Deal split the once solidly Republican Negro vote. The trend, however, had set in. Negro voters in Chicago, who in his first campaign gave President Roosevelt less than a quarter of their votes, cast 49 per cent of their ballots for him in 1936. In Cleveland they went over the top, turning in a 62-per-cent majority. The four predominantly Negro wards in Philadelphia each gave the President majorities of more than five thousand. In city after city, across the country, the Negro citizenry rallied to the Roosevelt banner. Of fifteen wards in nine cities studied by Myrdal, Roosevelt carried nine in 1936. In his first election he had carried only four. In 1940 only one of these fifteen wards remained in the Republican column.[1]

The Negro's precipitant response to the invitation to board the Roosevelt band wagon gave added pungency to the oft-repeated adage: "Politics makes strange bedfellows." Never a stranger or more uncomfortable menage huddled under the same political blanket than the miscellaneous brood which looked to Franklin D. Roosevelt for guidance, leadership, and salvation. There were the Bourbon Southerners, Democrats by tradition, who, chastened by their unhappy defection of 1928, returned to the party of their fathers in 1932. There were the northern big-city Democratic machines thirsting for federal patronage and disdainful of the religious bigotry of their southern associates. There were the millions of workers, organized and unorganized, unemployed or underemployed, insecure and fearful of each tomorrow. There was business, big and small, on the brink of disaster. There were the independents and the liberals eager for reform. And then there were those onetime Republican loyalists—the Negroes starving for recognition.

Of all these various and conflicting elements who followed the Roosevelt banner, perhaps none felt more uncomfortable than the anti-labor and anti-Negro Southerner. Nor was the Negro too happy to be linked with the party of Rankin, Bilbo, and Talmadge. He was quick to renounce that company and to affirm that his conversion was to the Roosevelt New Deal rather than to the Democratic party, which in Alabama still bore the imprint of "white supremacy" upon its official ballot. But the Southerner was the unhappiest. He felt somehow betrayed when, by the time of the 1936 election, he woke up and found among his assorted political bedfellows the unwanted Negro. He felt not only betrayed but also frustrated, because, unlike big business, he could not "take a walk." The big fellows, once they had been rescued from ruin by President Roosevelt, were free to return to their ancient opposition. The Southerners, however,

---

[1] Gunnar Myrdal, *An American Dilemma* (New York: Harper & Bros., 1944), p. 496.

were caught in a booby trap of their own making—the one-party system which they had devised for the express purpose of forever forestalling the political miscegenation which was now taking place before their very eyes. Little wonder that they squirmed uncomfortably!

It was in 1936, too, that the South was stripped of the veto power which for many years it had exercised over the choice of the presidential nominee at the Democratic National Convention. This authority, cherished as a safeguard by the South, was secured by a rule requiring a two-third majority for the nomination. The South had been able to control a sufficient number of votes at the convention to prevent the selection of any candidate whose views were deemed unacceptable. The abrogation of that rule deprived the South of this veto power. As a sop to the "pouting southern delegates," a recommendation was made to the National Committee to work out a bonus plan by which states voting heavily Democratic would be rewarded with additional delegates. "Not until they got home did the southern delegates realize that the pacifying offer was poisoned," reports George C. Stoney. "If representation at the national convention was based, as was recommended, upon the number of Democratic voices cast, instead of on the number of congressional representatives the state has, as is the present practice, the South's voice would be reduced to a whisper."[2]

The southern reaction to the new Negro vote was not immediate nor unanimous. Indeed, in the early days of the first Roosevelt administration most of the Southerners in both houses of Congress supported the New Deal measures. There were, of course, such conservative Democrats as Senators Harry F. Byrd and Carter Glass of Virginia, Ellison D. Smith of South Carolina, Walter F. George of Georgia, and Kenneth D. McKellar of Tennessee; and Representatives Martin Dies of Texas and E. E. Cox of Georgia, who consistently opposed legislation sponsored by the President to improve the social and economic status of low-income groups. On the other hand, among the more ardent New Deal supporters of that day was the notorious anti-labor, anti-Negro Senator Theodore G. Bilbo of Mississippi. But as the outlines and objectives of the Roosevelt program became clearer, resistance among southern politicians mounted. It was the inclusive character of that program which irked the Southerners. It sought to raise the living standards of the depressed masses. Negroes, being disproportionately concentrated in

[2]*Survey Graphic*, March 1940.

the low-income group and among the unemployed, naturally reaped a share of the benefits of such New Deal agencies and legislation as social security, Work Projects Administration, CCC, National Youth Administration, public housing, minimum wages, National Labor Relations Act, work and home relief, farm loans and security, and school lunches. These programs also opened up new job opportunities for trained Negroes in technical and administrative capacities as well as for unskilled labor. Indeed, in some of these programs, notably public housing, Negroes received a larger share of the benefits than their population ratio warranted, though not greater than their relative need.

Government under the New Deal ceased to be an abstraction enshrined in remote Washington. It was brought to the threshold of practically every home in America. Government was no longer merely the concern of the politicians and the vested interests. It became the concern of the people. It assumed as a national responsibility the welfare and security of the people. And because it was broad-based and humanitarian, it recognized the disadvantaged Negro minority as an integral part of the American people. At no time since the curtain had dropped on the Reconstruction drama had government focused as much attention upon the Negro's basic needs as did the New Deal. The Negro masses recognized that this new concept of government provided a means by which they could accelerate their progress toward full and unqualified citizenship. Accordingly, they voted repeatedly to retain and strengthen the New Deal.

The southern reactionaries also recognized the meaning of the Roosevelt reforms in terms of race relations. They began to resent and take serious exception to the provisions of that program. Some, of course, were opposed to the reforms because they believed their own vested interests, political and economic, were endangered. Like their counterparts in the North, they wanted a return to the status quo ante with unrestricted privileges of exploitation. They used the race issue to conceal their real motives in opposing the program of the head of their party. Others may have been willing to accept the reforms had they been labeled "For Whites Only" in conformity with the southern pattern of Jim Crow. Rallying their forces against the New Deal, many Southerners abandoned their avowed pretensions of chivalry and launched an incredibly slanderous attack upon Mrs. Roosevelt because of her open championship of equal rights. Her role in Washington was made a South-wide issue by the President's enemies. "The emotionalism of the professional Southerner was perhaps stirred more by the democratic speeches and attitude of Mrs. Roosevelt than by the acts of the New Deal Administration," commented Louis Martin, Detroit publisher. "To him she became a sinister figure because she dared to express some positive beliefs on racial equality."[3]

The emergence of the Negro as a voter in the Democratic column worried many a Southerner who feared that the Negroes would demand more and more recognition from the Roosevelt administration. John Temple Graves, the Alabama journalist, expressed this fear in an article in the *American Mercury:* "Perhaps the most significant political event below the Potomac since Lincoln freed the slaves was the winning of the Negro vote above the Potomac by the Democrats in 1936 and its retention in 1936 and 1940. It means from now on the Democratic Party will be competing for what has heretofore belonged to the Republicans. And because the vote represents something near a balance of power in balance-of-power states, it means also that Northern Negroes may become more important than Southern whites in the party of the white South's long allegiance."[4]

Southern resistance to the progressivist features of the New Deal came to a head in 1944 with the organization of the anti-Roosevelt Texas Regulars. Determined to prevent the re-election of the President, the Texas Regulars sent delegates to the Democratic National Convention to halt his renomination. Thwarted at the convention, they entered a slate of unpledged electors in the general election, where again they were decisively defeated. Elsewhere in the South, futile and less well-organized attempts were made to repudiate the President. The antipathy of these malcontents was evidently not shared by the rank and file in the South, who, despite a barrage of hate propaganda, refused to join in the hue and cry against the New Deal which had served their basic purposes well.

"The white masses in the South are still Democrats because they are poor and believe the Democratic party to be the poor white man's party," William G. Carleton observes. "And significantly, the fact that the Negro is now for the most part in the Democratic party has not altered this fundamental faith . . . today fear of the Negro in politics is diminishing in the South. The relative decline of the Negro population, the spread of the racial views of the New Deal, in spite of protestations to the contrary, and educational ad-

[3]*Opportunity,* July 1943.
[4]*American Mercury,* April 1943.

vances are softening the old prejudices. The cry of 'Nigger,' employed to divide the liberal forces, is losing its old magic. That cry was raised against Senator Claude Pepper in the 1944 Florida primary, but it was raised in vain. It was raised against Senator Lister Hill in the 1944 Alabama primary, but to no avail. Even in South Carolina the old Red Shirt slogans could not save 'Cotton Ed' Smith from defeat."[5] Smith, who had indignantly (and irreverently) stalked out of the Democratic National Convention in Philadelphia in 1936 when a Negro clergyman was called on to offer prayer, had counted on this well-publicized stunt to gain him votes in the senatorial campaign. The trick succeeded in 1938, but six years later he was defeated after spending long years in the Senate. Opposing minimum-wage legislation, he had expressed the opinion that the workers of South Carolina could live on fifty cents a day. They didn't believe him.

Although they were among the beneficiaries of the continued Negro support of Roosevelt, southern members of Congress chafed under their obligations to the black minority whose votes helped them to retain the chairmanships of the most important congressional committees. Southerners headed seventeen of the thirty-three standing Senate committees in the Seventy-ninth Congress, including such important assignments as the committees on agriculture and forestry, appropriations, expenditures in executive departments, finance, foreign relations, manufactures, rules, and the District of Columbia. Twenty-five of the forty-eight standing committees of the House were chaired by southern Democrats. Important among these were the committees on agriculture, appropriations, banking and currency, civil service, education, elections, expenditures, judiciary, naval and military affairs, public buildings and grounds, and veterans. These posts were held by virtue of the seniority rule and the Democratic majority in both houses of Congress, a majority which in 1944 could hardly have been attained without the Negro vote. Discomforted by this knowledge, some of the Southerners felt compelled to express their ingratitude. Senator John H. Overton of Louisiana, then chairman of the Committee on Manufactures, invited the Negro out of the Democratic party during the course of the following Senate debate on a petition for cloture to allow a vote on the FEPC bill:

Mr. OVERTON: But, Mr. President, the question I wish to ask the Senator is whether the National Democratic Party realizes that

[5] *The Virginia Quarterly Review*, Spring 1946.

ultimately the Negro is going to come to the conclusion that his permanent friend, his steady friend, his fast and certain friend is, not the Democratic Party, but the Republican Party? Is not the Negro going to come to the conclusion that out of a sense of gratitude he owes fealty to the Republican Party? Was it not the great emancipator, Abraham Lincoln, who broke the shackles from the Negro's wrists and gave him freedom? Was it not the Republican Party which placed in our Constitution the 15th amendment, giving the Negro the right of suffrage? Was it not the Republican Party, that, following the War Between the States, undertook to place and did place the Negro in political power in the Southern States? Is the Negro going to forget his obligation to the party which made his race free, which gave it political power, and which gave it political prestige? Is he going to go astray and worship after false idols and false gods? Is he going to surrender the birthright and heritage of his race, politically for a mess of pottage which might be thrown out by the present National Democratic administration?

As a Democrat whose forebears have been Democrats and whose democracy cannot be impugned, I wish to say that it would be infinitely better for the Negro to adhere to the Republican Party.

MR. HOMER E. CAPEHART (*Republican, Indiana*): Mr. President, are we to understand from the able Senator from Louisiana that the Democratic Party does not wish to have the vote of the Negro?

MR. OVERTON: So far as the southern Democrats are concerned, I can say "Yes"—unquestionably so, so far as the great majority of southern Democrats are concerned. We do not want the Negroes in the party. They do not belong in the Democratic Party.

MR. CAPEHART: Mr. President, I wish to say that I see no connection between wanting the vote of the Negroes and the question before the Senate at the moment. Let me say that we in the Republican Party want the votes of the Negroes of America because they are Americans.

MR. OVERTON: You want them because they are votes. That is why you want them, and this is the only reason.

MR. DENNIS CHAVEZ (*Democrat, New Mexico*): Very well. If the Negro did not vote the Democratic ticket in Ohio, Illinois,

Indiana, Pennsylvania, and other States, what the Senator from Louisiana has stated might be correct, namely, that some other persons might be elected. But we want the Negroes to vote the Democratic ticket in Indiana and in all the other States, so that we may be able to have a majority of the Senate on this side of the aisle and be able to re-elect the Senator from Tennessee as President pro tempore of the Senate. I want the Senator from Tennessee to be chairman of the Committee on Appropriations. I am satisfied with the Senator from Texas [Mr. Connally] as Chairman of the Committee on Foreign Relations. But how are we going to obtain a Democratic majority in the Senate and have the Senators who now hold them retain their chairmanships unless we get the votes of the Democrats in the North?

Mr. OVERTON: The Senator means to say "unless we get the Negro vote."

Mr. CHAVEZ: Very well; unless we get the Negro vote.

Mr. OVERTON: We are indebted for these chairmanships to the Negro votes from the North, and that is the reason why this bill is here. Let us be perfectly frank about it. If it were not for the political issue involved, this bill would not be on the floor of the Senate of the United States.

Mr. CHAVEZ: I tell the Senator again that I am for this bill because I honestly believe in fair play for everyone. That is the way I feel about the matter. I am not questioning the motives or integrity or sincerity of purpose of anyone who may oppose the bill, but I believe in the bill because I believe it will apply to all; I believe that opportunity should be afforded to all; I believe there should be equality of opportunity for all persons. The Negro is only an incidental consideration in connection with the bill. In the South there has never been any trouble, and there we had no trouble during the war.

Mr. TOM STEWART (*Democrat, Tennessee*): But we will have trouble if this bill is passed.

Mr. CHAVEZ: Oh, no; that is merely politics on the part of Tennessee. We can also be accused of playing politics. But, Mr. President, suppose politics is involved, and suppose we Democrats do not work for liberal rule, for equality of opportunity for others.

Then I would not blame the Negro for going back to the party of his fathers. If a few Senators can keep the majority of the Senate from expressing its opinion one way or the other, then I do not blame the Negro for being resentful. Then he would say, "Mr. Senator, we elected you for this particular seat in the Senate and we know that you are for us, but you cannot do anything about it. Eighteen or 19 other Senators can keep you from voting. So we are going to go back to the party of our fathers."

That is what would happen, and I would not blame the Democratic National Committee chairman, if he did something about it. I wish he would. I have been complaining because he has not done anything about it. The Senator from Tennessee complains because he is supposed to have something to do with it. I have not heard from him. I wish I would. I think it would be in the interest of the political job he is holding.

MR. STEWART: I have not complained about political votes, if the Senator has been directing his remarks to me. The Senator was addressing the Senator from Louisiana upon that point. Of course, this bill does not affect the right of suffrage of anyone. It affects the matter of employment, or is supposed to. So far as the Negro vote is concerned, Negroes vote in most parts of the State of Tennessee.

MR. CHAVEZ: Personally, I hope they vote the Democratic ticket in Tennessee.

MR. STEWART: I wish to say to the Senator from New Mexico, the Senator from Louisiana, and all other Senators that, as they remember, the Negro voter left the Republican Party when he became hungry under a man named Hoover. That would drive anyone out of a party.[6]

It was just this sort of billingsgate in the halls of Congress that soured many Negroes on the Democratic party. It was grist for the Republican mill. "It is certain that the Dixie gentlemen (Messrs. Bilbo, Rankin & Co.) who preach race hate with Hitler venom will probably win more Negro votes for the Republicans than the combined efforts of a half dozen Deweys," commented the Democratic Chicago *Defender.* The Pittsburgh *Courier,* which in 1936 expressed the belief that "the South is rising to a dignity commensurate with the de-

[6] *The Congressional Record,* February 4, 1946.

mands of our era," later demanded the election of a Republican Congress in order to deprive the Southerners of the committee chairmanship which they controlled and used to impede legislation for a Fair Employment Practices Commission, anti-poll-tax and antilynching bills.

Resentment against the maneuvers and verbal abuse of many southern congressmen continued to mount among northern Negro voters. The White House seemed powerless to halt these tactics or to stop this vile flow of vituperation. Once, in 1938, the President vainly tried to get rid of some of the more insidious anti-Negro propagandists in his attempted purge of reactionary congressmen. Although the President did not cite the racial attitudes of these southern reactionaries as a reason for retiring them, both Senators Walter F. George of Georgia and Ellison D. (Cotton Ed) Smith of South Carolina made use of the race issue in their successful campaigns for re-election. The purge, they shouted to the wool-hat boys, was a New Deal conspiracy to take over the Democratic party and, at the behest of northern Negroes, push through anti-lynching legislation, which they termed "an insult to the South." Attacking the NAACP's fight for anti-lynching legislation, George appealed: "When Walter White sat in the Senate gallery for nearly six long weeks directing the parliamentary maneuvers on the floor of the Senate, I know you did not want me to follow Walter White's leadership." The President was soundly beaten in this direct attempt to get the southern voters of his party to sustain his request for co-operation.

Despite the hateful antics of many of his Democratic supporters, President Roosevelt was able to retain the support of the bulk of Negro voters. Their confidence in him stemmed from the conviction that he was trying to facilitate their long hard struggle to attain full citizenship. Nor was this support due solely to the relief program. Indeed, Gosnell's study of the Negro vote in Chicago reveals that the greatest shift from the Republican to the Democratic columns occurred in those areas where rents and income were highest and unemployment least. Between 1928 and 1934, the Democratic vote in the better areas doubled, whereas, in the precincts where the relief rolls were biggest, it increased only one and one half times. To a people in need, relief is certainly an important factor. The unemployed are no more likely to vote to cut their relief than stockholders to eliminate their dividends. Roosevelt's appeal, however, was much broader. After the deadening inertia of the Hoover administration, the New Deal provided a sorely needed intellectual and spiritual stimulant.

Among the hundreds of eager young reformers and idealists which the administration brought to Washington was a small group of non-political Negro appointees. Known generally as racial-relations advisers, the members of this group were assigned the task to make the New Deal program a living reality to the masses of Negro citizens, to see that they were not by-passed in the administration of the program. Early in the New Deal, the entering wedge was made by the Rosenwald Fund, which prevailed upon the Secretary of the Interior, Harold L. Ickes, to appoint Clark Foreman, a young southern white liberal, to the newly created post of Adviser on the Economic Status of Negroes. Foreman was soon succeeded by his Negro assistant, studious young Robert C. Weaver, just down from Harvard with a Ph.D. in economics. The group gradually expanded and included, in addition to the designated racial-relations advisers, other Negroes in professional, administrative, or technical positions. While their function, duties, and responsibilities varied from agency to agency, "all [were] primarily concerned with the racial aspects of public relations. It is not merely that they seek to interpret the agency's program to minority groups and the reactions of the minority groups to the agency; they seek also to influence the basic policy of the agency in such manner that its program will provide for equitable participation of minority groups in all its phases—in responsibilities and administration as well as in benefits."[7]

Most distinguished of this group, and one who already had attained national prestige prior to appointment, was the matriarchal Mary McLeod Bethune, friend of Mrs. Roosevelt, president of Bethune-Cookman College in Daytona Beach, Florida, and founder of the National Council of Negro Women. Others of this able group, in addition to Weaver and Mrs. Bethune, included William H. Hastie, urbane and brilliant, later appointed governor of the Virgin Islands; alert, keen-minded Frank S. Horne, still with the National Housing Agency; Alfred Smith of WPA, steady and unhurried; the eloquent R. O'Hara Lanier, now United States Minister to Liberia; Clarence R. Johnson, skilled negotiator out of the ranks of organized labor; the Christian militarist, Colonel Campbell C. Johnson; hard-working William Trent; the veteran Lawrence A. Oxley; Robert R. Taylor, the breezy, confident businessman from Chicago; Ira De A. Reid, scholarly and fluent; Ted Poston of OWI,

[7] Henry Lee Moon, in *Phylon*, First Quarter, 1943.

famed as an enterprising newspaperman and matchless raconteur; the seasoned social worker, T. Arnold Hill; the quiet and industrious Booker T. McGraw; and, youngest of them all, Truman K. Gibson, up-and-coming lawyer from Chicago. And then there was that bizarre, bearded character, Edgar G. Brown, the political chameleon from Chicago, who, when his job with the CCC was terminated, hastened to join the Republican attack upon his former benefactors.

What was the value of the work of this group composed, for the most part, of intelligent, honest, competent, and industrious personnel who believed in, and worked hard for, the over-all objectives of the New Deal? To southern reactionaries they were a sinister and powerful group driving the New Deal into a fight against all forms of segregation. Congressman Joe Starnes of Alabama, then a member of the House Appropriations Committee, repeatedly sought to have funds for the Racial Relations Office stricken from the budget of the United States Housing Authority. He branded this personnel as "special propagandists" engaged in efforts "to promote the idea that racial discrimination is being practiced" and whose chief objective was to make white and Negro families "live together under the same roof." To many Negro critics this group was useless because it "had no power" and served merely as buffers between the agency and Negro representatives. "In actual practice, race-relations advisers perform very little, if any, useful service to the agency in which they are employed or to the people whose special interests they are supposed to serve," complains Louis Lautier, Washington correspondent for the National Negro Publishers Association.

Both the southern and the Negro critics have taken extreme and untenable positions. The advisers did not have the power ascribed to them by the southern reactionaries, nor were they as useless as some Negro critics maintain. They did serve a useful purpose and got some things done. To the friendless Negro in some distant community they were ofttimes helpful in overcoming some discrimination, and to such individuals they represented a direct and friendly link to the government in Washington. In the public housing program the office of racial relations did not succeed in breaking down Jim Crow but was able to get a number of projects in eastern, northern, and western cities established on a democratic integrated basis. Moreover, largely through efforts of this personnel, about one third of all low-rent public housing went to Negro families.

The steady work of the similar office in the War Department contributed to the relaxation of some of the segregation and dis-

criminatory policies in the armed services. Whatever of value was
accomplished by these advisers was incalculably aided by the organized pressure of Negro groups, both national and local, and the
Negro press. The plea of Negro critics for the complete elimination
of these offices rests upon the premise of an equality in status which
the Negro in America has not yet attained, the Constitution not
withstanding. This, of course, is not a matter of capacity, but rather
of opportunity. One of the objectives of the racial-relations offices
was to make real and commonplace the Negro's legal status of
equality. Underlying the New Deal program was this basic equalitarian objective.

The administration often had to run the gantlet between the
various opposing factions which supported it, but the crossfire between the southern reactionaries and the Negro New Dealers was
perhaps the most grilling because the differences were the most irrec-
oncilable. Mr. Roosevelt needed the Negro vote in the North more
than he needed the southern vote. But the Southerners kept two
aces up their sleeves. First, they had vast influence and power in the
nominating Democratic National Convention in which the Negro
was practically voiceless. True, they had no one whom they could
run against the President to win either the nomination or the election, but they did have a formidable vote in the convention. Second,
Roosevelt needed their support in both houses of Congress in order
to get through his legislative program. They could, and frequently
did, kill legislation which they disapproved, usually with the connivance or open collaboration of the Republican minority. Indeed,
Congress developed a three-party system: the Republicans, the
Roosevelt New Dealers, and the southern Democrats. The coalition
between the southern Democrats and the Republicans became so
consistent and so flagrant that New Deal Senator Joe Guffey of
Pennsylvania openly denounced it as "an unholy alliance." The
Republicans, in return for support of issues they considered vital,
permitted the southern Democrats to filibuster to death the FEPC,
anti-poll-tax and anti-lynching bills.

In the pre-war defense period and during the war, the pressure
upon the President increased and he tended to retreat from his
earlier reforms and finally announced himself as "Dr. Win-the-War"
at any cost. He had, meanwhile, under the mass pressure of Negroes
led by A. Philip Randolph, signed Executive Order 8802 establishing the Fair Employment Practices Committee to gain compliance
with the government policy of non-discrimination in employment in

the expanding war industries. During the long period of his leadership, observes Edgar E. Robinson, "Mr. Roosevelt was not one man
with one program, but several men with several programs. But
whereas his leadership appealed at times to reformers, to radicals, to
labor leaders, to businessmen, to 'internationalists,' rarely did it appeal to all of them. At no time did it have a particular appeal to the
leaders in the area from which he was seen to draw basic Democratic support, that is, the South."[8]

Negro voters were ardently wooed by both parties in 1936 and in
1940, but it was not until 1944 that their votes became of really
crucial importance. Mr. Roosevelt had won so handily in 1936 that
his victory would have been unimpaired if he had lost the entire
Negro vote as well as the total vote of the late Confederate states.
Winning better than 60 per cent of the total popular vote, he carried
46 of the 48 states with a total of 523 electoral college votes. In an
effort to retain Negro support in 1940, the Democrats, for the first
time, incorporated a frank appeal for that vote in the party platform. Other conventions of the party had affirmed the right of all
citizens, regardless of race, creed, or color, to equal justice and the
protection of the Constitution, but this was the first time the Negro
was mentioned by name in a Democratic party platform. At the
Chicago convention that year the following plank was adopted and
received with the applause of the assembled delegates:

> *Our Negro citizens have participated actively in the economic and
> social advances launched by this Administration, including fair
> labor standards, social security benefits, health protection, work re-
> lief projects, decent housing, aid to education, and the rehabilitation
> of low-income farm families. We have aided more than half-a-
> million Negro youths in vocational training, education and employ-
> ment. We shall continue to strive for complete legislative safeguards
> against discrimination in government service and benefits, and in the
> national defense forces. We pledge to uphold due process and the
> equal protection of the laws for every citizen, regardless of race,
> creed or color.*

Opposing President Roosevelt that year was Wendell Willkie, the
big corporation lawyer and businessman. Little was then known of
his attitude toward race. He was an officer of a public utility com-

---

[8]Edgar Eugene Robinson, *They Voted for Roosevelt* (California: Stanford
University Press, 1947), p. 184.

pany, and such companies have been most discriminatory in employment practices, although Mr. Willkie claimed, "We have a great number of them [Negroes] working for Commonwealth and Southern. I don't know exactly how many, or in what categories, but I know we have a great many." Immediately following his nomination he told reporters from the Negro press: "I want your support. I need it. But irrespective of whether Negroes go down the line with me or not, they can expect every consideration. They will get their fair proportion of appointments, their fair representation on policy-making bodies. They'll get the same consideration as other citizens." It was not until after his defeat, in his few remaining years, that the world learned that Mr. Willkie had meant what he had said—and much more. Meanwhile, Negro voters, unmoved by the anti-third-term propaganda, gave to Mr. Roosevelt a larger percentage of their vote than in 1936. The President was again reelected by a safe margin.

By 1944 the President was absorbed in and burdened down by world problems and engaged in directing the all-out effort to win the war. At home he had lost ground politically, while abroad he was looming ever bigger as the biggest of the Big Three in the Anglo-Soviet-American coalition against the Fascist powers. But at home, having abandoned reform, he was losing ground among many who formerly had supported him ardently. There was increasing resentment among Negroes against the hoary limitations imposed upon them in the midst of a war shrilly acclaimed as a life-and-death struggle for the Four Freedoms. Segregation, discrimination, and humiliation within the armed services were deeply and bitterly resented. Although there had been a noticeable upswing in employment in the war industries, owing to man-power shortages and the work of the FEPC, there was still widespread denial of equal opportunity, particularly in skilled, technical, and administrative jobs and positions. The difficulties of many Negro migrants were augmented by a general, though not universal, policy of exclusion from most of the war housing projects developed with federal funds. These continuing disabilities caused many Negro newspapers which had formerly supported the President to sour on him and his administration during the war period. At a time when Negro support was most sorely needed, a distinct break with the administration seemed imminent.

In answer to these complaints, the administration lifted some of the restrictions imposed upon Negroes in the armed services. The

WAVES, the naval auxiliary, and the SPARS, attached to the
Coast Guard, were opened to Negro women on an unsegregated
basis. Segregation in transportation and recreational facilities on
Army posts was ordered banned. The Navy announced the training
and acceptance of Negro officers and nurses. Negro troops were
ordered into combat service. And, most dramatic, the White House
sent troops into Philadelphia to back up the FEPC and to quell the
hate strike of white transit workers who objected to the promotion
of Negroes to jobs as motormen and conductors. During the course
of the campaign the President came out for a permanent FEPC and
for the abolition of racial and economic restrictions on the ballot. All
these moves had a political impact upon Negro voters who wanted
to believe in the President's good intentions.

The campaign for Roosevelt had to overcome two vital weaknesses: the ditching of Henry A. Wallace and the inadequacy of the
plank on Negro rights in the Democratic platform. Though his positive contributions to the advancement of the Negro were vague and
illusive, Wallace had become the symbol of the struggle for the
rights of the common man of whatever race, color, or creed. His
open challenge to reaction in the South at the Democratic National
Convention endeared him to Negroes who had become weary of
pussyfooting on these issues. Wallace's ringing words were widely
repeated. "The future," he had declared, "belongs to those who go
down the line unswervingly for the liberal principles of both political
and economic democracy regardless of race, color, or religion. In a
political, educational, and economic sense there must be no inferior
races. The poll tax must go. Equal educational opportunities must
come. The future must bring equal wages for equal work regardless
of sex or race. Roosevelt stands for all this." This was the kind of
talk Negroes liked to hear from high places and directed to the
people most in need of it—the southern delegates. The convention's
subsequent rejection of Wallace's bid for renomination as vice-
presidential candidate alarmed and depressed colored citizens
throughout the country. Nor were they satisfied that Roosevelt had
done all that he might have in behalf of his faithful co-worker.

The so-called racial plank in the Democratic platform was so inadequate that Walter White angrily denounced it as a mere
"splinter." It declared:

*We believe that racial and religious minorities have the right to
live, develop, and vote equally with all citizens and share the rights*

*that are guaranteed by our Constitution. Congress should exert its
full constitutional powers to protect these rights.*

Clearly a compromise with southern reaction, the plank said nothing about FEPC, anti-poll-tax or anti-lynching legislation, or discrimination in the armed services. The watered-down racial plank
and the rejection of Wallace made Roosevelt's colored supporters
most unhappy. The Republicans were gleeful and hopeful, for their
platform declarations, though by no means satisfactory, were fuller
and more promising. These developments made more difficult the
task of mobilizing Negro sentiment behind Roosevelt.

In addition to the National Democratic Committee, the administration had the support of the newly organized Political Action
Committee of the Congress of Industrial Organizations. Under the
leadership of Sidney Hillman, the PAC conducted an intensive drive
in all the major industrial centers. Not only did the PAC reach the
half million Negro members of CIO unions, but it also conducted a
vigorous campaign among non-trade unionists in the various communities. The influence of PAC among Negro voters was enhanced
by the reports of its effective role in the retirement of Senator
"Cotton Ed" Smith of South Carolina, Congressman Joe Starnes of
Alabama, and other congressional Negro haters. The Roosevelt
record in the early days of the New Deal was recalled and widely
publicized both by PAC and the organized Democrats. While the
Pittsburgh *Courier,* the Baltimore *Afro-American,* the New York
Amsterdam News, and other Negro publications supported the
candidacy of Governor Thomas E. Dewey, the Chicago *Defender,*
the Michigan *Chronicle,* the St. Louis *Argus,* the Norfolk *Journal
and Guide,* and the *People's Voice* of New York, among others,
advocated the re-election of the President. The New York *Age,* one
of the oldest of the Negro newspapers and long a Republican stal-
wart, came out for "Roosevelt whose statesmanship is proven" and
"whose ideals and ideas on the masses have already been demonstrated in peace and in war." The Negro voter, as an American,
was, of course, concerned in the over-all vital problems which confronted the nation as a whole. The completion of the war, establishment of a just and enduring peace, and the planning for a post-war
period of full and fair employment were as vital to the Negro as to
any other citizen. These considerations were important factors in
determining his vote.

The President's fourth-term candidacy also drew the support of a galaxy of prominent Negroes who had no personal political ax to grind and who were on the pay roll of no political organization. Among these were Channing H. Tobias, an independent Republican and at that time an executive of the national YMCA. Tobias had broken with Governor Dewey because of the latter's failure to act upon the recommendations of his own committee which had called for the establishment of a New York State FEPC. "As a Negro," Dr. Tobias said, "I shall support President Roosevelt because his philosophy of government and the generally progressive course that he has followed for the past twelve years have vested the common man of every race, creed, and color with a dignity and inspired him with a hope that he has never known before."

The race's veteran protagonist, W. E. B. Du Bois, after "looking carefully at the record," was convinced "without the slightest doubt that Franklin D. Roosevelt has done more for the uplift and progress of the American Negro than any president since Abraham Lincoln." Joining Tobias and Du Bois in support of the President were such other Negro spokesmen as Bishop R. R. Wright of the A.M.E. Church, Paul Robeson, Mrs. Mary McLeod Bethune, William H. Hastie, Robert C. Weaver, Willard S. Townsend, Charles S. Johnson, Metz T. P. Lochard, John Sengestacke, Carter Wesley, Gordon Hancock, P. B. Young, and J. E. Mitchell, representing a cross section of Negro leadership.

While the organized work of the Democratic National Committee, the PAC, and the contributions of individual leaders were important factors in holding the bulk of the Negro vote for Roosevelt, there was another consideration of equal importance. The masses of the race were unconvinced that the ills of which they complained would be corrected by a Republican victory. They realized that all the discriminations which irked them had persisted under Republican administrations. Roosevelt, they knew, had not created their difficulties; he had simply inherited them.

A post-election analysis by Herbert Brownell, Jr., chairman of the Republican National Committee, claimed that "a shift of 303,414 votes in fifteen states outside of the South would have enabled Governor Thomas E. Dewey to capture 175 additional electoral votes and to win the presidency with an eight electoral-vote margin." In at least eight of the fifteen states listed by Brownell, the Negro vote exceeded the number needed to shift in order to place them in the Republican column. In Maryland the 50,000 votes which Negro citizens in Baltimore alone cast for F.D.R. were more than double his 22,500 state plurality. Negro voters of five New Jersey cities gave the President a total of 28,780 votes to assure him a winning margin of 26,540. Michigan, which Roosevelt lost in 1940 by the narrow margin of 6,926 votes, was carried by 22,500, with the colored citizens of Detroit casting 41,740 votes for him. Negro voters in Kansas City and St. Louis accounted for 34,900 of the President's margin of 46,180 in Missouri. In Chicago, 121,650 voters in predominantly Negro districts contributed to the 140,165 margin by which the President carried the state of Illinois. The black belts of New York City and Buffalo accounted for 188,760 Roosevelt votes or more than half his state plurality of 316,000. The combined American Labor and Liberal party tickets for which many Negroes voted gave the President a total of 825,640, enough to overcome the Republican lead over the Democratic slate and hold New York's 47 electoral votes. The President carried Pennsylvania by 105,425 votes, to which Negro voters in Pittsburgh and Philadelphia contributed no less than 52,000. These seven states account for 168 votes in the electoral college and were essential to the Roosevelt victory. In addition, Negro votes contributed substantially to the Roosevelt lead in West Virginia, Kentucky, and Delaware. The outcome in any one of these ten states could have been reversed by a shift of less than 5 per cent of the total popular vote. In Michigan and New Jersey a shift of less than 1 per cent would have placed those states in the GOP column.

President and Mrs. Roosevelt were greatly admired by the masses of Negroes, who loved them for the enemies they made—the most infamous of southern reactionaries—as much as for the positive benefits derived from his administration. The President, however, was not without critics among Negro citizens, some of whom pointed out that he never openly challenged the southern reactionaries on issues vital to the Negro. In this he was less bold than his successor, President Harry S. Truman, who demanded of the House Rules Committee the release of the bottled-up FEPC bill. Although in 1933 Roosevelt had condemned "that vile form of collective murder— lynch law," he had not pressed for an anti-lynching bill and made no public condemnation of the disastrous Detroit riot of 1943. He got some things done, some important things for racial advancement, but he often moved too slowly for a people too long held in patient restraint. The gains made under Roosevelt were tangible and lasting: the 66,850 new low-rent dwellings made available for low-income Negro families who formerly were compelled to live in slums; the hospitals, schools, and recreational centers built with federal aid, the training of thousands of young Negroes in the programs of the National Youth Administration and the Civilian Conservation Corps, the aid to more than half a million Negro farmers, the opening up of new employment opportunities in government and in private industry, the stimulation of a progressive non-discriminating labor movement, the breaking down of some of the barriers in the armed services and in the merchant marine, the elimination of Jim Crow in most government cafeterias and bureaus, and, perhaps most important, the appointment of a liberal Supreme Court which vindicated the Negro's basic rights and, by banning the white primary, opened the way to mass Negro voting in the South.

While there was just cause for much of the Negro criticism of the Roosevelt regime, some of the attacks upon the President were certainly politically inspired. There were critics who assailed Mr. Roosevelt as if he had originated segregation and discrimination and foisted these practices upon an unwilling nation. They accused of him of being a timid, if not willing, tool of the South. "The South is running the government, it dominates the White House, it controls the Army and Navy, all because President Roosevelt is too weak and probably feeble to do anything to stop them. He has failed to defend his wife or his close friends and party associates from the calumny of southern race hatred," complained W. O. Walker in his column, "Down the Big Road," published in the Cleveland *Call and Post.*

"Thousands of Negroes, who distrust the Democratic party but who have confidence in President Roosevelt, are finding that even the great office of the President has not been able to cope with the malignant influence of the South when the Democratic party is in power," the Pittsburgh *Courier* warned. The *Courier's* acidulous and widely read columnist, George S. Schuyler, believed that "if Roosevelt were an angel from Heaven on high, his criminal surrender of the Negro soldier and sailor to the jim-crow system of the unreconstructed (and Democratic!) South was enough to damn him in the eyes of every red-blooded Negro with any feelings of pride." To Schuyler the President was "a man who could speak systematically about the tortured Jews of Europe, but was too callous or too cowardly to speak likewise about the tortured Negroes of America." Edgar G. Brown, who had for years fed at the New Deal trough, called for a "revolt against President Roosevelt's raw deal" in 1944 and accused him of "failing the Negro on vital issues of race equality."

While the critics condemned Roosevelt for his manifest failings, the masses of black folk intuitively recognized, as did the masses of common people the world over, his essential humanitarianism and applauded his championship of a world order of freedom, peace, and security for all mankind.

CHAPTER II

Votes for Sale

THAT THE NEGRO VOTE IS SINGULARLY IGNORANT, VENAL,
and corrupt is a widely held generalization in American politics. Indeed no other segment of the American electorate has been so consistently maligned with the charge of vote selling. Professed liberals
and confirmed conservatives alike share this appraisal of the Negro's
political morality and frequently express it in such a manner as to
convey the impression that venality is a uniquely racial trait practically unknown among voters of other races. The supporters of the
party or candidate *against* whom the bulk of the Negro vote may be
cast can be depended upon to raise this cry. It has proved to be a
much easier way of accounting for the preferences of the Negro
voters than an honest examination of the failings of the repudiated
faction, party, or candidate. A common complaint of a defeated candidate in any community where there is a sizable Negro vote is his
lack of funds to "buy" that vote.

Certainly some Negroes have sold their vote for cash or other considerations. There is, however, no evidence that this practice has been
more common among Negroes than among other voters. Corruption
in American politics antedates large-scale Negro suffrage and reached
its climax just at the period when mass voting by Negroes was being
introduced following the ratification of the Fifteenth Amendment.
Tammany Hall and other local and state machines perfected the
tricks of buying and stealing votes long before the Negro became a
positive factor in American politics. Recent investigations indicate
that the practice continues in many communities. And yet, while
Negroes in many urban centers are important cogs in machine politics, they are not the majority or controlling element in any dominant
political organization in the country today. Nevertheless, the stigma
sticks.

"The Negro vote is notoriously venal," Dorothy Thompson, the newspaper columnist, sneers. "Ignorant and illiterate, the vast mass of Negroes are like the lower strata of the early industrial immigrants, and like them are 'bossed' and 'delivered' in blocs by venal leaders, white and black. . . . The Negro is a voter who can be bought."[1] Miss Thompson only baldly expresses the prevailing American concept of the Negro vote. Politicians, reformers, historians, editorial writers, radio commentators, and others have reiterated her charge. At their charitable best they are prone to look apologetically upon the Negro vote as a necessary evil in a democratic system. Thus the tendency to isolate and stigmatize the vote of the Negro as a corrupt and venal factor in American politics persists. Commentators who would not dare make a similar charge against any other specific group of Americans do not hesitate to assail the Negro voters.

Miss Thompson's rash charge stems directly from the anti-Negro propaganda which sought to justify the overthrow of the Reconstruction governments. In order to create an attitude in the North that would sustain their subversion of the war amendments, the southern Bourbons had to discredit the Negro voter. They did this by a systematic and passionate propaganda associating Negro suffrage with fraud and corruption. They were out to demonstrate that Negro suffrage would not work and they were in no wise scrupulous about the method they used to make their case. Not only was the Negro a venal voter, but his very participation in the electoral process was a corrupting influence, they contended. There was no disposition to discriminate among Negro voters—to separate the venal from the unpurchasable, the ignorant from the intelligent. Rather the objective was to lump them all together as undesirable citizens whose constitutional rights had to be curbed in order to restore the old order of life in the South. Senator James K. Vardaman, the Mississippi demogogue, expressed this point of view starkly. He was "opposed to Negro voting; it matters not what his advertised mental and moral qualifications may be. I am just as much opposed to Booker T. Washington as a voter, with all his Anglo-Saxon re-enforcements, as I am to the cocoanut-headed, chocolate-colored, typical little coon, Andy Dotson, who blacks my shoes every morning. Neither is fit to perform the supreme function of citizenship."[2]

Henry W. Grady, the cavalier apostle of the New South, shared the

---

[1] New York *Herald Tribune,* August 11, 1936.

[2] Quoted by Lewinson, *Race, Class and Party* (New York: Oxford University Press, 1932), pp. 84–85.

opinion of Vardaman, his plebeian counterpart. The Negro vote, he maintained, if not quarantined, "would invite the debauching bid of factions, and drift surely to that which was the most corrupt and cunning." To Grady, "the worst thing that could happen is that the white people of the South should stand in opposing factions, with the vast mass of ignorant or purchasable Negro votes between. Consider such a status. If the Negroes were skillfully led—and leaders would not be lacking—it would give them the balance of power, a thing not to be considered."[3] To Carter Glass, the Virginian, Negro suffrage was a "crime" and the 146,000 Negro voters of his state "ignorant."

Citing allegations of wholesale vote buying in an election in Augusta, Georgia, in 1878, Alexander H. Stephens, the vice-president of the late Confederacy, asserted: "It is needless to add that the votes which were so openly sold in the market were chiefly, if not entirely, those of the lowest class of the colored race." According to a current newspaper account of the election, quoted by Stephens: "Money was freely exhibited and offered for votes and as freely and as openly taken. The price of a vote ranged from ten cents to five dollars, according to the desire of the purchaser to obtain the vote and the estimate put by the seller upon the value of the franchise. Hundreds of votes were thus openly disposed of in plain view of everybody."[4]

"Both Republicans and Democrats had to buy [Negro votes] and it made it quite expensive," a delegate to the Alabama disfranchising convention of 1901 recounted. "He himself had never bought a vote, but he had chipped in to the campaign fund. Negro voters had gone to ten dollars apiece, and, Mr. President, it makes it awful on our people. . . . The Republicans . . . are as anxious to get rid of the Negroes as we are."[5]

Curiously enough, the charge of mass venality did not become widespread even in the South until the period of unrest which led to the Populist revolt. That the Negro vote was ignorant and controlled, and Negro legislators corruptible, the southern Bourbons maintained throughout the Reconstruction period; but it was not until later that they joined in a chorus of unqualified condemnation of all Negro voters as purchasable. Even Stephens, in his contribution

[3]Quoted by Ralph W. Wardlaw, *Negro Suffrage in Georgia, 1867–1930* (Phelps-Stokes Fellowship Studies, No. 11, 1932), p. 50.

[4]*North American Review*, March 1879.

[5]Birmingham *Age-Herald*, July 26, 1901. Quoted by Lewinson, op. cit., pp. 89–90.

to the *North American Review* symposium on Negro suffrage in 1879, restricted his charge of venality to "the lowest class of the colored race." Wade Hampton of South Carolina and L. Q. C. Lamar of Mississippi, also participants in the discussion, did not directly raise the issue. Hampton, even before the ratification of the Fifteenth Amendment, had advocated a restricted franchise for the freedmen based upon education and property holdings—a vote which he hoped his planter class would be able to control. In his contribution to the symposium, the South Carolinian observed that "as the Negro becomes more intelligent he naturally allies himself with the more conservative of the whites, for his observation and experience both show him that his interests are identified with those of the white race here. . . . I will venture the assertion that in every locality he [any investigator] will find as earnest, as active and as consistent Democrats among the colored people as among the whites, and these colored Democrats are generally among the more intelligent of their race." Stephens and Hampton, unlike Grady, Glass, and Vardaman of the succeeding generation, recognized individual variation in quality and character within the race.

Contributing to the same discussion were James G. Blaine, James A. Garfield, Thomas A. Hendricks, Montgomery Blair, and Wendell Phillips. Of these, only Blair, the counsel for Dred Scott in that historic case and member of Lincoln's Cabinet, repudiated the Negro's right to vote. Even the Southerners accepted the permanence of Negro suffrage. It was Phillips, however, who, with the burning zeal of his Abolitionist days, was most challenging in his defense of enfranchisement. "Though his voting has been crippled and curtailed throughout a large part of the South during half the time he has been entitled to vote," Phillips wrote, "the Negro has given the best evidence of his fitness for suffrage by valuing it at its full worth. Every investigation of southern fraud has shown him less purchasable than the white man. He has wielded his vote with as much honor and honesty—to claim the very least—as any class of southern whites; even of those intellectually his superiors. . . . Negro suffrage gave the helm to the Republican party when it represented a principle— that was intelligent. It stood firmer against bribery than other southerners—that was honest. It vindicated the Negro's fitness for legislation—that scattered the fogs about Negro inferiority. It educated the Negro more and more every day, and was fast bringing him to a level with the whites of the best class—that was death to southern dreams of future rule and treason."

After the rout of Republicanism in the South, the Negro voter became, as Lamar pointed out, "a power between Democrat and Democrat." It was during this period that the charges of wholesale vote selling became the dominant note in anti-Negro propaganda. Opposing factions of Democrats were accused of "hauling in great loads of Negroes and paying them for their votes."[6] Wardlaw, in his study of *Negro Suffrage in Georgia,* asserts that "at these times it [the Negro vote] was no more than any other economic good, to be bartered for, bought, and sold to the highest bidder." Charges of "Negro venality" replaced the earlier fear of "Negro domination" as the rallying slogan to consolidate the whites and eliminate the Negro voter. The South set out to "purify" the electoral process through the elimination of the Negro vote.

What have been the results? George C. Stoney, in his *Memorandum on the Suffrage in Georgia,* raises these questions and gives his own answers based on a study of selected counties. "Has the elimination of the Negro from political power resulted also in the hoped for elimination of corrupt practices and the elevation of the electorate?" he asks. "Are white citizens as well as Negroes excluded from the polls as a result of the election laws? Has the position of the entrenched machine politicians been strengthened as was feared? The answer to the first question, if our counties are a fair sample, must be 'no'; to the last two a qualified 'yes.' "

As evidence of the type of corruption which followed the elimination of Negro suffrage, Stoney cites the city of Savannah, in which a political machine "has been in uninterrupted control since 1924. Among the sources of the funds which it uses to maintain itself in power are collections from large industries to whom it gives special favors in the form of lowered tax valuations, etc., and rake-offs from the underworld to which it gives protection in illegal activities. This machine has its roster of faithful henchmen kept in line partly by small favors in the form of positions as vote gatherers and poll watchers at election times, when they in return bring in family and neighbors to vote for their bosses. . . . The machine uses a substantial part of the funds realized from the sources described above to keep a large number of voters' poll taxes continuously paid up. . . . The buying of votes in addition to the payment of taxes is quite customary." During the entire twenty-two years that this ma-

[6]Cullen B. Gosnell, *Government and Politics of Georgia* (New York: Thomas Nelson & Sons, 1936), pp. 64–65.

chine controlled the city of Savannah there were probably never more than 1000 registered Negro voters. In 1940 there were only 725 qualified Negro voters in the city, and these, being barred from the Democratic primary, usually had no effective voice in the selection of city officials. The machine-paid poll taxes were those of white voters. The machine-purchased votes were the votes of white men and women.

This corrupt machine was kept in power by the votes of white citizens until 1946, by which time Negro registrants accounted for 20,000 qualified voters out of a total of 50,000. The vastly expanded Negro vote was the result of the elimination of the poll tax, the voiding of the white primary, the lowering of the voting age to eighteen, and an intensive registration drive conducted by able local Negro leadership. This new electorate was an important factor in the decision of the machine bosses to withdraw from the contest, leaving the field to two new contending factions, both of which openly and actively sought the support of colored voters. In this election there were no charges of vote selling leveled at the new Negro voters.

Following grand-jury investigations in 1929 and 1930, several Atlanta councilmen and other municipal officers were tried and convicted on charges of bribery and extortion. They were fined and given chain-gang sentences. This was at a time when there were no more than 500 Negroes qualified to vote in the city elections. The Atlanta thieves had been elected by the white voters of that city. Apparently corruption recognizes no color line.

Elsewhere in the South the elimination of the Negro vote contributed no more to the purification of politics than in Georgia. The corruption, stealing, fraud, and vote buying of the Huey Long regime in Louisiana and Bilboism in Mississippi merely high-light the degeneration of the electoral process in the deep South. While machine politics in the South is apt to be more local and less notorious than in the North, it is no less corrupt. The county courthouse ring usually controls local politics and in turn is likely to be controlled by vested interests, often foreign not only to the county but to the state and region as well. It has been common practice for millowners and large landlords to pay the poll taxes of their white workers and tenants and to see that they vote for the "right" candidates. The widespread absence of the secret ballot, the power of the local registrars and the small electorate all contribute to controlled elections in many sections of the South. It is in the operations of the courthouse gangs, Ralph Bunche found, that "the real venality of southern politics is revealed."[7]

The Negro has not lacked defenders of the integrity of his ballot. Answering Miss Thompson's rehashed charge of venality, Elmer A. Carter, then editor of *Opportunity* magazine, concluded that "a careful and impartial study of Negro political action will reveal in every instance that what appears to be particular is common to other groups similarly placed. In some instances there may be lacking an exact historical parallel but the reaction of the Negro to the dominant economic and social forces in America is exactly the same as the white."[8]

In his declining years Frederick Douglass was able to look back over a long and active life and find hope "in the fact that colored men are strong in their gratitude to benefactors, and firm in their political convictions. They cannot be coaxed or driven to vote with their enemies against their friends. Nothing but the shotgun or the bulldozer's whip can keep them from voting their convictions."

Bunche observed that "the Negro voter in the mass, like the white voter in the mass, tends to follow the guidance of his leadership. In some instances this Negro leadership is independent and honestly devoted to the welfare of the group. In other instances it is machine controlled, venal and selfishly opportunistic." His extensive study of Negro suffrage revealed no evidence that the Negro vote is any more purchasable than the white vote. "As a matter of fact," he reported, "in many of the southern communities today, the small Negro vote is the most independent and free from purchase in the electorate."[9]

The new Negro vote in Georgia, Ira De A. Reid remarked, "is different from any other known in fifty years in Georgia politics. It is interested in issues and welfare; its leaders are not to be tempted by the promise of spoils. . . . Only once in forty years has a candidate for a state or national office come to a Negro group in Georgia and talked over the political issues of the moment. That candidate was elected."[10]

The character of this vote is further attested by Ralph McGill, editor of the Atlanta *Constitution*. "It is interesting," he wrote, "to observe the comments over the State with regard to the Negro vote in those sections where they have participated. In not a single in-

[7]Ralph J. Bunche, *Memorandum on the Political Status of the Negro.* Unpublished MSS. prepared for the Carnegie-Myrdal study, 1940.

[8]*Opportunity,* October 1936.

[9]*Bunche,* op. cit.

[10]Ira De A. Reid, "Georgia's Negro Vote," *The Nation,* July 6, 1946.

stance have they voted in any number on the side of bad government or in behalf of racketeers. They have voted each time with the
reform, or so-called 'better elements.' A lot of persons are beginning
to see, too, that those who are pushing racial prejudice the most are
certainly not representative of good government now or any time in
their careers. They always have stood with gangsterism, with the
worst sort of corrupt machine politics."

Despite the persistent coupling of Negro suffrage with political
corruption, some Negro voters, almost from the beginning of their
enfranchisement, were to be found on the side of reform, even though
the reformers have generally offered Negro citizens even less in the
way of recognition than the corrupt machines. Indeed, about the
only reform movements which sought to advance the Negro politically were the Tom L. Johnson administration in Cleveland, Ohio,
the Roosevelt New Deal, and the La Guardia regime in New York
City. Many of the "law and order" civic reformers have been
too property-conscious to be concerned about the human rights and
employment opportunities of a disadvantaged minority.

Nevertheless, Negroes were enlisted in reform movements as early
as Reconstruction times. "There was not a single reform movement,
a single step toward protest, a single experiment for betterment in
which Negroes were not found in varying numbers," Du Bois records.
"The protest against corruption and inefficiency in South Carolina
had in every case Negro adherents and in many cases Negro leaders."[11] General Hampton, who in 1876 overthrew the Republican
regime in South Carolina, boasted of his Negro following as "earnest,
active, and consistent Democrats." Analyzing the election of a so-
called reform administration in Louisiana, Senator Thomas A.
Hendricks, Democrat of Indiana, credited the Negro with the success of this ticket. The new governor, he reported, "in his canvass
for the office addressed the colored voters in the language of argument and of patriotic appeal. He and his cause proved stronger than
the party control. They came to his support. They contributed to his
election. Without their help no change could have occurred. The
reform that followed was complete."[12] During the era of the Populist
revolt, the Southern Negro vote was split with substantial segments,
particularly in North Carolina and Georgia, allied with the agrarian
rebels. Even before the abolition of the white primary, Negroes ef-

---

[11]W. E. B. Du Bois, *Black Reconstruction* (New York: Harcourt Brace & Co.,
1935), p. 411.
[12]Thomas A. Hendricks, *North American Review*, March 1879.

fectively supported reform tickets in general and non-partisan municipal elections in Savannah, Georgia; Nashville, Tennessee; Galveston and Fort Worth, Texas; and Raleigh and Durham, North Carolina.

The average reformer's cavalier unconcern for the welfare of the race, his remoteness from the day-to-day problems which confront Negroes, and his post-election forgetfulness all present hazards to the Negro voter who may desire to support certain reforms. Half a century ago Du Bois discerned this dilemma in his study of the Philadelphia Negro. Then a young man of high ideals, he was shocked and disturbed by the commonplace political bargaining through which the machine controlled the city. Even so, "the paradox of reform" was clear to him. "Suppose," he ventured, "the Municipal League or the Woman's School-board movement, or some other reform is brought before the better class of Negroes today; they will nearly all agree that city politics are notoriously corrupt, that honest women should replace ward heelers on schoolboards, and the like. But can they vote for such movements? Most of them will say No; for to do so will throw many worthy Negroes out of employment: these very reformers who want votes for specific reforms will not themselves work beside Negroes, or admit them to positions in their stores or offices, or lend them friendly aid in trouble. Moreover Negroes are proud of their councilmen and policemen. What if some of these positions of honor and respectability have been gained by shady 'politics'—shall they be nicer in these matters than the mass of the whites? Shall they surrender these tangible evidences of the rise of their race to forward the goodhearted but hardly imperative demands of a crowd of women? Especially, too, of women who did not apparently know there were any Negroes on earth until they wanted their votes? Such logic may be faulty, but it is convincing to the mass of Negro voters."[13]

Most Negroes would agree with Gunnar Myrdal that they "are grossly discriminated against in what they get from politics just as they are in their exercise of the right to vote."[14] From the reformers, at least until the advent of Franklin D. Roosevelt in the White House, they got practically nothing—or, too often, a post-election kick in the face. What little they have obtained in the way of benefits has come most generally from machine politicians—often the

[13]W. E. B. Du Bois, *The Philadelphia Negro* (Philadelphia: University of Pennsylvania publication, 1899), pp. 383–84.

[14]Myrdal, op. cit., p. 497.

heads of corrupt machines—all the way from Republican President U. S. Grant to Democratic Mayor Ed Kelly of Chicago. To a people such as the American Negro, socially circumscribed and economically depressed, the most important spoils of politics are job opportunities in both public and private employment and on varying levels, protection of civil rights, equality of access to public facilities, and adequate provisions for housing, health, schools, and recreation. For a small but often politically influential group there is the added demand for protection of illicit practices, most frequently policy and other forms of gambling, and soft penalties for infractions of the law.

In terms of these objectives, the Negro probably attained his greatest recognition under the lush administrations of Big Bill Thompson of Chicago, 1915–23 and 1927–31. It was generally acknowledged that Mayor Thompson leaned heavily upon the Negro vote for his repeated victories at the polls. He discharged his obligation to this electorate to such a conspicuous extent that his political enemies—and they were many and powerful—dubbed the City Hall "Uncle Tom's Cabin." Unabashed, the mayor "did not hide his colored appointees in the back rooms but he gave them the regular places to which their positions entitled them. As the size of his majorities in the Black Belt increased at each election, so the amount of recognition he gave this section in the form of patronage also increased."[15]

Under Mayor Thompson's administration the Negro forged ahead politically as he had not done anywhere since Reconstruction. This was not alone a measure of the mayor's attitude or his political sagacity. It was primarily the result of an exceptionally astute Negro leadership which knew what it wanted and how to go about getting it. In Edward H. Wright the Negro community had a skilled and seasoned politician. Associated with him were others who, under his guidance, quickly learned the art and science of ward politics at a time when they could turn this knowledge to effective use. Thompson came to power during the period of accelerated expansion of the black belt. Attracted by the high industrial wages of World War I and driven from their homes by discrimination and lynch terror, tens of thousands of southern Negroes flocked to Chicago during the decade 1910–20. This influx more than doubled the black belt population, which rose from 44,103 to 109,458. In the next decade the Negro population continued to grow, expanding by 114 per

---

[15]Harold F. Gosnell, *Negro Politicians* (Chicago: University of Chicago Press, 1935), p. 55.

cent—to 233,903. It was these new voters, Republican by tradition, who, crowded into the black ghetto, supplied the base of operations for the Negro politicians and gave to the latter power in the city's politics through solid support of the Thompson faction in the Republican party.

The eagerness with which these migrants turned to political action gave ample refutation to the charge that their acceptance of disfranchisement in the South was an expression of apathy. Organized on a ward and precinct basis, they responded to the exhortations of their new leaders, who developed an enviably effective political machine. As a result, 77 per cent of the potential Negro vote was registered in 1920 as compared with 68 per cent for the city as a whole. This heavy registration gave to the Negro leaders the necessary bargaining power. In four primaries Thompson received more than 80 per cent of the Republican vote in the Second Ward, in which most of the Negroes were concentrated. In the 1927 primary he received 94 per cent of the party vote in that ward. This support was essential to his nominations and elections. Negro support of Thompson, Gosnell reports, survived "political landslides, economic depressions, graft revelations and other ground swells that affected voters in other parts of the city."[16]

It was not mere loyalty to the party of Lincoln and Thompson which consolidated the Negro vote behind the mayor. It was the conviction that Negroes were getting something out of this political solidarity. The ambitious young men were finding a new outlet for their talents. Thompson appointed Bishop Archibald E. Carey to the Civil Service Commission and Wright as assistant corporation counsel. These were just the opening appointments. In the various legal departments of the city, county, and state, Negroes were represented, not by one, but, in many instances, by several appointees. The number of Negro police, teachers, and other public servants was greatly increased and opportunities for promotion facilitated. Young Negro women who previously had but little opportunity to use their training as stenographers and clerks found openings in the civil service. Negro candidates, running on the Thompson ticket, were elected to the Board of Alderman and to both houses of the state legislature. One became the first Negro judge in the North elected on a city-wide basis. And finally it was in this period that, with Thompson's aid, Oscar De Priest was elected to Congress in 1928 as the first Negro representative since 1901.

[16]Ibid., p. 43.

What else did Negroes get out of their support of Thompson, whose regime has been widely publicized as the acme in corrupt machine politics? It was Thompson's boast that he started the playground movement in America when he established the first public playground in a predominantly Negro neighborhood. Yet recreational facilities for Negroes remained woefully inadequate. It was during one of Mayor Thompson's administrations that the disastrous race riot of 1919 occurred. Contributing to this outbreak were the insufficiency of recreational outlets, the lack of adequate housing to meet the needs of the swelling Negro population, as well as the economic fears and tensions which were the aftermath of the war. Thompson's regime further offered the protection which the Negro underworld demanded, but the activities of these black parasites were neither as vicious nor as remunerative as those of white gangsterdom which flourished in the Chicago post-war era. While the Negro made gains under Thompson, his regime was not an unmixed blessing.

Evaluating Mayor Thompson, two competent Negro social scientists concluded: "If Thompson was not a 'second Lincoln,' as enthusiastic supporters sometimes called him, at least he had treated his Negro followers more fairly than they had ever been treated before. If he allowed the community to be corrupted and had put into power Negroes connected with the underworld, he had nevertheless given recognition to the entire Negro population and offered it a hope for the future. If for the entire city he had been a buffoon and a corrupt politician, for Negroes he had made possible their own organization into ward machines which could and did demand concessions in return for support."[17]

What was the impact of this consistent support of the corrupt Thompson machine upon the political morality of the Negro community? Was venality and fraud any more conspicuous and widespread in the predominantly Negro Second and Third Wards than elsewhere in the city? "The impression is current that bribery and election corruption are prevalent in the sections inhabited largely by Negroes," Gosnell answers. "It is common for candidates to say that they lost in the 'Black Belt' because they did not spend money there. However, recounts, special investigations, and the records of prosecutions show that corruption and ballot thievery are as common in white as in colored neighborhoods. It is true that money is used on

[17]St. Clair Drake and Horace R. Cayton, *Black Metropolis* (New York: Harcourt, Brace & Co. 1945), p. 351.

election day in the near Southside wards, but most of this money is spent to pay election workers. . . . This practice extends over the entire city, and the money used for such purposes is usually furnished by the central headquarters of the party. . . . As to actual buying of votes and the paying of precinct election boards to falsify the returns, the evidence is meager and inconclusive."[18]

The temptation to irregularity was certainly present, but it was not always a matter of pecuniary gain. The Negro voter certainly has been no less hesitant than other citizens to align himself with corrupt political machines in his group interest. Thus in the Democratic primaries in 1946, Negro voters supported the Pendergast machine of Kansas City, Missouri, in a successful effort to retire Representative Roger C. Slaughter. The Missouri representative, as a key member of the important House Rules Committee, had been, perhaps, the one person most responsible for the refusal of that committee to submit to the House the bill for a permanent FEPC. He had boasted: "I sure as hell opposed the bill for a Fair Employment Practices Commission, and I'm proud of the fact that my vote [in the Rules Committee] was what killed it." The labor movement, through the CIO-PAC, joined in the fight against Slaughter. President Harry S. Truman personally intervened to assure the defeat of the man who had held up legislation which the President had expressed a desire to have enacted.

In the Fifth Congressional District which Slaughter represented there were 21,000 potential Negro voters, constituting approximately 15 per cent of the total vote. In the 1944 general election, Slaughter had been re-elected, with the support of the Pendergast machine, by a margin of 5193 votes. In view of the strength of the Negro vote in his district, his open hostility to FEPC seemed to indicate that Congressman Slaughter did not care for this vote or that he did not believe colored citizens were intelligent enough to vote in their own interest. In the next election he was defeated by a margin of 2783, with 7000 Negro votes cast against him. His vote in the thirty predominantly Negro precincts was negligible. In two of these precincts he received not a single vote, and the highest was 35. This solid Negro vote was the decisive factor in the defeat of Slaughter. In the subsequent general election, the Democratic nominee was defeated by the Republican candidate. Later, charges of fraud in the primary election were made. To the Negro voter, however, the important thing was the retirement from public life of a man who

[18]Harold F. Gosnell, op. cit., pp. 145-46.

sought to deny them equality of job opportunity, their paramount demand today.

Except for Chattanooga and Memphis, Tennessee, and San Antonio, Texas, Negroes have not been an important factor in recent years in the political machines of any southern city. What they have been able to get out of these political organizations is far less than what their brothers have been able to get out of political machines in Chicago, New York, Philadelphia, or Cleveland. While in San Antonio the Negro vote has been for years vital and, indeed, at one time the virtual political boss of the city was a Negro, little recognition has been given to the race in the form of patronage. The chief reward has been in the form of protection for the illicit practices of the Negro boss and his fellow gamesters. In Memphis, Negro supporters of Boss Crump point with pride to the overcrowded colored schools (better equipped and more numerous than elsewhere in the South), the recreation center, the shabby Negro park, the paved streets in the ghetto, the flourishing Negro businesses as evidences of Crump's beneficence and the opportunities for racial development afforded by his control of that city. In none of these cities have reform movements been able to make any appreciable headway, in part at least, because they have been unable or unwilling to offer Negro voters even as little as they now get from the machine. In Memphis, reformers commonly begin their attack upon Crump by focusing attention upon and discrediting his Negro supporters. This does not make for votes in the Negro community, even though many of its citizens may be dissatisfied with the present regime. Maury Maverick made this mistake in San Antonio in 1938 and alienated potential Negro support.

What is the price of the Negro's vote? What does he demand for it and what has he been able to buy with it? The price he can command depends upon a number of factors: the number and strategic location of qualified colored voters; the type of leadership and the degree of organization; the possibilities for favorable alliances, as with a labor or progressive group, or a political machine; the extent of division prevailing in the community at large and the competition for his ballot; the local political climate; the presence or absence of race as an issue in the campaign, and the degree of integration into the existing party structures. These are the factors which determine the value of the Negro's vote. How much can he buy with it? In general, he has not been able to get as much for his vote as have members of other groups. However, in some instances, as Bunche points out, the Negro population "has been given an opportunity to exert a political influence often far in excess of its numerical strength in the particular locality." Nowhere, however, has he been able to use the ballot to solve his basic social and economic problems. Amelioration—yes. Solution—no.

Challenging Representative Arthur W. Mitchell's charge on the floor of the House that the Republicans were "trying to buy back the Negro votes," Congressman Hamilton Fish queried: "I want to know whether the gentleman believes that the Negro vote is for sale." The Negro Democrat responded: "I may say to the gentlemen that every vote in the United States is for sale, not for money but for rights and privileges."

These rights and privileges, the Chicago *Defender,* one of the more influential Negro newspapers, set up as the price of the Negro vote: "We want an assurance of jobs in a free America. We want the right to vote for millions of our brethren disfranchised in Dixie. We want the 'freedom from fear' that the President spoke of in the Atlantic Charter and that to Negroes means total war upon lynching. We want the right to fight and die without the humiliation of segregation and discrimination in the armed forces. . . . Yes, the Negro vote in 1944 is for sale—but for a high price. No more will a measly dollar or two-dollar bill on a street corner buy our ballot. Today we can be bought only with post-war jobs and ballot rights. Today we cast our ballots for the men and the party that will give us the genuine political emancipation that we won only in part in 1865. Today we strike for full freedom."[19]

In placing a price on his ballot, the Negro does no more than any other voter. The operators of the coal mines and the stockholders in United States Steel are not likely to vote for candidates who run on a platform calling for nationalization of basic industries, however beneficial such a program might be for the common welfare. Nor are the directors of the light and power companies among the advocates of public ownership of power, as exemplified in the Tennessee Valley Authority. No more can the Negro be expected to vote for candidates whose program means curtailment of their economic opportunities or civil and political rights. The American people are apt to vote in the interest of the group with which they feel most closely identified, and they all fondly believe that the interests of their particular group are identical with the national welfare. And they fix the price of their ballot accordingly.

[19]Chicago *Defender,* July 13, 1944.

CHAPTER III

Experiment in Democracy

ALTHOUGH NEGRO SUFFRAGE IS AS OLD AS THE NATION, IT was not established as a national policy until the ratification of the Fifteenth Amendment in 1870. At one time or another free men of color were permitted to vote, if otherwise qualified, in each of the thirteen original colonies. The Constitution, under which the independent colonies were federated into a single nation—the United States of America—left to the several states the determination of the basic electoral qualifications. Indeed, the Constitution originally recognized the presence of the Negro only indirectly. It provided, as a compromise measure, that "representatives . . . shall be apportioned among the several states . . . according to their respective numbers, which shall be determined by adding to the whole number of free persons . . . three-fifths of all other persons," namely, the black slaves. Thus the heavy slaveholding states started off with an inflated representation in Congress based upon a large body of non-voting residents.

Even before the Revolution the movement to disfranchise the free Negro got under way. South Carolina disqualified Jews and Negroes in 1716. Virginia, in 1723, followed with a law depriving all Negroes, Indians, and mulattoes of the right to vote in any election. Georgia restricted voting to white males in 1761. Not until three quarters of a century later did this ban become general in the states of the new nation. As the profits from slave labor soared, the institution became more firmly rooted in the cotton states of the South. At the same time the fear of slave insurrections grew, particularly after the successful revolution of the enslaved blacks in Haiti in 1801. Meanwhile the hope, entertained by some of the leaders of the American Revolution, that slavery would gradually die out faded and the nation headed steadily toward the "irrepressible conflict" of 1861–65.

State after state restricted suffrage to white males: Delaware in 1792; Kentucky in 1799; Ohio in 1803; New Jersey in 1807; Maryland in 1810; Louisiana in 1812; Connecticut, alone among the New England states, in 1814; Tennessee in 1834, and North Carolina in 1835, four years after Nat Turner's bloody and fear-inspiring revolt in Virginia. Pennsylvania followed in 1838 and Florida in 1845. New York, in 1821, demanded of Negro voters a property qualification not required of white voters. The newly admitted states, northern as well as southern, banned Negro voting.

"Thus," says Albert Bushnell Hart, "in the 84 years from the Revolution to the Civil War, from Negro suffrage in all but two out of thirteen commonwealths, things had come to the point where he could vote only in five New England states, and (under special restrictions) in New York."[1]

The vote of the free Negro was everywhere small and in most places insignificant. It was a limited though growing class, numbering in 1860 nearly half a million throughout the country. Free persons of color accounted for something over 10 per cent of the total Negro population. Within the ranks of this group was a wide range of economic and cultural levels. While most of the free Negroes were poverty-stricken and poorly schooled, though by no means entirely illiterate, there were many who had attained property (including human property), education, and culture.

North Carolina was the last of the original slave states to ban voting by free Negroes. Sentiment against disfranchisement was so strong, especially in the mountainous western counties, that the measure was barely passed by the constitutional assembly of 1835 by a vote of 66 to 61. A switch of three votes would have retained the ballot for the free Negroes of that state. This constitutional provision disfranchised several hundred colored men who were credited with voting "prudently and judiciously." Their vote had been eagerly sought, and in some communities they were reported as holding a balance of power. Politicians had wooed the Negro vote as ardently as any other. "The opposing candidates," a contemporary recalled, "for the nonce oblivious to social distinction and intent only on catching votes, hobnobbed with the men and swung corners with dusky damsels at election balls."[2]

[1] Albert Bushnell Hart, "Negro Suffrage," Boston *Transcript*, March 24, 1906, reprinted as pamphlet by Niagara Movement.

[2] Judge Buxton, *Reminiscences of the Bench and Fayettesville Bar*, quoted by John Hope Franklin, *The Free Negro in North Carolina* (Chapel Hill: University of North Carolina Press, 1943), p. 106.

Resistance to Negro suffrage, both North and South, continued throughout the Civil War and into Reconstruction. Proposals for extending the right to vote to Negroes were defeated in Connecticut, Wisconsin, and Minnesota in 1865; in Nebraska in 1866; in Ohio in 1867, and in Michigan in 1868. The South, defeated, demoralized, and bitterly opposed to the recognition of the free status of the Negro, pointed to these actions by northern states as additional justification for withholding the ballot from the freedmen. With such sentiment in the North, the South might have averted or postponed the Fifteenth Amendment had not the Black Codes, enacted by eight states between 1865–67, made plain the intent to re-establish the status quo ante, to retain the conditions of slavery even after the abolition of the institution.

Reconstruction was something new in American history, an eventuality entirely unanticipated by the Constitution. There were no precedents, no established rules to follow, nothing to guide the nation in readjusting to the aftermath of the Civil War. The war had destroyed the old order irrevocably and created a political vacuum. Despite anti-Negro sentiment in the North and Lincoln's early insistence that the sole purpose of the war was to maintain the Union, with or without slavery, it soon became apparent that emancipation was inevitable. The South from the beginning drew the issue clearly. The Confederate states were fighting to maintain the South's "peculiar institution," to protect the slaveholders' property rights in human chattel. The slogan, "States' Rights," had no other meaning than the planters' right to hold slaves. All the conciliatory protestations from the North that slavery was not the issue were realistically discounted.

As the war drew to a close, enlightened leaders of the Confederacy recognized that, whatever the military outcome, slavery was at an end. The great American anachronism could not be continued. In response to a proposal that the Confederacy arm the Negroes to fight against the North on promise of freedom for those who enlisted, General Robert E. Lee wrote: "We should not expect slaves to fight for prospective freedom when they can secure it at once by going to the enemy, in whose service they incur no greater risk than in ours. The reasons that induce me to recommend the employment of Negro troops at all render the effect of the measures I have suggested upon slavery immaterial, and in my opinion the best means of securing the efficiency and fidelity of this auxiliary force would be to accompany the measure with a well digested plan of gradual and general emancipation. As that will be the result of the continuance of the war, and will certainly occur if the enemy succeeds, it seems to me most advisable to do it at once, and thereby obtain all the benefits that will accrue to our cause."[3]

Urged by Abolitionists and confronted with military necessity, Abraham Lincoln issued the Emancipation Proclamation on January 1, 1863, and five days later the enlistment of black men in the Union Army was formally authorized by the Secretary of War. Before the war's end nearly 200,000 black fighting men had enrolled in the armed services of the United States. It was then no longer possible to subordinate the slavery issue. It was not an abstraction, or a theory of government, or a remote principle for which these men fought. They fought for freedom. And their leaders, at least, knew that freedom could be maintained only through a recognition of their civil and political rights as citizens.

The assassination of Lincoln placed Andrew Johnson in the White House. President Johnson was a representative of that paradoxical class of anti-slavery, anti-secession, and anti-Negro poor whites of the South. This class hated slavery and the planter slaveholders on economic rather than ethical grounds. But most of all they hated the black slaves whose competition they feared in a bountiful land in which scarcity had been artificially created by the economic and political monopoly tightly held in the genteel hands of the southern oligarchy. The war crushed this monopoly and might have permanently destroyed it had Johnson and his fellow poor whites measured up to the opportunity confronting them.

Dismayed by the evident intention of the embittered planters to retain the essence of slavery even without its form, the Abolitionists, who composed the left wing of the triumphant Republican party, and the Negro leaders pressed for suffrage rights for the freedmen. Johnson clung tenaciously to his provincial prejudices, insisting that black men could have no part in Reconstruction. His stand brought him into bitter conflict with the Republican Congress in which Charles Sumner of Massachusetts, in the Senate, and Thaddeus Stevens of Pennsylvania, in the House, were leading the fight to take control of Reconstruction out of the President's hands.

Meanwhile, on February 7, 1866, Frederick Douglass, the great Negro leader, headed a delegation of eminent colored men to urge the President to support the fight to extend the franchise to the freedmen. The President was blunt in his rejection of the proposal

[3]Quoted by W. E. B. Du Bois, *Black Reconstruction* (New York: Harcourt, Brace & Co., 1935), p. 118.

and, after pre-empting most of the interview period, refused to listen to any reply from the Negro spokesmen. Douglass, who was no stranger to the White House, resented Johnson's unpolitic refusal to consider seriously the case for the Negro. Lincoln had received him cordially and sought his advice. Stung by President Johnson's unqualified rejection of the proposals, the delegation responded in an open letter prepared by the ex-slave leader.

"The first point to which we feel bound to take exception," their statement challenged, "is your attempt to found a policy opposed to our enfranchisement, upon the alleged ground of an existing hostility on the part of the former slaves toward the poor white people of the South. We admit the existence of this hostility and hold that it is entirely reciprocal. But you obviously commit an error by drawing an argument from an incident of slavery and making it a basis for a policy adapted to a state of freedom. The hostility between the whites and blacks of the South is easily explained. It has its root and sap in the relation of slavery, and was incited on both sides by the cunning of the slave masters. Those masters secured their ascendancy over both the poor whites and blacks by putting enmity between them. They divided both to conquer each. . . . Now, sir, you cannot but perceive, that the cause of this hatred removed, the effect must be removed also. Slavery is abolished. The cause of this antagonism is removed, and you must see, that it is altogether illogical to legislate from slaveholding and slave-driving premises for a people whom you have repeatedly declared your purpose to maintain in freedom. Besides, even if it were true as you allege, that the hostility of the blacks toward the poor whites must necessarily project itself into a state of freedom, and that this enmity between the races is even more intense in a state of freedom than in a state of slavery, in the name of Heaven, we reverently ask how can you, in view of your professed desire to promote the welfare of the black man, deprive him of all means of defense and clothe him whom you regard as his enemy in the panoply of political power?"[4]

Johnson expressed this same distrust and fear of the Negro to a fellow Tennessean, warning that "the Negro will vote with his late master, whom he does not hate, rather than with the non-slaveholding white man, whom he does hate."[5] The President seemed unable to discard the prejudices of his class. He was bitter against the

[4]Frederick Douglass, *Life and Times* (Hartford: Park Publishing Co., 1882), pp. 391–92.

[5]Paul Lewinson, *Race, Class and Party* (New York: Oxford University Press, 1932), p. 24.

big planters, some of whom, like Wade Hampton of South Carolina, threatened to "vote" the Negroes if enfranchised. He would have placed the power formerly held by the planter class into the hands of the poor whites. To have achieved and secured such an objective would have required the collaboration of the hated blacks. There were Negro leaders who recognized this imperative, if the planters were to be permanently displaced as the political mentors of the region. But not Johnson, and, indeed, very few of his class.

Johnson, claiming Reconstruction as an executive prerogative, plunged stubbornly ahead with his plan. However, it soon became evident that the leaders of the old South were still in the saddle, arrogantly refusing to recognize the dawn of a new day. The Negroes were kept in a state of subjection and denied all civil and political rights. Nor were Johnson's poor whites, ill prepared for political control, making any appreciable headway. They turned their backs upon their natural allies, the black workers, and, despite political antipathies, joined the planter class in the suppression of the freedmen.

Finally Congress, under leadership of Sumner and Stevens, took control, asserting congressional responsibility for Reconstruction. A series of Reconstruction Acts was passed in 1867, dividing the late Confederacy into five military districts and providing for a constitutional convention in each of the ten unreconstructed states. (Tennessee had previously been re-admitted to the union.) The conventions were to be elected by universal male suffrage, disqualifying only those who refused to swear allegiance to the government of the United States. Democracy, sustained by federal authority, was at long last to be given an opportunity in the South. Never before had an election in the South been based on so broad a suffrage. Even more than ratification of the Thirteenth Amendment did the Reconstruction Acts dramatize the end of the blighted era.

"The South was aghast," Lewinson recounts. "According to an estimate in the Senate, 672,000 Negroes had been enfranchised, as against a total possible white electorate of 925,000. But some 100,-000 of these whites had been disfranchised, and 200,000 disqualified for office."[6] Immediately the South prepared to invoke its traditional weapon against democratic encroachment—nullification.

Meanwhile, the black freedman, protected by federal troops and guided by the agents of the Freedmen's Bureau (a post-war federal employment, welfare, and educational agency bitterly resented by

[6] Lewinson, op. cit., p. 41.

the white South), prepared for the first mass voting by black men in the history of the nation. This was the beginning of a new era in which the former slaves were to achieve recognition as men and to be endowed with the political instrument for the protection of their new status as American citizens. Stripped of their shackles, the black men of the South stood ready to embark upon a noble experiment in democracy.

Sulking and embittered, the white South set about the task of sabotaging the constitutional conventions. A boycott of the elections was proposed. Failing to carry through with a successful boycott, the former slaveholders voted against calling the conventions. As a result of these tactics, the number of registered Negro voters exceeded the whites in five of the ten states under military government —South Carolina, Alabama, Florida, Mississippi, and Louisiana. In Georgia the white voters outnumbered the registered freedmen by the slim margin of 1165. In Virginia, North Carolina, Arkansas, and Texas the white majorities were more substantial. For the first time in the South, ballots were cast by more than a million voters, including 703,500 Negroes and 660,200 whites. In the last preceding general election in 1860 there had been 722,000 voters, all white.

"The elections which reconstructed the South under the Congressional plan were fair and honest elections," Du Bois asserts, "and probably never before were such democratic elections held in the South and never since such fair elections."[7] Despite the Negro majorities in five states, only in South Carolina did black men constitute a majority of the delegates to the constitutional convention. The Louisiana delegation was, by agreement, evenly divided. In the other eight states the conventions were controlled by white majorities ranging from 60 to 90 per cent. There was no evident attempt on the part of the freedmen to impose "Negro domination" on the South. They did not pick the candidates by race, but voted for those whom they believed best able to represent honestly their interests.

The conventions drafted new constitutions and set up governments in conformity with the requirements of the congressional plan for Reconstruction. State government in the South was liberalized not only by the elimination of the slave codes and other discriminatory legislation, but also by the inclusion of long-overdue reforms. Under these new governments public schools were established, election requirements broadened, and women's rights recognized. Civil-rights legislation was passed. The Fourteenth and Fifteenth Amend-

[7]Du Bois, op. cit., p. 372.

ments were ratified. Land reform, through the breakup of big plantations, was proposed. Wage legislation was sought.

The demand for land, for "forty acres and a mule," as a necessary concomitant of emancipation, had been stimulated by military orders during the course of the war, under terms of which the ex-slaves were granted certain rights to the land on which they and their forebears had been settled for generations. In Congress, Sumner and Stevens sought to make permanent and secure the war-time orders and to open up new lands for settlement and ownership by the freedmen. In legislative halls, in conventions, in the press, and on the land the Negroes themselves voiced this demand. "The main question to which the Negroes returned again and again was the problem of owning land," Du Bois records. "It was ridiculed as un-reasonable and unjust to the impoverished landholders of the South, and as part of the desire for revenge which the North had."[8] In the end the plans fell through. There was too much resistance in the North to the idea of confiscation of the lands of the former slave-holders and to aiding small farmers with federal grants. Negro fami-lies who had settled on the land in accordance with military orders were dispossessed and faced freedom as an uprooted, landless group of displaced persons.

The concept of federal aid to education was introduced by the Reconstruction legislators. Booker T. Washington later remarked: "Even as a youth, and later in manhood, I had the feeling that it was cruelly wrong in the central government, at the beginning of our freedom, to fail to make some provisions for the general education of our people in addition to what the states might do, so that the people would be the better prepared for the duties of citizenship."[9]

The effort was made to establish a new equalitarian order. This forlorn attempt immediately became the object of bitter and unre-lenting attack which continues even to this day—three quarters of a century after the overthrow of the Reconstruction governments by counterrevolutionary forces. To justify this subversion of congres-sional Reconstruction, a great volume of legend and myth has been evolved to distort and discredit the attempt of a poor and disad-vantaged people to participate in the government under which they lived. Tales of the horrors of "black domination" have become a part of the folk material of the white South and are now widely

[8]Ibid., p. 368.
[9]Booker T. Washington, *Up from Slavery* (New York: Doubleday, Page & Co., 1924), p. 83.

propagated as "history." Charges of wholesale corruption, wild extravagance, and criminal inefficiency have been accepted with little challenge. That these "black-and-tan" Reconstruction governments were perfect is not here maintained. Of corruption and incompetence there was doubtlessly aplenty, but the freedmen had neither the political know-how nor the audacity to match the corrupt practices of their contemporary, Boss Tweed of New York, nor their successors, Huey Long of Louisiana and Theodore (The Man) Bilbo of Mississippi. Yet no one seeks to establish the incapacity of the white race for self-rule by pointing to the failures of some of its representatives. While historians have sought to blame black politicians for Reconstruction failing, there is ample evidence that this propertyless class played a minor role in the corrupt practices of the post-war period in which there was nationwide relaxation of standards of political morality. Corruption in the South was part of a current national pattern in which a new and ruthless capitalism was engaged in wholesale bribery of federal, state, and local legislators, administrators, and judges, in which buccaneers of the era competed among themselves for the purchase of legislative and judicial favors for their railroad building and corporate schemes. Their agents were everywhere corrupting whomever they could. But the bribes, as well as the prizes, were bigger in the North and West than in the South.

William Hannibal Thomas, the caustic critic of his own race, exculpates the black politicians, of whom he was one in South Carolina. "When the civil governments of the South were finally reconstructed," he recorded, "the white people of that section and their political sympathizers of the North sought to discredit them with the cry of Negro domination. It was a baseless charge. . . . Its sole plausibility lay in the fact that Negroes were voters, and held various subordinate offices under the new order of things. . . . The Constitutions of the reconstructed states were framed by white men, under the direction and with the approval of the best legal intelligence of America. The majority of state executive offices and the most important were always filled by white men. The congressional delegations were composed of the same class of individuals. The leading men in both branches of every state legislature were representatives of the dominant race. . . . These white men planned and directed the financial and civic policy of their several states. It was they who created a bonded indebtedness, negotiated loans, and levied and collected taxes, disbursed revenue, and therefore they, and they alone, were responsible for the good or evil wrought by a government of unique exigencies. The Negro had a place in this non-descript scheme, but his place was that of a registering factor of the schemes of white men whom he blindly trusted and for whose culpability he is now vindictively execrated."[10]

In his study of the Negro in the reconstruction of Virginia, Taylor concludes: "The Negroes of Virginia, however, can not be charged with the mistakes in the reconstruction of that state. White men, the majority of whom were Virginians, were the officeholders during Reconstruction. The number of Negroes elected to office never became sufficient to determine any definite policy of the government, except in a few cases of exercising a balance of power between militant factions. Those Negroes who attained office, moreover, were generally persons of intelligence or common sense and gave a good account of themselves."[11]

Sharing the blame with the black politicians were the white Northerners who had migrated South after the war and came to be known as "carpetbaggers." That some of these were self-seeking opportunists is undoubtedly true. But among them also were men whose high aim was to introduce democracy into an area in which such concepts of government had been alien. The historian, Albert B. Hart, exonerates the carpetbaggers, who, he says, "though powerful in organization, were but a few hundred in number; and the worst features of these governments were due to the southern white voters, born on the soil, acting in conjunction with the worst element of the Negro vote. It was not a savory period in American politics. From 1869 to 1871, Boss Tweed had his serpent grip on New York City and squeezed out more millions than were stolen in the entire South."[12]

The articulate white South, the defeated planter class, loudly objected to the Reconstruction governments, denouncing the freedmen as unlettered and uncouth barbarians, the northern carpetbaggers as vultures preying upon the prostrate body of the South, and the southern collaborators, the scalawags, as base renegades to their race and culture. Thus these new governments were launched and conducted in an atmosphere of hate and hostility. Every obstacle was thrown in the way. Everything was done to assure failure. "The

[10]William Hannibal Thomas, *The American Negro* (New York: Macmillan Co., 1901), pp. 307–08.

[11]Alrutheus A. Taylor, *The Negro in the Reconstruction of Virginia* (Washington: Association for Study of Negro Life and History, 1926), p. 285.

[12]Hart, op. cit.

former slaves," Myrdal, the Swedish sociologist, observes, "started their new life as free citizens with a solid mistrust against them, which was crystallized into an elaborate political philosophy, powerful even in its partial disorganization. The very idea of awarding Negroes suffrage was, to the average Southerner, preposterous. The white South *wanted the Negroes to fail as freedmen* and saw in their failure a confirmation of their own wisdom and the Northerners' folly."[13]

What of the black men who served their respective states and the nation as officeholders in that period? Unquestionably many of them were ill prepared for the tasks they undertook. None of them had had any experience in government. Some of them were unlettered. Others were susceptible to bribe offers. But some of them were men of exceptional quality—intelligent, well trained, poised, and principled. Men like Francis L. Cardoza and Robert Brown Elliott of South Carolina, Hiram Revels and B. K. Bruce of Mississippi, P. B. S. Pinchback and Oscar J. Dunn of Louisiana, J. T. Rapier of Alabama, Henry Turner and Tunis Campbell of Georgia, Jonathan Gibbs of Florida, James H. Harris, James Walker Hood, and George W. White of North Carolina, and Norris Wright Cuney of Texas. Of the twenty-two Negroes who served in Congress, ten were college-trained. These shared with less able men an intense desire to advance the status of the freedmen, to make him a citizen in fact as well as in name.

The early Negro legislators were totally lacking in vindictiveness toward the former slaveholders. Indeed, they were among the advocates of amnesty for the defeated leaders of the Confederacy. According to one historian, "The legislation proposed and discussed by the Negro congressmen concerned not only the removal of the political disabilities of the former secessionists, the abrogation of undesirable laws or privileges in the investigation of the political methods used in certain states, but also the direction of attention to conditions which merited legislative enactment—such as granting civil rights to the Negro, protection of economic interests, state and local improvements, appropriations for the construction of buildings, the promotion of public works and racial welfare, and also national aid for the educational development of black and white."[14]

While the South harped upon the ignorance and incapacity of

---

[13]Myrdal, op. cit., p. 445.
[14]William F. Nowlin, *The Negro in American National Politics* (Boston: The Stratford Co., 1931), p. 20.

the Negro, the greater fear was of intelligence and ability, Dunning and Du Bois agree. "The Negroes were disliked and feared," Dunning asserts, "almost in exact proportion to their manifestation of intelligence and capacity."[15] And Du Bois: "If there was one thing that South Carolina feared more than bad Negro government, it was good Negro government."[16]

No longer legally empowered to hold the Negro in economic and political bondage, the white South devised other means to thwart the orderly development of democracy in that region long ruled by the slave oligarchy. The die-hard white Southerners resorted to gangsterism. They went underground and developed a subversive organization. Its purpose, the overthrow of constituted authority. Its method, terror and murder. Its legacy, blight and Hitlerism. The records of the congressional investigation of this gang, known as the Ku-Klux Klan, reveal one of the foulest stories in American history. It is a record of fraud, deceit, intimidation, arson, raiding, kidnaping, mayhem, and violent death to innocent men, women, and children. The methods used were the same as those which later enabled Mussolini to seize power in Italy and Hitler to overthrow the Weimar Republic; the motivations and objectives, essentially the same.

In the face of this assault, and with diminishing support from the North, the Reconstructionists were forced to yield ground. Supplementing the undercover work of the Klan was the organization of a so-called Conservative or "white man's party" whose ranks were swelled by amnesty acts restoring citizenship to ex-Confederates. The party entered into the political arena and won elections after large numbers of Negro voters had been intimidated by Klan violence. In South Carolina and Louisiana dual governments were set up following the "elections" of 1876. The combined violence of the Klansmen and the virulent anti-Negro propaganda of the Conservatives threatened a renewal of the war—this time a war between the races in the South. There were no limits to which certain elements in the South would not go in order to eliminate the Negro as a political factor and to restore as nearly as possible the old order.

The southern experiment in democracy was doomed by the fateful compromise of 1877—a compromise between northern and southern white folk, with democracy and the Negro as the sacrificial victims. Following the disputed Hayes-Tilden election of 1876, a deal was

[15]William A. Dunning, *Reconstruction,* quoted by Lewinson, op. cit., p. 36.
[16]Du Bois, op. cit., p. 428.

made between northern Republicans and white southern leadership by terms of which federal troops were to be withdrawn from the South and the white people of that region permitted to handle the question of Negro rights and suffrage in their own wanton fashion. Samuel J. Tilden of New York, Democrat, and Rutherford B. Hayes of Ohio, Republican, were the rival claimants of the presidency. An arbitration commission finally awarded to Hayes the disputed electoral votes of four states, which gave him the office.

This compromise, writes Paul H. Buck, "pleased those northerners who still dreaded the prospect of a national Democratic administration, by placing Hayes in the White House to purify the Republican party. Hayes was tacitly committed to the restoration of white rule in the South, and southerners seemed perfectly satisfied with their share of the spoils. . . . The Federal troops were removed from the South. Carpetbag governments toppled. White men governed from Virginia to Texas, a vast Democratic area, anti-Republican in politics, in which the Negro became again what he had been in 1860, the ward of the dominant race."[17]

What was the meaning of Reconstruction?

To the Bourbon white South it was a tragic era. A period of regional humiliation. To substantiate their position, white Southerners fabricated tales of "black terror." While expressed in terms of race, this propaganda concealed basic economic motives and ageless psychological considerations which stemmed from a deep-seated tribal resentment of the fact that Negroes possessed the franchise rather than from any actual deeds of Negro officeholders. The southern reaction reflected the restless foreboding and bad conscience of the South for past crimes against the Negro. Even today the distorted memories of the period are, according to Myrdal, "in a sense cherished. They serve a vital defensive function to the white South. . . . They are, in fact, symbols of regional allegiance."[18]

To the Negro it was a noble experiment—the one period in American history in which a serious attempt was made to make democracy work, to bring the national practices in line with the national ideals. Du Bois, the eloquent defender of the Negro's role in those years, defines the historic period as follows:

"Reconstruction was an economic revolution on a mighty scale and with world-wide reverberation. Reconstruction was not simply

---

[17]Paul H. Buck, *The Road to Reunion* (Boston: Little, Brown & Co., 1937), pp. 100–02.

[18]Myrdal, op. cit., p. 446.

a fight between the white and black races in the South or between master and ex-slave. . . . It was much more subtle. . . . It was a vast labor movement of ignorant, earnest, and bewildered black men whose faces had been ground in the mud by three awful centuries of degradation and who now staggered forward blindly in blood and tears amid petty division, hate and hurt, and surrounded by every disaster of war and industrial upheaval. Reconstruction was a vast labor movement of ignorant, muddled and bewildered white men who had been disinherited of land and labor and fought a long battle with sheer subsistence, hanging on the edge of poverty, eating clay and chasing slaves and now lurching up to manhood. Reconstruction was the turn of white northern migration southward to new and sudden economic opportunity which followed the disaster and dislocation of war, and an attempt to organize capital and labor on a new pattern and build a new economy. Finally, Reconstruction was a desperate effort of a dislodged, maimed, impoverished and ruined oligarchy and monopoly to restore an anachronism in economic organization by force, fraud and slander, in defiance of law and order, and in the face of a great labor movement of white and black, and in bitter strife with a new capitalism and a new political framework."[19]

To the North it was all a sentimental mistake to be forgotten and forgiven. The Republicans who sponsored the Fifteenth Amendment and congressional Reconstruction were divided into two distinct groups: first, the exponents of abolition-democracy, who believed that all men were "created free and equal" and sought to implement that idea in national politics; and second, the minions of Big Business, who wanted to secure control of the national administration in order to expand, unhampered as in ante-bellum days, by the political obstruction of the South's feudal economy. Having succeeded in this latter objective through coalition with southern reaction, northern Republicanism is content to let Reconstruction lie dead, buried, and forgotten.

[19]Du Bois, op. cit., pp. 346–47.

CHAPTER IV

The Great Blackout

IN THE YEAR OF THE GREAT COMPROMISE—1877—
Frederick Douglass, then sixty years old, accepted an appointment
from the new President, Rutherford B. Hayes. He became, to the
utter dismay of the old-line Washingtonians, United States marshal
of the District of Columbia. At that time Douglass had been for a
generation the great Negro leader through the Abolition crusade and
the Reconstruction experiment. With Wendell Phillips, Arthur and
Lewis Tappan, and William Lloyd Garrison, he had campaigned
for Abolition. He had urged President Lincoln to admit Negroes
into the armed services and to declare emancipation as a war aim.
He had counseled Sumner and Stevens in the drive to push through
the war amendments. Though he had refused to go South and run
for Congress, as he had been urged, he had become the leading
politician of the race. To him was attributed the oft-repeated warning: "The Republican party is the ship; all else is the sea."

As early as 1865 Douglass had demanded "immediate, uncon-
ditional and universal enfranchisement of the black men, in every
state in the Union." Prodding the Massachusetts Anti-Slavery
Society, which had given evidences of having become laggard in this
demand, Douglass pleaded: "I fear that if we fail to do it now, if
Abolitionists fail to press it now, we may not see, for centuries to
come, the same disposition that exists at this moment. Hence, I say,
now is the time to press for this right. . . . Without this, his [the
Negro's] liberty is a mockery; without this, you might as well almost
retain the old name of slavery for his condition; for, in fact, if he is
not the slave of the individual master, he is the slave of society, and
holds his liberty as a privilege, not as a right. He is at the mercy of
the mob, and has no means of protecting himself."

If, in 1877, Douglass made any indignant outcry against the compromise which subverted all that he had struggled for throughout his free life, he failed to record it in his autobiography. Not until years later, in the last edition of his *Life and Times,* did he castigate the Republican party for its appeasement of the southern Bourbons. And even then he remained loyal to the party. Reconstruction had been abandoned, its goal unattained. And the Negro in the South left alone to carry on an uneven contest. The policies of abolition-democracy had been ditched and its leading advocates, Charles Sumner, Horace Greeley, and Carl Schurz, had bolted the Republican party, which under President U. S. Grant became more openly the vehicle of Big Business. Douglass remained loyal and helped to hold the new Negro voters in line for Grant in the 1872 election because "there was no path out of the Republican party that did not lead directly into the Democratic party—away from our friends and directly to our enemies."[1]

Out in a West Virginia village, Malden, a young Negro was, in 1877, in his second year of teaching other eager colored youths the A B C's of living as well as of the alphabet. He had only recently finished his training under General Samuel C. Armstrong at Hampton Institute in Virginia. Now, back in his home town, he was beginning his life's work. He was Booker T. Washington, earnest, youthful, and ambitious, who, like Frederick Douglass, had been born a slave. As Douglass had been the leader during the early struggles of the Negro in the ante-bellum years and during the period of the aborted Reconstruction, Washington was destined to be the leader during the period of the Great Blackout.

The blackout of the Negro's political activity in the South did not descend suddenly and dramatically with the consummation of the compromise. The controlling interests of the nation had given the white South the green light. His support from the North withdrawn, the unschooled Negro faced the bitter test alone.

"Negroes did not surrender the ballot easily or immediately," Du Bois affirms. "They continued to hold remnants of political power in South Carolina and Florida, Louisiana, in parts of North Carolina, in Texas, Tennessee and Virginia. Black Congressmen came out of the South until 1895 and black legislators served as late as 1896. But it was a losing battle, with public opinion, industry, wealth, and religion against them. Their own leaders decried 'politics' and preached submission. All their efforts toward manly self-assertion

[1]Frederick Douglass, op. cit., p. 424.

were distracted by defeatism and counsels of despair, backed by the
powerful propaganda of a religion which taught meekness, sacrifice
and humility.

"But the decisive influence was the systematic and overwhelming
economic pressure. Negroes who wanted work must not dabble in
politics. Negroes who wanted to increase their income must not
agitate the Negro problem. Positions of influence were only open to
those Negroes who were certified as being 'safe and sane,' and their
careers were closely scrutinized and passed upon. From 1880 on-
ward, in order to earn a living, the American Negro was compelled
to give up his political power."[2]

At first the white South did not challenge the legality of Negro
suffrage. Evasion of the law, rather than repeal, was the tactic. It
was not until fifteen years later that the movement to eradicate this
electorate through the adoption of new state constitutions got under
way. But there was always steady and unrelenting pressure to nullify
the Negro's vote. Terror became established as an instrument of the
electoral process. After the Bourbons had things well in hand they
began to develop other devices to repress, discount, and eliminate
Negro voting. Violence and economic pressure were not the only
instruments used to establish and maintain "white supremacy." All
the old anti-democratic devices were refurbished and new frauds
spawned.

To achieve their objectives, the Bourbons revived the ancient
gerrymander, redistricting election areas in such a manner as to
dissipate the Negro's voting strength. Elaborate schemes of keeping
the colored voter away from the polls were employed. The persistent
and lucky ones who arrived at the right polling place (which may
have been relocated overnight without any warning to Negro voters)
were confronted with other difficulties. They were required to produce their registration certificates which had been issued six months
before the election. If these tests were met they were hurried into
the election booth, if any, and given two minutes to mark a complicated ballot. As the election machinery was in the hands of the
dominant whites, the counting of the ballots was their responsibility.
The rest was easy.

New disabilities, aimed at alleged weaknesses of the Negro, were
imposed as restrictions upon registration and voting. Arrest and conviction for such offenses as petty larceny and wife beating disqualified prospective voters. Then, as now, it was easy to get convictions

[2]Du Bois, op. cit., pp. 692–93.

against Negroes on flimsy evidence. Registration was made a complicated ordeal, requiring not only literacy but above-average intelligence to fill out the forms. White voters were assisted by registrars and other election officials. There was no one to assist the Negro voters. Witnesses—white, of course—were required to attest the "good character" of the applicant.

It remained for South Carolina to devise the most bewildering trick to confuse Negro voters. This state, in which Negro political power was most firmly established, was among the last in which the white counterrevolution succeeded. From 1868 until 1873 there were Negro majorities in the state legislature, although the whites, throughout Reconstruction, retained majorities in the state Senate. As late as 1878 there were 62 Negroes and 78 whites in both houses. The white majority in the Senate, however, was 14 to 4. After the triumph of the counterrevolution, South Carolina not only adopted the devices commonly used in other states of the late Confederacy, but also developed the notorious eight-ballot-box trick. Under this law a separate ballot was required for each office, and the voter was required to place each ballot in the right box for the office voted. Thus, if there were eight offices to be filled, there were eight different ballots and eight different ballot boxes. A ballot in the wrong box was void. The boxes were supposed to be properly labeled. It was, however, an easy matter to shift the boxes or the labels upon the approach of Negro voters.

These devious devices, supplemented by economic pressures, intimidation, and violence, succeeded in drastically reducing the number of Negro voters. Dunning estimated that by 1884 only half as many Negroes were voting in South Carolina as in 1876. In Louisiana a third of the Negro voters had been eliminated during that eight-year period, and the number of Negro voters in Mississippi had been reduced by 25 per cent. By 1900, he concluded, the Negro vote had practically disappeared in the South.[3]

Though reduced and repressed, the Negro vote had not been entirely eliminated. Rather it had been quarantined by the closed ranks of the majority race. In order to re-establish what they called "white supremacy," class interests were submerged. The poor whites, beguiled into believing that some magic superiority attached to their pale complexions, joined with others of their "blood"—the Bourbon planters and the burgeoning industrialists—in pushing the Negro back into the political and economic ditch from which he was striv-

[3]William A. Dunning, *Undoing*, quoted by Paul Lewinson, op. cit., p. 68.

ing to emerge. As long as this united front held, the quarantine was effective. The Negro in the South was isolated and rendered politically impotent.

No sooner had the South achieved its primary objective—the repression of Negro suffrage—than the white façade began to crack. "By the middle 1890's the acquiescence of the white Southern masses was at an end," writes William G. Carleton. "The hard times, the deflation policies of the federal government, and the cumulative effects of a too-rapid industrialization of the country goaded them into passionate rebellion. They could no longer be silenced by the old conservative cry of 'Nigger.' In some areas of the South, Populism spread like a prairie fire. In others, the small farmers and poor whites bored within the Democratic party and gained control of the party organization."[4]

The rise of Populism created competition for votes. Both the Bourbon Democrats and the leaders of the new poor man's party realized that, once in the ballot box, the vote of a Negro was indistinguishable from that of a white man. With both groups bidding for his vote, the Negro again became a balance-of-power factor in southern politics. The laws which had been enacted to prevent this development proved inadequate in the face of the political schism within the ranks of the white voters. In some states Populism made a real, if short-lived, effort to effect a fundamental political coalition of white and black workers. In North Carolina a fusion of Populists and Republicans (composed chiefly of Negroes and poor whites in the mountainous western counties) gained control of both houses of the state legislature. Before the tide receded, North Carolina, in 1896 and again in 1898, sent to Congress George H. White, who was the last Negro elected to Congress from the South. In Texas, Norris Wright Cuney, the astute Negro leader, first opposed but later threw his support to a Populist candidate for governor.

The Populists, reversing the southern tradition, sought political equality for the Negro, Carleton observes. He quotes Tom Watson, the leader of the party in Georgia: "The accident of color can make no difference in the interests of farmers, croppers, and laborers. . . . You are kept apart that you may be separately fleeced of your earnings."[5] Later Watson turned his venomous rhetoric against the Negro. During this decade the Negro vote was divided between the

[4]William G. Carleton, "The Conservative South—A Political Myth," *Virginia Quarterly Review*, Vol. 22, No. 2.
[5]Ibid.

Bourbons and the Populists. While many, comprehending the need for a coalition with their fellow white workers, supported the Populists, others harbored the old hostility, fears, and suspicions of the poor whites. Lacking the vitality to withstand the onslaughts of the Bourbons, the coalition collapsed. The poor whites were again seduced by the blandishments of the white supremacists.

Alarmed by the Populist revolt, the southern politicians renewed their efforts to eliminate the Negro as a voter. But now it was no longer fear of the Negro vote which motivated the Bourbons. It was something bigger and, potentially, far more revolutionary. "The repressive activities against the Negro of the 90's and the early 1900's," Bunche points out, "were stimulated no longer by fear of the Negro, but by fear of the unity of the Negroes with whites. The Negro, by this time, was no longer a menace."[6] The little people of the South shared with the western farmers a distrust of and antagonism toward the economic and political dominance of Wall Street. To give effective political significance to this resistance required the joint efforts of Negro and white voters. To avert this eventuality required drastic measures.

These drastic measures were embodied in new constitutions adopted by eight southern states between 1890 and 1910. Most of the old statutory limitations were incorporated in the new constitutions and new provisions added. The poll tax, which as a voting requirement had been abandoned during Reconstruction in all the southern states except Georgia, was reintroduced. Payment of the tax was required months in advance of the election, at which the tax receipt had to be presented. Property qualifications were also revived. Voters were required to read, understand, and interpret the state or federal constitution to the satisfaction of the election officials. The notorious "grandfather clause" was spawned, under terms of which persons who were eligible to vote in 1860 and their male descendants were exempt from the educational and property qualifications required by the new constitutions. This was an endeavor to permit voting by illiterate poor whites while excluding Negroes. Registration was made more difficult and residence requirements tightened.

In Louisiana these measures assured the blackout of Negro voting. It was almost 100 per cent effective. "For the 1896 national election, the last before the disfranchising code, there were registered in the state 130,344 Negroes," Lewinson records. "Negro registrants were

[6] Ralph J. Bunche, op. cit.

in the majority in 26 parishes. For the 1900 national election, two years after the adoption of the new constitution, there were only 5320 Negroes registered, and no parishes showed a majority of Negro registrants. While Negro registration fell off by 125,000—96 per cent—white registration decreased by only 30,000."[7] In Virginia the Lynchburg *News* reported that the number of qualified Negro voters dropped from 147,000 to 21,000 following the disfranchising convention of 1902. While reliable figures are not available for other states, there are indications that the results were equally as devastating.

The sponsors of poll-tax legislation everywhere affirmed their purpose to exclude Negroes from polling booths. There were also open indications in the debates in Alabama of a willingness to disfranchise the poor whites. "The purpose of the suffrage clause is to eliminate the unfit or unqualified," asserted William C. Oates, a delegate to the Alabama Constitutional Convention, ". . . if such a rule strikes down a white man as well as a Negro, let him go." Reviewing the proceedings of the Alabama convention, Francis G. Caffey stated the issue baldly in an article in the *Political Science Quarterly*, March 1905: "How to get rid of the venal and ignorant among the white voters was a far more serious problem than how to get rid of the undesirable among the Negroes as voters. While it was generally wished by leaders in Alabama to disfranchise many unworthy white men, as a practical matter it was impossible to go further than was done. The long sway of one party had naturally put undue political power into the hands of unworthy white men."

To assure the effectiveness of the poll tax as a disfranchising agent, three obstructive provisions were generally included in the legislation. The tax was made voluntary, with no effort to enforce collection. It was made cumulative. In Alabama it accumulated over the entire period from the age of twenty-one through forty-five, amounting to a total of thirty-six dollars. Payment of the tax, ranging from one dollar to two dollars annually, had to be made from two to ten months in advance in order to qualify to vote in an election. Everything was done to discourage voting. In the end, the poll tax disfranchised more whites than Negroes. Of the estimated ten million potential voters penalized by the tax, six million are white. The poor whites, succumbing to the Bourbon racial appeal to maintain "white supremacy," succeeded in disfranchising themselves as well as the bulk of potential Negro voters.

[7]Lewinson, op. cit., p. 81.

But the new constitutions with their poll tax requirements could not completely remove the Negro from politics. The leaks in the barriers erected by the constitutions were most effectively plugged by the one-party system with its white primary. Having isolated the Negro voter in a defunct and moribund southern Republican party, the Bourbons fashioned the Democratic party in the South as an exclusive white man's association, within the ranks of which all governmental functions were determined. The general election was relegated to complete insignificance. All policies and candidacies were to be settled in the Democratic primary, from which Negroes were excluded. Only in the mountain areas of Tennessee, Virginia, North Carolina, and Alabama did the Republicans retain the vitality to enter candidates in the general elections. In those areas the party consisted mainly of poor whites, the descendants of the anti-secessionist mountaineers. Elsewhere in the South the party consisted of the remnants of Negro voters and white job holders greedily feeding at the federal trough.

The white primary was not an altogether new device. It had originated during Reconstruction with the Conservative or "white man's party," which was the open political arm of the undercover, violent counterrevolution. While there was still an active Republican party, the exclusion of Negroes from the Conservative party did not disfranchise them. But with the withdrawal of the Republicans from the political arena in the South and the consequent development of the one-party system, the exclusion of Negroes from the Democratic primary provided the *coup de grâce* by which Negro suffrage was nullified from Virginia to Texas.

True, some Negroes continued to vote in general elections in ever-dwindling numbers. But this was a gesture of defiance—or perhaps of hope. Because voting ceased to be effective, it no longer was important. Negro candidates no longer ran for public office. The triumphant white South permitted this gesture, for it could neither elect nor defeat any candidate. With the collapse of Populism, Negro voters were no longer permitted to exercise a balance of power between two candidates for Congress or between two state parties. "They might vote for a man who would be elected without their aid," Professor Hart observed in 1906, "or for a man in a safe minority, but in the essential quality of a vote that may go to convert a minority into a majority, the Negroes have for years been hopelessly disfranchised."[8]

[8] Hart, op. cit.

In the midst of the South's bitter campaign to drive the Negro back into political bondage, Frederick Douglass died, a mellowed old man, in February 1895. He had epitomized in his life the revolution in the status of his race. The hope for the future of his people which he had earlier found "in the fact that colored men are strong in their gratitude to benefactors, and firm in their political convictions," faded in his declining years as he saw the Republican party steadily retreating and withdrawing federal protection from the freedmen. He had held that as long as the Constitution guaranteed the Negro's right to vote, "somebody in the South will want that vote and will offer the terms upon which that vote can be obtained." The deepening blackout of Negro suffrage and the return to power of the former Confederates disturbed him greatly, both as a Negro and as a Republican. Under Presidents Hayes and Arthur, he recalled, "the spirit of slavery and rebellion increased in power and advanced towards ascendancy. At the same time, the spirit which had abolished slavery and saved the Union steadily and proportionately declined, and with it the strength and unity of the Republican party also declined. . . . Under President Hayes it took organic, chronic form, and rapidly grew in bulk and force. . . . When the Republican party ceased to care for and protect its Southern allies, and sought the smiles of the Southern Negro-murderers, it shocked, disgusted, and drove away its best friends."

Douglass was not alone in his disillusionment. The rout of the Republicans spread dismay among Negro voters. The party's failure to provide any effective rear-guard defense left the southern Negro exposed and endangered. Negro politicians throughout the South echoed Douglass's protest. From Texas, Norris Wright Cuney, national Republican committeeman, complained in 1888: "It does seem to me that our friends in the North are asleep on this southern question. They have not had time to consider it or they certainly would understand the purposes of this southern oligarchy. The South has ceased to be a democracy as far as the Negro is concerned." That purpose, as Cuney saw it, was to rule not only the South, but the entire country.

The passing of Douglass coincided with the rise of Booker T. Washington, who, in 1881, founded an industrial school for Negroes in the heart of Alabama's black belt. Washington had, as a youth, lived through Reconstruction in Virginia. He had developed a distaste for politics and had arrived at the conviction that "the general political agitation drew the attention of our people away from the more fundamental matters of perfecting themselves in the industries at their doors and in securing property." Emerging as the new Negro leader, Washington advocated a conciliatory attitude toward the white South and acquiesced in the southern contention that the race was not prepared for the franchise. After his famous speech at the Atlanta Exposition in September 1895, his role was charted and his place assured. The man, the time, and the place had met.

In this speech, sometimes called the "Atlanta Compromise," Washington did not disavow the Negro's right to vote. He derided political activity and subordinated it to industrial training, the acquisition of property, and co-operation with southern whites. To the founder of Tuskegee Institute, first things came first, and politics was avowedly not at the top of his list. He did, however, send memorials to the Alabama and Louisiana constitutional conventions opposing discriminatory measures against Negro voters. But his support of the Negro's right to vote was always with qualifying reservations.

"As a rule, I believe in universal, free suffrage," he wrote in his classic autobiography, *Up from Slavery*, "but I believe that in the South we are confronted with peculiar conditions that justify the protection of the ballot in many of the states, for a while at least, either by an educational test, a property test, or by both combined; but whatever tests are required, they should be made to apply with equal and exact justice to both races. . . . I do not believe that the Negro should cease voting, for a man cannot learn the exercise of self-government by ceasing to vote any more than a boy can learn to swim by keeping out of the water. . . . I do not believe that any state should make a law that permits an ignorant and poverty-stricken white man to vote, and prevents a black man in the same condition from voting. Such a law is not only unjust, but it will react, as all unjust laws do, in time; for the effect of such a law is to encourage the Negro to secure education and property, and at the same time it encourages the white man to remain in ignorance and poverty."

Contemporary Negro critics looked upon Mr. Washington's pronouncements as equivocal. To them the Negro could be assured of the right to an education and security in his possessions only through the ballot. Extremists bitterly denounced him as a compromiser; more moderate critics felt compelled to voice their grave concern at his "submission and silence as to the civil and political rights" of the Negro. The foremost dissenter, W. E. B. Du Bois, charged: "Mr. Washington distinctly asks that black people give up, at least for the present, three things—first, political power; secondly, insistence on civil rights; and thirdly, higher education for Negro youth."[9] It is doubtful that Washington at any time explicitly made these demands upon his race, but they are implicit in his program and career. Certainly Negroes came to believe that Booker T. Washington thought it best for the race to eschew politics.

Washington, of course, could not have stemmed the rising tide of counterrevolution, no matter how militant he might have been in demanding full suffrage rights for Negroes. But by belittling the importance of voting, his leadership encouraged apathy and undermined the southern Negro's will to continue the fight for the right to vote. Such a fight involved physical and economic hazards. Mr. Washington made it appear that the ballot was not worth these hazards. As a consequence, the number of Negro voters continued to dwindle. This was true not only among the ill-prepared masses but also, and more fatefully, among the growing class of trained men who were prepared to pass the rigid electoral tests and to give leadership to the masses in the struggle for citizenship. "The better class of Southern Negroes," Du Bois asserts, "stopped voting for a generation." They abandoned the fight to participate in politics.

Paradoxically, Mr. Washington, who did not like politics, who believed that "the race troubles in the South could be solved by education rather than by political measures"—this Mr. Washington became, during the period of the blackout, the leading Negro politician. This may not have been of his choosing. But his pre-eminence as *the* Negro leader placed this responsibility upon him and brought him in contact with the outstanding political figures of his time. He was acquainted with every President from Grover Cleveland to William Howard Taft. It was to him that they turned, and particularly after the passing of Douglass, for counsel on racial policy and for endorsements of political appointments. To his office at Tuskegee came both Negro and white office seekers from all over the South to get his support for federal appointments. He wielded wider political influence than any of the avowed Negro politicians of his time. He became the only Negro leader with national prestige.

While the Negro, during Washington's ascendancy, was practically eliminated as a positive factor in southern elections, he retained for a number of years an important role in Republican politics of that region. Negroes were seldom able to elect Republicans to

---

[9]W. E. B. Du Bois, *Souls of Black Folk* (Chicago: A. C. McClurg & Co., twenty-second edition, 1940), p. 53.

Congress and were no longer able to swing any southern state for the party in a presidential election. Nevertheless, they continued for years to be the base of the skeleton Republican party in the South, to share in its leadership, and to participate in the selection of Republican nominees at the party's quadrennial national conventions. This gave to the remaining political cliques a voice in the selection of presidential candidates for whom they could deliver no decisive votes in the general election. The delegates elected to represent these state cliques at the national conventions became handy tools for ambitious candidates seeking the Republican presidential nomination. Although there were some principled state leaders, like Cuney of Texas, who were unpurchasable, others, with little to look forward to in the event of a Republican victory, traded their votes at the conventions for immediate rewards.

The Republican party in the South was from the beginning biracial in its composition. It was never an all-Negro party, although in certain localities and states Negroes were at times in control of the party. The Bourbons sought unceasingly to stigmatize it as the "Black" Republican party. They brought social and economic pressure upon white men who affiliated with the Republicans and branded them as "renegades." Confronted with these pressures, southern white Republicans could either withdraw from the party or conspire to eliminate the last vestiges of Negro control in the vain hope of attracting enough white voters to make the Republican party an effective political instrument in the South. As many of them were federal job holders and, accordingly, had a vested interest in the party, they were reluctant to withdraw.

As early as 1884 certain white Republicans in Texas began to chafe under the leadership of the resourceful Cuney. By 1888 they were in open revolt. They organized "White Republican Clubs" in various counties for the purpose of sending their own delegates to the state convention with the intent of seizing control and eliminating Negro leadership. Cuney, one of the ablest of the avowed politicians during the blackout, outgeneraled and beat the white opposition, whom he derisively dubbed "lily-whites." This, apparently, was the origin of the term which has come to designate the movement to eliminate the Negro from the Republican party in the South. Cuney, of course, had white supporters; and the lily-whites had their discontented Negro adherents. The fight originally was against Negro leadership. It became ultimately a movement to eliminate the Negro voter. Starting in Texas, where the wily Cuney was able to hold it at bay until, in 1896, he was tricked out of his leadership by Mark Hanna because of his refusal to support the candidacy of William McKinley, the lily-white Republican movement spread throughout the South.

Denouncing this maneuver, Cuney declared: "The lily-white movement is incoherent, having no principle to back it, and it is based entirely on racial prejudices. It must therefore pass away, leaving no signs of its present existence save a sulphurous name." At the 1892 National Republican Convention the petition for recognition by the Texas lily-whites was rejected and the movement termed "un-American and un-Republican." History, however, has controverted Cuney's optimistic prophecy. Lily-white Republicanism, encouraged by prominent northern Republicans, continued to grow in the South, where today it is in control in practically every state except Mississippi. However, in its avowed objective of increasing the party's prestige and following among southern whites, lily-white Republicanism has failed. In reality, it was a fight for control of federal patronage in the South. The lily-whites did not want to see Negroes holding or controlling important government jobs in the South.

If at the dawn of the twentieth century there was widespread gloom, despair, and apathy among Negro Americans, there was ample cause. Within the brief span of a generation they had been robbed of their basic citizenship rights. They were being lynched at the rate of more than one hundred per year, while the lynchers went free to go unpunished from one mob murder to another. The Supreme Court in 1883 had handed down a decision invalidating the Federal Civil Rights Law of 1866—a decision bitterly assailed by Frederick Douglass and other militant Negro leaders as "a deed done for slavery, caste, and oppression." Other narrow interpretations by the Supreme Court further restricted the validity of the war amendments. Jim Crow laws had been passed in all the southern states. Everywhere in the South the Negro was being denied the respect and dignity universally accorded to a human being. The apathy of Negro voters in the South was real, but its genesis lay outside the race. It was the apathy of the inmates of a concentration camp to the selection of their guards.

"The Negro is now passing through the most distressing stage of his political experience," Kelly Miller, Howard University dean and pamphleteer, dolefully observed. "He stands listlessly by as his political rights are denied, his privileges curtailed, and the current of public feeling grows cold and chilly. The constitutional amendments in the reconstruction states have been and are inspired by the purpose of eliminating the black factor from the governmental election. . . . These disfranchisement measures, harsh and severe as they are in many features, meet with little or no opposition from the nation at large . . . there is no moral force in the nation at present that will lead to their undoing, and no political exigency seems to demand it."

Progress, of course, had been made. Schools had been established throughout the South and were turning out sorely needed trained men and women. Most of the northern colleges and universities were open to the select group of young Negro men and women able to attend. The property holdings of the race had expanded enormously. Negroes had entered business, operating shops, small banks, and insurance companies. They had entered the learned professions. At the same time they had lost ground in certain of the skilled trades in the South, owing in part to the racial restrictions imposed by a short-sighted labor movement. Thousands had acquired ownership of farms which they were operating. They had created a Negro press to articulate their demands. All this progress had been made within a generation. Indeed, by 1900 there was already emerging a small middle class among southern Negroes—a class of people with training and property.

Nevertheless, there was gloom, because they had been stripped of the only democratic means by which they could protect their lives and make their possessions secure. Denied the ballot, they were easy prey for white intimidation and exploitation. Meanwhile, in the South there had been no improvement in the quality of legislative representation as had been forecast by the white purists who won their unholy war to purge the voting lists of Negroes. The representatives whom the white South sent to Congress during the Great Blackout were certainly not superior to the black Republican representatives of the Reconstruction period. Nor was there any less corruption in the electoral process. Votes, white votes, were bought and sold as freely as black votes had ever been traded. Moreover, with the elimination of the Negro, there had been a steady decline in the number of white voters, so that it became possible to elect a man to Congress with no more than 3 per cent of the potential vote. The restrictions imposed upon black voters had their reactions upon white voters. After the virtual elimination of the Negro as a voting citizen there was a real diminution in the proportion of eligible white voters who took the trouble to pay poll taxes, register, and go to the polls on election day. As late as 1944 only 18.31 per cent of the potential voters in the eight southern poll-tax states participated in the presidential election as compared with 68.74 per cent in the forty tax-free voting states. Years ago Booker T. Washington had said: "You can't keep a man in the ditch without staying in there with him." The whole South wallowed in the muck and mire of the political ditch into which the white majority had thrust and sought to hold the black minority.

As the blackout settled over the South attention began to be focused on the North, where, since ratification of the Fifteenth Amendment, Negro suffrage had ceased to be an issue. It was the destiny of the northern Negro voter, his forces steadily augmented by recruits from the South, to start the race back on the road to equal suffrage throughout the nation.

CHAPTER V

Refuge in the North

AT THE BEGINNING OF THE TWENTIETH CENTURY LESS than 10 per cent of the nearly 9,000,000 Negroes in the country were living beyond the borders of the former slave states. Pennsylvania continued to lead the northern states in Negro population with a total of 157,000. New York followed with 100,000. There were 97,000 in Ohio, 85,000 in Illinois, 70,000 in New Jersey, 57,500 in Indiana, and 52,000 in Kansas. Only two cities in the North had as many as 50,000 Negro inhabitants—Philadelphia with 62,600 and New York with 60,700. Detroit, in 1900, had only 4100 Negroes.

Although this was before the day of the great migrations, the vanguard of freedom-seeking Negro families had already penetrated the North. This early movement, particularly westward into Kansas, was an inspired and organized exodus away from southern terror. It reached such proportions as to attract national attention. Senator D. W. Voorhees of Indiana introduced a resolution in the United States Senate to investigate the causes. "The movement, however, could not be stopped and it became so widespread that the people in general were forced to give it serious thought," Carter G. Woodson asserts in his *Century of Negro Migration*. Negro leadership was divided on the advisability of such a movement. Frederick Douglass thought it ill-timed, while others, like Richard T. Greener, the first Negro Harvard graduate, endorsed it. This was the first significant movement out of the South since the flight of the fugitive slaves in the ante-bellum days.

The great migrations, however, were yet to come. The over-congested ghettos in New York, Philadelphia, Detroit, Chicago, Cleveland, Pittsburgh, Cincinnati, and Los Angeles were still in the future. Also in the future was the concentration of Negro voting strength—the natural and inevitable outgrowth of the residential segregation which the white property owners imposed upon the in-migrating Negro workers. Meanwhile, the old settler and migrant alike found that, with the ratification of the Fifteenth Amendment, Negro voting had ceased to be an issue in the North. The Negro voter in the North, unlike his brother in the South, was not "compelled to wade to the ballot box through blood." His vote was sought and counted even though his numbers were small.

As early as the 1880s this small Negro vote in the North was conceived of as a balance-of-power factor in national elections. Maud Cuney Hare's biography of her father, Norris Wright Cuney, the Texas Negro leader, expressed the conviction that the northern Republicans would not sustain lily-white Republicanism in the South, because to do so would be politically costly to the party in such states as Ohio, Indiana, Illinois, and perhaps New York, which would go "overwhelmingly Democratic" without the Negro vote. Even Frederick Douglass believed that the northern Negro vote could "turn the scale for or against one or the other of the parties in doubtful Republican states." With Negroes casting a very small percentage of the total votes in any northern state, they could be a decisive factor in only the closest of elections, the results of which could be changed by a shift of less than 3 per cent of the total vote. They did not constitute a majority in a single ward in any major city in the North. W. E. B. Du Bois, in his study of the Philadelphia Negro, estimated in 1897 that "the Negro vote has never exceeded 4 per cent of the total registration" in that city, which then had the largest Negro population in the North. Chicago, which, with a Negro population of 14,300, ranked third among the northern cities, had only 3000 Negro voters in 1890.

Nevertheless, the Negro was not alone in contending that his vote in the North represented a balance-of-power factor. Governor Joseph B. Foraker of Ohio, later a United States senator, conceded when he was running for re-election in 1885 that "the Negro vote was so large that it was not only an important but an essential factor in our consideration. It would not be possible for the Republican party to carry the state if that vote should be arrayed against us."[1] The governor had expressed concern about a report his political enemies were circulating branding him as "anti-Negro."

Du Bois, evaluating the early Negro voters in Philadelphia,

[1]Wendell P. Dabney, *Cincinnati's Colored Citizens* (Cincinnati: Dabney Publishing Co., 1926), p. 84.

idealistically grouped them into three categories: "a large majority of voters who vote blindly at the dictates of the party and, while not open to direct bribery, accept the indirect emoluments of office or influence in return for party loyalty; a considerable group, centering in the slum districts, which casts a corrupt purchasable vote for the highest bidder; lastly, a very small group of independent voters who seek to use their vote to better present conditions of municipal life. The political morality of the first group of voters, that is to say, the great mass of Negro voters, corresponds roughly to that of the mass of white voters, but with this difference: the ignorance of the Negro in matters of government is greater and his devotion to party blinder and more unreasoning."

With evident disgust Dr. Du Bois describes the workings of ward politics among Negro voters in Philadelphia at the close of the nineteenth century. "Next to this direct purchase of votes," he discovered in his detailed social study of the community, "one of the chief and most pernicious forms of bribery among the lowest classes is through the establishment of political clubs, which abound in the Fourth, Fifth, Seventh, and Eighth Wards, and are not uncommon elsewhere. A political club is a band of eight or twelve men who rent a clubhouse with money furnished them by the boss, and support themselves partially in the same way. The club is often named after some politician . . . and the business of the club is to see that its precinct is carried for the proper candidate, to get 'jobs' for some of its 'boys,' to keep others from arrest, and to secure bail and discharge for those arrested."

In Chicago politics was no purer, as Harold F. Gosnell points out in his volume, *Negro Politicians*. In the 1890s, when, under the leadership of Edward H. Wright, Negro voters were beginning to exert political influence, the city was controlled by "the caucus, the convention, rough-and-tumble politics, and 'boodle' aldermen." In New York, Tammany Hall, then at its malodorous worst under the notorious Boss Tweed, was wooing the incredulous Negro voters by much the same tactics as the Republicans used in Philadelphia— clubhouses and protection for petty criminals and illicit practices.

Negro suffrage in the North had endured indifference and attack. Free men of color had voted on equal terms in all the northern colonies prior to the Revolution. By the time of the Civil War they were permitted to vote only in Maine, Vermont, New Hampshire, Massachusetts, Rhode Island, and, with special property qualifications, in New York. The restrictions imposed in New York followed too active participation by Negro voters in behalf of the Federalists, according to Roi Ottley in *New World A-Coming*. "When the Democrats were returned to power in 1821," Ottley asserts, "they immediately started action to disqualify Negro voters," with the result that a discriminatory property qualification of $250 was required of these voters. Disfranchisement of Pennsylvania Negroes in 1838 was demanded by politicians after a Negro candidate in Bucks County narrowly missed being elected to the state legislature.

The right to vote carries with it, in this country, the right to run for office. The unnamed candidate in Bucks County was possibly the first Negro to offer himself for election to public office. The first successful candidates were Edward G. Walker and Charles L. Mitchell, who were elected in 1866 to the lower house of the Massachusetts legislature from Boston. John Jones, a free-born Negro tailor, was elected to the Cook County Board of Commissioners by Chicago voters in 1871. New York State, in 1872, named Frederick Douglass a presidential elector to cast the state's ballot for President Grant. Four years later John W. E. Thomas, a Chicago schoolteacher, became the first Negro to sit in the Illinois state legislature. In 1881 John P. Green, who previously had been elected justice of the peace in Cleveland, was sent to the Ohio legislature, initiating Negro representation in that body. After serving two terms in the lower house, he was elected to the Ohio state Senate in 1890, the first Negro to be elected to the upper house of any state legislature in the North. Green, who sponsored the official recognition of Labor Day, received wide support from organized labor and became known in Ohio as the "Daddy of Labor Day." Meanwhile Negroes in Boston, Chicago, and Philadelphia were receiving minor political appointments in local, state, and federal services.

All of these earlier Negro candidates were elected primarily by white votes. Thomas, the Illinois legislator, received 11,532 votes in his first election at a time when Chicago's Negro population was less than 7000. Likewise the number of votes cast for Green in his various elections exceeded the total Negro population in Cleveland. When Walker and Mitchell were sent to the Massachusetts legislature the maximum Negro vote in Boston was less than 1000. For twenty years thereafter Negro representation in Massachusetts was maintained by "the outflowing favor of the other race." This generosity on the part of white voters, John Daniels maintains in his volume, *In Freedom's Birthplace*, "was the potent factor in the appointment of Negroes to many respectable posts and their election to the City Council and the State Legislature. Not till about 1885 did they themselves reach the point where, by virtue of having become so numerous in the West End as to comprise over half of the voters in the Republican majority of old Ward 9, they were in a position effectually to demand representation. But though, thereafter, their numbers constituted the most apparent reason for their political prosperity, the continued though diminishing favor of the whites was still its underlying cause." The political advantage gained by the increasing concentration of Negroes in Ward 9 was lost in 1895 when the city was redistricted and the ward split.

Although in many localities white persons continued to vote for Negro candidates nominated by their party, the sentimental era came to an end about the turn of the century. From that time on the success of Negro candidates, with few exceptions, depended primarily upon a basic backlog of Negro voters. Party loyalty on the part of white voters was still necessary to elect Negro candidates in areas where they may have had a substantial but not majority vote. But the Negro had to stand on his own political base.

While in the North Negro suffrage was accepted by both Democrats and Republicans, there was a growing disposition to look upon the aftermath of the Civil War in the South as a horrible mistake. White Republicans in the North, who not only encouraged Negro voting but also voted for Negro candidates, were all too eager to close their ears to the anguished cries of their persecuted fellow Republicans in the deep South. In respectable Republican circles it was no longer in good taste to speak of enforcing the Fifteenth Amendment. Mrs. Hare, a loyal Republican, voiced her pained surprise that the Michigan state chairman of the GOP should, in 1890, "declare that the party had done enough for Negroes and call them insolent for requesting recognition." Douglass was no less pained by this "degeneracy in the Republican party" which led it to "despise and reject the hand that had raised it to power."

Long before 1900 it had become plain, even to the most loyal Lincoln disciple, that the Republican party, as a political organization, was no longer interested in the fate of its black adherents south of the Potomac and Ohio rivers. Indeed, the party was intent upon unloading the southern Negro, while at the same time seeking the votes placed by black hands into ballot boxes in the North. The Republicans actively campaigned for Negro support in Pennsylvania, New York, Illinois, Ohio, Indiana, Kansas, and the border states of Kentucky and Missouri. Invoking the memory of Abraham Lincoln, they continued to hold this vote, particularly in national elections, for the Party of Emancipation. It was, however, not alone the Lincoln legend which stabilized the Negro vote. More important was the aggressive anti-Negro policies and objectives of the southern Democrats—policies and objectives too seldom challenged by northern Democrats.

The Democratic party, in national affairs, had consistently supported the South throughout the bitter pre-Civil War days and on through Reconstruction and the Great Blackout. The party, then as now, was composed of conflicting elements. In the South the Bourbon planters controlled. In the North it was largely the workingman's party into which the bulk of the immigrant population was lured by the favors and protections afforded by Tammany Hall. Slavery in the South was detrimental to free white labor in the North and had the potentiality of completely undermining the northern workers' living standards. Slaves could be trained to produce in factories as well as to pick cotton. Already they had established an enviable record in the building trades, which they monopolized in many southern cities. But a considerable segment of the white working class in the North, like the poor whites in the South, hated the slaves more than they feared the institution of slavery. So politically they supported the slaveholding class through adherence to the Democratic party.

But the realistic leaders of the Democratic machines in northern cities realized that "a vote's a vote," and no sooner had the enfranchisement of the Negro been affirmed than they sought that new vote. Indeed, even before the ratification of the Fifteenth Amendment, the Democrats in the Boston area got busy. Walker, who in 1866 became one of the first two Negroes elected to a legislative body in this country, represented the District of Charlestown, which had not then been annexed to Boston. It appeared to Daniels "that his affiliation in that town had been with the Democrats and that his nomination came from them." In New York City, Boss Tweed, no stickler for ideological niceties, lost no time in trying to line up the Negro vote through his black henchman, Hank Anderson. It was votes that he wanted; he didn't care how he got them, nor from whom. In the judiciary election of 1870, Gustavus Meyers reports in his *History of Tammany Hall,* the Democrats sent white repeaters into a ward in which there were 1100 registered Negro voters and had them cast the ballots of 500 black men. Going later to the polls, the Negroes found that they had already been "voted" and when they protested were promptly arrested as "repeaters." In Chicago, Democratic Mayor Carter Henry Harrison I campaigned assiduously for the Negro vote. As a result of his efforts he won the support of many of these voters, some of whom split away from the Republicans and organized the Colored Democratic League of Cook County.[2]

The Boston Democrats had from the first favored Negro candidates, sponsoring Walker in 1866 for the state legislature and Paul C. Brooks in 1890 for the Common Council. It was not, however, until 1895 that a serious effort was made to organize the Negro Democratic vote. In that year a Democratic club was organized among Negro voters in Ward 11. Six years later a similar club was organized in Ward 18. As a result of this organizational drive "a goodly number of Negro votes" went to the Democratic candidate for mayor in 1905. From a quarter to a third of the Negro vote is reported to have been cast for the Democratic candidate for governor in 1910. The Negro vote was probably the decisive factor in electing a Democratic district attorney who won by the narrow margin of 3211 votes in the 1908 election.[3]

Under Richard Croker, who became its leader in 1886, Tammany Hall renewed its efforts to corral the Negro vote in New York City. On promise of jobs in the various city departments, Croker was able to induce a large number of Negro voters to support Tammany candidates. He organized the United Colored Democracy of Tammany Hall and designated as its leader "Chief" Edward F. Lee, a shrewd and ingratiating Negro hotel bellman. Failing to deliver the promised jobs, Croker lost the support of Negro voters.[4]

On the local level, the Democratic party was making some inroads on the solid phalanx of Republicanism among Negro voters. But in national politics, although distressed by the failure of the GOP to enforce the war amendments, the bulk of Negro voters continued their support of the Republican party. In view of the unabated virulence of the southern Democrats' anti-Negro attack, this was a sane decision. Nevertheless, some of the northern Negro voters in doubtful states "began to advocate the withdrawal of their support from the old party by which they were made citizens and to join the Democratic party. Of this class I was not one," Frederick

[2]St. Clair Drake and Horace R. Cayton, *Black Metropolis* (New York: Harcourt, Brace & Co., 1945), p. 344.

[3]John Daniels, *In Freedom's Birthplace* (New York: Houghton Mifflin), pp. 296–97.

[4]Roi Ottley, *New World A-Coming* (Houghton Mifflin, 1943), pp. 210–11.

Douglass averred. "I knew that however bad the Republican party was, the Democratic party was much worse. The elements of which the Republican party was composed gave better ground for the ultimate hope of the success of the colored man's cause than those of the Democratic party."

The election of Grover Cleveland to the presidency in 1884 as the first Democrat to occupy the White House since the Civil War spread dismay through the black masses, particularly in the South, where it was feared an effort would be made further to deprive Negroes of such rights as they had gained under the war amendments. The Democratic party was the party of the South, the party of the slaveholders and the terror-spreading night riders. Its victory in a national election could not but alarm the freedmen. Douglass admitted that he "shared in some measure the painful apprehension and distress felt by my people at the South from the return to power of the old Democratic and slavery party." The election further stimulated the steady out-migration of southern Negroes. The South was no place to be caught under a backward-looking Democratic administration. Had not things been bad enough under the Republicans?

The alarm turned out to be unwarranted. President Cleveland was more interested in civil service reform, the platform upon which he campaigned and was elected, and in reduction of the tariff than in the repression of the Negro citizenry. Indeed, the latter did not at any time appear to be an objective of his. In defiance of the southern Democrats, he continued the practice of appointing a few Negroes to federal positions. He did not immediately remove Douglass from his post as Recorder of Deeds for the District of Columbia. He appointed a Boston Negro, James M. Trotter, Registrar of the Treasury, and offered a position to John R. Lynch, a former congressman from Mississippi during Reconstruction. Lynch, a loyal Republican to the bitter end, declined the offer. No new restrictions or handicaps were imposed upon the race. The progress of the Negro was in no way retarded by President Cleveland's administration.

Northern-born and onetime governor of New York, Cleveland evinced no sympathies for the rank prejudices of his fellow Democrats from the South who frowned upon his friendly overtures to Negroes. He defied the Bourbons not only by appointing Negroes to office but by inviting Douglass and his white wife to official White House receptions. Douglass, unfaltering Republican though he was, felt constrained to praise Cleveland, whom he found to be "a robust, manly man, one having the courage to act upon his convictions, and to bear with equanimity the reproaches of those who differed from him." Booker T. Washington was even more laudatory in his appraisal of the President: "Judging from my personal acquaintance with Mr. Cleveland," he wrote in *Up from Slavery,* "I do not believe that he is conscious of possessing any colour prejudice. He is too great for that. . . . As soon as I met him I became impressed with his simplicity, greatness and rugged honesty." To the Negroes of the country, President Cleveland was a new kind of Democrat, the like of which was not again to occupy the White House for a full half century.

Politically the Negro was trapped. His disillusionment with the Republican party was steadily mounting. But despite Cleveland's conciliatory gestures, the Democratic party remained primarily the party of the South. The South—the white South—as everyone knew, was openly committed to the elimination of the race from politics. But what of the Republicans, the party which had sponsored the Negro's demand for recognition as a citizen? That party was no longer concerned with such principles. Indeed, it showed increasing signs of being embarrassed by the race issue. The party platform still carried some pious affirmation of intent to assure Negroes of their citizenship rights; but the party in power did nothing to implement its platform declarations with regard to the Negro.

In vain quest of an illusory white Republican vote in the South, the party continued the purge of Negroes from its inner circles. In 1892 there were 120 Negro delegates at the National Convention. Texas, Mississippi, Florida, and the District of Columbia were represented by Negroes on the National Committee. The number of colored delegates steadily declined to 65 in 1912, 35 in 1916, and 27 in 1920. This objective was accomplished by a reduction in the representation from southern states and a concomitant attempt to purge these delegations of Negro members. Contending against the threat of reduction in the southern delegations, former Congressman Lynch of Mississippi, at the convention in 1884, countered with a proposal accepting reduction on the basis of the number of votes cast for Republican candidates in the state or congressional district, "provided the convention would agree to change the national law, as they had a right to do under the Fourteenth Amendment, so as to reduce the representation in Congress and in the Electoral College of States that disfranchised voters as they do in the South." Not until 1904, when Theodore Roosevelt was the presidential candidate, did the Republican platform embody a "demand that representation in Congress and in the electoral college be proportionately reduced as directed by the Constitution of the United States." This platform pledge was never carried out.

Section II of the Fourteenth Amendment vests in Congress the constitutional authority to reduce representation of any state which restricts the franchise of qualified citizens. Since the day of its ratification this provision has remained a dead letter, never once having been enforced and seldom invoked as a threat. It provides that "when the right to vote at any election for the choice of electors for President and Vice-President of the United States, representatives in Congress, the executive and judicial officers of a state, or the members of the legislature thereof, is denied to any of the male inhabitants of such state being twenty-one years of age, and citizens of the United States, or in any way abridged, except for participation in rebellion or other crime, the basis of representation therein shall be reduced in the proportion which the number of such male citizens shall bear to the whole number of male citizens twenty-one years of age in such state."

Year after year Negro leaders vainly urged the Republicans to put through Congress legislation reducing southern representation in accordance with this article. Although a pledge to invoke this provision was included in the party platform, action to this end never got beyond the talking stage on the floor of Congress. In 1870 Congress had passed a "force" act providing federal protection for all citizens in the exercise of their civil and political rights under the Constitution. In later years Representative George H. Tinkham of Massachusetts sought congressional sanction for reduction of representation from states with restricted suffrage.[5] The Republican party was not prepared to take this drastic action, though failure to do so gave to each southern voter a bloated ballot, far outbalancing that of any voter in the North.

Resentment against abandonment by the Republican party continued to grow among northern Negro voters. William Monroe Trotter, the radical and uncompromising leader of Boston, opposed William Howard Taft in 1908 and advised Negroes to vote for William Jennings Bryan. Taft, then the protégé of the retiring President Theodore Roosevelt, was reported to have remarked that

[5]Bernard Nelson, "The Negro before the Supreme Court," *Phylon,* Vol. VIII, No. 1.

Negroes were "political children, not having the mental stature of manhood."[6] Taft was suspect, although he had given lip service to the enforcement of the Fourteenth and Fifteenth Amendments, as did the Republican platform of that year. Bryan and the Democratic platform were silent on this issue. In his inaugural address President Taft committed himself against the appointment of a Negro to any federal post in a locality in which the white people raised objection. "This suggestion," Kelly Miller commented, "is sufficient to invite the fiercest antagonism to the appointment of a Negro to a federal office in any community in the United States." The President did, near the end of his term, appoint William Henry Lewis, of Boston, Assistant United States Attorney General. Taft obviously was following the pattern, set by Roosevelt, of limiting the quantity of Negro appointees while attempting to improve the quality.

Not until the campaign of 1912 was a serious attempt made on a national scale to channel the Negroes' discontent into positive political action against their original sponsors. In the spring of 1911 a national convention of Negro Democrats was held in Indianapolis. The convention "urged colored voters of the United States to note the conditions surrounding them, to cease following any one party to their detriment, and thus divide their votes." Reaffirming its allegiance to the Democratic party, the assembly further urged "the intelligent, honest, law-abiding colored citizens to organize together in Democratic clubs for the election of 1912."[7]

There were three parties in the field in 1912 in addition, of course, to the Socialists, Prohibitionists, and what not. There was the Grand Old Party of Lincoln with the well-intentioned but weak Taft as its candidate. The Democrats named Woodrow Wilson, an austere academician turned political reformer, onetime president of Princeton University, and at the time of his nomination governor of New Jersey. The third was the Progressive party, which former President Roosevelt organized when he found he was unable to get the Republican nomination. Taft and Roosevelt were well known to colored voters. Both had been sparing in their appointments of Negroes to office. Neither wished to offend the southern whites. Indeed, Roosevelt, after having failed to swing the Negro delegates at the Republican convention, set up his Progressive party in the South as a lily-white organization and otherwise catered to prejudices of the white South.

[6]Daniels, op. cit., 294.
[7]William F. Nowlin, op. cit., p. 33.

This much Negroes knew about Woodrow Wilson: He was a
Virginian by birth. He had headed the only major northern university which excluded colored students. Though hailed as a liberal
reformer, he was evasive on the race question. Not a record to inspire confidence. Nevertheless, the restless, independent, and intellectual Negro leaders were in desperate straits. Taft and Roosevelt
had demonstrated their unacceptability. Wilson was their only hope.
Among the Virginian's liberal friends and supporters was Oswald
Garrison Villard, publisher of *The Nation* and the New York *Eve-
ning Post,* and grandson of the resolute Abolitionist leader, William
Lloyd Garrison. Carrying on in the tradition of his family, Mr. Villard was a foremost advocate of equal rights for Negroes and a
founder of the three-year-old National Association for the Advancement of Colored People.

The publisher's connections with the liberal Democrats and with
the Negro leaders made him the natural liaison between the two
groups. Largely under Villard's prodding Wilson assured Negro
voters "that should I become President of the United States they
may count upon me for absolute fair dealing and for everything by
which I could assist in advancing the interests of their race in the
United States." He further expressed his "earnest wish to see justice
done them in every matter; and not mere grudging justice, but justice executed with liberality and cordial good feeling." He was
hesitant to go further and became alarmed after the Reverend J.
Milton Waldron, a Negro leader, released a statement to the effect
that the Democratic nominee had indicated in an interview that
his party "wanted and needed" Negro votes.

Although the candidate was unduly jittery, the Democratic party
was definitely out for the Negro vote in the three-way fight of that
year. Hoping to capitalize upon the Negro's resentment against the
Republican party and against Taft and Roosevelt, the Democrats
sponsored the organization of the National Colored Democratic
League and other political outfits among Negro voters in the North.
The party's campaign expenditures for that year included the sum
of $52,256 used for the purpose of swinging the Negro vote.[8] They
sent speakers to address Negro groups and advertised in the Negro
press. There had been reports that in the 1910 congressional races
20 to 40 per cent of the northern Negro vote went to Democratic
candidates. It was, however, an uneasy and restrained association,

---

[8]Arthur S. Link, "The Negro as a Factor in the Campaign of 1912," *Journal
of Negro History,* Vol. XXXII, No. 1, January 1947.

almost clandestine. The Democrats, fearful of possible reaction in the South, were careful about making public commitments. Already, in the pre-convention campaign, Tom Watson of Georgia and other Dixie demagogues had branded Wilson as a "nigger-lover."[9] Moreover, Roosevelt, with his lily-white program, was striving to make inroads in the Solid South. He was handicapped, however, by his record as President and his effort to get Negro votes in the North. Wilson himself was exceedingly wary both out of a sense of expediency and because of his own provincial racial attitude. He was southern by origin and outlook. Despite his later acclaim as the champion of the New Freedom and of international democracy, he was never able to purge himself of his provincial prejudices.

The Negro leaders were full of qualms. The suppression of the Negro in the South by the Democratic party in that region was a real and present danger to the race. Of this the Negro intellectuals were aware, but they vainly hoped that Wilson, as a "cultivated scholar" and a professed liberal, would rise above his origin and party. W. E. B. Du Bois, who had left his post at Atlanta University to become editor of *The Crisis,* the organ of the newly organized NAACP, did not "believe that Mr. Wilson admires Negroes." Nevertheless, he brought himself to the "conviction that Mr. Wilson will treat black men and their interests with far-sighted fairness. He will not be our good friend, but he will not belong to the gang of which Tillman, Vardaman, Hoke Smith and Blease are the brilliant expositors."[10] Also in Wilson's corner were such Negro leaders as William Monroe Trotter and the Reverend J. Milton Waldron, representing the National Independent Political League, and the leaders of the National Colored Democratic League, Robert N. Wood and Bishop Alexander Walters of the A.M.E.Z. Church. They conducted a campaign throughout the North in an effort to win for the Democratic candidate the Negro vote in that region, estimated by Dr. Du Bois at 500,000. Meanwhile, of course, the Republicans and the Progressives were campaigning to hold these votes.

The split in the Republican ranks assured Wilson's election. There was restrained rejoicing among his Negro supporters. Dr. Du Bois was "gratified that at least 100,000 black votes went to swell the 6,000,000 that called Woodrow Wilson to the presidency. We do not as Negroes conceal or attempt to conceal the risk involved in

[9]Link, op. cit.
[10]*The Crisis,* Vol. 4, No. 4, August 1912.

this action." In light of the number of Negroes living outside or the former slave states, Dr. Du Bois's estimate of 500,000 Negro voters in those states and 100,000 black ballots for Wilson appears inflated. The importance of the Negro vote in that election is "questionable," according to Link, in view of the large pluralities Wilson won in all of the more populous northern states.[11]

The rejoicing was of short duration. President Wilson did not follow the example of his Democratic predecessor, Grover Cleveland. The President had not been in office six months before segregation was introduced, reputedly upon the instigation of Mrs. Wilson, in the various departments of the federal government. This discriminatory innovation, which remained uncorrected until the next Democratic President came to office twenty years later, stunned Negroes throughout the country and was likewise disturbing to Wilson's liberal white supporters. In an open letter to the President, Dr. Du Bois expressed the faint hope that this move was initiated without the knowledge or authority of the White House. "Sir, you have now been President of the United States for six months, and what is the result?" the Negro leader queried. "It is no exaggeration to say that every enemy of the Negro race is greatly encouraged. . . . A dozen worthy Negro officials have been removed from office, and you have nominated but one black man for office, and he, such a contemptible cur, that his very nomination was an insult to every Negro in the land."[12]

Trotter took his protest to the White House in person and was assured by the President that the matter would be looked into. A year later, on November 12, 1914, the militant Bostonian returned as spokesman of a delegation sent by his National Independent Equal Rights League. He was forthright. "We have come to you, Mr. President," he said, as reported in *The Crisis,* "to set before you this definite continuance of race segregation against us a year after you heard our protest and seemed to heed our appeal to ask you to entirely abolish segregation of Afro-Americans in the executive departments." The President fell back on the hoary southern defense of segregation as a device for preventing interracial friction. He had discussed the issue with his Cabinet, he said, and it was agreed that this was the only purpose of the directives ordering segregation of the races in government departments. Negroes should accept this

---

[11]Link, op. cit.
[12]*The Crisis,* Vol. 6, No. 5, September 1913.

for what it was meant and not as a humiliation, the President insisted.

Face to face they argued—the white Princeton man from Virginia and the black Harvard man from Massachusetts. Exasperated by Trotter's rigorous rejection of this flimsy defense of Jim Crow, the schoolmaster turned President angrily moved to terminate the interview. "If this organization is ever to have another hearing before me it must have another spokesman," he warned. "Your manner offends me. . . . Your tone with its background of passion." It was the old story repeated. The clash of wills between President Andrew Johnson and Frederick Douglass half a century before. The incapacity of the tradition-bound southern white man to treat on equal terms with a black man.

Wilson made no move to end segregation in the federal service. The pattern was established. Later he appointed a few Negroes to office. Among them Emmett J. Scott, who had been Booker T. Washington's faithful assistant until the latter's death in 1915. Mr. Scott became adviser on Negro affairs in the War Department during World War I. Finally, in the midst of the war, the President spoke out against lynching, but only after publication of Kelly Miller's devasting pamphlet, *The Disgrace of Democracy,* an open letter to the President. The Democratic platform on which he ran for re-election in 1916 affirmed that "whoever, by arousing prejudices of a racial, religious or other nature, creates discord and strife among our people . . . is faithless to the trust which the privileges of citizenship repose in him and is disloyal to his country."

Wilson's double-cross killed the furtive affair of the Negro leaders with the Democratic party. Even though the Republican platform of 1916 made no reference to the problems of the Negro, the Negro voters, disillusioned by President Wilson's Jim Crow policies, returned en masse to the party of liberation. By the time of World War I, colored citizens, abandoned by the Republican party and disdained by the Democrats, were politically homeless. They were not, however, entirely hopeless. Their numbers in the principal northern industrial states had, in the twenty-year period since 1900, been almost doubled by wartime migration. This first wave of the great migrations gave political substance to the earlier claim of being an important balance-of-power factor in national politics. Meanwhile they were developing an influential press to articulate their demands and an effective organization to supplement their political action with a concerted legal attack upon disfranchisement.

CHAPTER VI

The Counterattack

THE PLIGHT OF THE NEGRO IN THIS COUNTRY, HIS ALMOST complete isolation from the main stream of American life, early compelled him to seek some organizational medium through which to express his needs, aspirations, and protests. The church and the conspiracy were the first outlets. The church not only gave spiritual guidance but also served as a center of Negro life. The conspiracy was his weapon of revolt against the slave system. It fomented the slave insurrections, inspired the slowdown strikes on the plantations, and recruited fugitives for the Underground Railroad. Its potential fury kept the slaveholders in a constant state of jitters.

Even before the Civil War free Negroes in the North held open conventions and church conferences at which ways and means of improving their conditions were discussed. They also participated actively in the anti-slavery movement. Frederick Douglass, Charles L. Redmond, Harriet Tubman, Henry Highland Garnett, David Ruggles, Sojourner Truth, and others were in constant demand as speakers and workers at conventions and meetings of Abolitionists. After the war, in the late sixties and early seventies, Negro conventions blossomed all over the country. Union Leagues and other societies were organized. State and regional conferences were held. National labor and political conventions were called in Washington, Cincinnati, and New Orleans. The newly emancipated blacks were striving for group expression. But all of these new organizations were short-lived, lacking in co-ordinated program and having little or no grass-roots support back in the cities and states from which the delegates came. The basic need for organization was not met by these loosely knit gatherings of that period. The freedmen had not learned the technique of efficient and permanent organization. And with the collapse of Reconstruction they received little assistance from sympathetic whites.

The need for organized resistance to the subversion of the war amendments became imperative during the period of the Great Blackout. And indeed, not until this need was at least partially met did the first rays of hope begin to penetrate the deep gloom that had settled over black America. Following the success of the white counterrevolution, the Negro struggle in America had been one of constant retreat. Step by step the great masses of black folk were being stripped of their basic citizenship rights and pushed back toward serfdom. In compensation they were being given something called "industrial training" and urged to pursue a chimerical goal—the creation of a separate life and economy, devoid of political rights and free expression.

To call a halt to this rout, Dr. W. E. B. Du Bois, then a young Harvard-trained professor of sociology at Atlanta University, proposed a conference of Negro leaders to foster "organized determination and aggressive action on the part of men who believe in Negro freedom and growth." In response to his proposal fifty-nine colored men from seventeen states signed a call for a meeting to be held in Buffalo, New York, in July 1905. The conference, attended by twenty-nine delegates from fourteen states, became known as the Niagara Movement. Among its objectives, as outlined by Dr. Du Bois in his autobiography, *Dusk of Dawn,* were the achievement of manhood suffrage and the abolition of all caste distinctions based simply on race or color.

Meeting the following year at Harpers Ferry, West Virginia, where John Brown had launched his abortive revolution to purge the land of the evil of slavery, this small group of inspired intellectual radicals hurled a futile reproach at an unresponsive nation. Their desperately bitter statement, prepared by Dr. Du Bois, denounced "the work of stealing the black man's ballot" and challenged the right of the "fifty and more representatives of stolen votes" to sit in the nation's Capitol. It demanded universal manhood suffrage. "First we would vote; with the right to vote goes everything: freedom, manhood, the honor of your wives, and the chastity of your daughters, the right to work, and the chance to rise, and let no man listen to those who deny this. We want full manhood suffrage, and we want it now, henceforth and forever," their statement cried. Enforcement of the Fourteenth and Fifteenth Amendments was demanded. "The failure of the Republican party in Congress at the

session just closed to redeem its pledge of 1904 with reference to suffrage conditions at the South seems a plain, deliberate and pre-
meditated breach of promise, and stamps the party as guilty of obtaining votes under false pretense."[1]

The movement met twice again, in Boston in 1907 and in Oberlin,
Ohio, the following year. The Niagara Movement was really no
movement. It was more an exclusive fraternity of righteous protest-
ers. There was plenty to protest, and the spokesmen were highly
articulate. But neither Dr. Du Bois, William Monroe Trotter, nor
any of their associates seemed able to reach the mass of black folk in
whose interests they were embattled. Their cause was just, their motives pure, their goals noble and practical; but they were perhaps
too far removed from the masses to inspire them to action—too
conscious of their own privileged position as black elite. Among the
limited intelligentsia they created a considerable stir, stimulating and
inspiring the young men and women of this class whom Dr. Du Bois
called the Talented Tenth. They failed, however, as completely as
earlier efforts, to build sustained support among any considerable
number of Negroes, the vast majority of whom were ground down
to the prosaic, day-to-day business of surviving in a hostile environment.

The Niagara Movement was finally absorbed in the newly created
National Association for the Advancement of Colored People
founded in 1909, the centennial anniversary of Lincoln's birth.
Though Trotter dissented and formed his own National Equal
Rights League, Du Bois and most of the others of the little band
came into the NAACP, which, unlike the Niagara Movement, was
initiated and supported by liberal whites in co-operation with the
advance guard of Negroes. Among the original sponsors of the or-
ganization were William English Walling, Mary White Ovington,
Bishop Alexander Walters, Dr. Henry Moskowitz, John Dewey,
Francis J. Grimke, Ida Wells Barnett, Charles Edward Russell, and
Dr. Du Bois.

"In the summer of 1908, the country was shocked by the account
of the race riot in Springfield, Illinois," Miss Ovington later recounted. "Here in the home of Abraham Lincoln, a mob containing
many of the town's 'best citizens' raged for two days, killed and
wounded scores of Negroes, and drove thousands from the city."
Walling, a southern-born white man, who covered the riot for *The*

[1]Du Bois, *Dusk of Dawn* (New York: Harcourt Brace & Co., 1940), pp.
88-91.

Independent, concluded that only through organized effort could the rising tide of mob murder and persecution of Negro citizens be halted. It was in response to this suggestion that Miss Ovington and others issued a call on Lincoln's birthday, 1909, for a conference to form such an organization. The call, issued shortly after Georgia had become the last of the southern states to ban Negro suffrage, charged that the United States Supreme Court "had refused every opportunity to pass squarely upon this disfranchisement of millions by laws avowedly discriminatory and openly enforced in a manner that the white men may vote and the black men be without a vote in their government." The political status of the Negro thus became one of the cardinal concerns of the new organization.

The new movement was destined to become the most effective instrument for protest and action since the liquidation of the Abolition movement upon attainment of emancipation. In time it attracted practically the entire leadership element within the Negro race as well as a large rank-and-file membership. Negro leadership served the Association either as board members, staff workers, legal consultants, leaders in the local branches, or members. Now an organization of more than half a million members in sixteen hundred branches located in forty-four states, the District of Columbia, and the Territory of Hawaii, the NAACP is easily the most influential agency working to enhance the citizenship status of the Negro and the race's most powerful political instrument.

From the beginning the Association recognized the need for legal defense, effective propaganda, and political action. In the initial issue of *The Crisis,* November 1910, Dr. Du Bois, who was the first editor of the Association's organ, urged Negro men to qualify and vote wherever possible. "Let every colored man who can, vote," the editorial implored, "and whether he vote the Republican, Democratic or Socialist ticket, let him vote it, not because his father did or because he is afraid, but because, after intelligent consideration, he thinks the success of that ticket best for his people and his country."

In order to guide the Negro voters, the Association early developed the questionnaire which it submitted to candidates for public office in an effort to determine their attitude toward legislation affecting the welfare of the race. Particularly were congressional candidates questioned. At first many candidates either ignored the questionnaires or responded with evasive or indifferent answers. Over the years, as the Association continued to grow, responses were more prompt and enlightening. The political strength of the organization was gaining recognition.

The political objectives of the Association were baldly stated in its *Ninth Annual Report,* 1918. "The Association is striving to become so strong in numbers and so effective in method," the report asserted, "that no President, no governor, North or South, no member of Congress of any party and no mayor or a city will dare commit any indignity against colored people without realizing that the legitimate and constitutional rights of the race will be defended in the press, on the platform, at the ballot box and in the courts." The previous year, the report had suggested that "Negroes pursue this line of action, even perhaps to the extent of organizing a Negro party."

On the legal front the Association opened its offensive in behalf of the Negro's political rights with an attack upon the notorious "grandfather clause" which had been incorporated in the 1910 Constitution of Oklahoma. This clause, which both Mississippi and Louisiana claimed to have originated, was a trick which permitted indigent and illiterate whites to vote while excluding Negroes of the same class. It provided that an otherwise unqualified citizen might vote if his ancestor had voted prior to 1866; that is, before the enfranchisement of Negroes. Even this provision had a loophole, as Lewinson points out in his *Race, Class and Party.* Quoting an Alabama newspaper, he records: "There are in Alabama, as in all the States, large numbers of Negroes who perhaps would be unable to establish legitimacy of birth, but could nevertheless easily establish the identity of white fathers or grandfathers," and under the law would be entitled to a vote.

In the Oklahoma case, a Negro voter brought about the indictment of certain election officials for refusing him the right to vote. The NAACP filed briefs in support of the suit. In a decision handed down in June 1915 and written by the Louisiana-born Chief Justice Edward D. White, the Court invalidated the "grandfather clause" in the following words: "It is true it contains no express words of an exclusion, from the standard which it establishes, of any persons on account of race, color, or previous condition of servitude prohibited by the Fifteenth Amendment, but the standard itself inherently brings that result to existence, since it is based purely on a period of time before enactment of the Fifteenth Amendment and makes that period the controlling and dominant test of the right of suffrage."

Still intent upon circumventing the clear meaning of the Fourteenth and Fifteenth Amendments, the state of Oklahoma, soon after this decision, passed a law providing that all who were already registered should remain qualified voters, but all others would have to register within a twelve-day period or remain forever barred from voting. A Negro citizen who was denied the right to register after this period brought a suit which eventually reached the Supreme Court. In 1939 the New Deal Court, in an opinion written by Justice Felix Frankfurter, rejected this law, declaring that "the Amendment [Fifteenth] nullifies sophisticated as well as simple-minded modes of discrimination. It hits onerous procedural requirements which effectively handicap the exercise of the franchise by the colored race although the abstract rights to vote may remain unrestricted as to race."

While the legal basis of disfranchisement was being undermined step by step, two other important developments were taking place. First, the economic and cultural status of the Negro was advancing rapidly. The old excuses of ignorance and poverty were wearing thin. Negro illiteracy, which in 1870 was 80 per cent, was down to 16 per cent by 1930. The property holdings of the race had, by that time, risen to $2,600,000,000. While the median educational and economic status of the Negro was still below that of the white race, there were millions of white persons, particularly in the South, whose education and wealth were far below that of a vast number of Negroes. It was no longer possible to use these tests to exclude Negroes as a race. Secondly, there was the continued and accelerated migration not only out of the South, but from rural areas to urban centers within that region. Whereas at the turn of the century not more than a tenth of the race lived outside the borders of the former slave states, nearly a quarter was living in northern and western states by the end of the third decade of the century. While these migrants encountered segregation, job discrimination, residential restrictions, and sometimes violence, they did not meet obstacles to their voting rights in the North and West. Crowded into black ghettos, they augmented the Negro's political strength and made the race an increasingly important factor in local, state, and national elections.

The vote of the Negro in the North became of vital importance to the Republican party. Yet because of the anti-Negro attitude of southern Democrats this vote could not exercise influence within the ranks of the national Republican party commensurate with its importance. The double-cross by Woodrow Wilson still rankled deep in the hearts of Negro voters. It served also as a convenient whiplash in the hands of the Republicans. "If you don't behave, the bad, bad Democrats will get you!" Mindful of the biased Wilson administration, Negro voters were wont to heed the dire Republican admonitions. Meanwhile the Democrats, by devious indirections, continued to seek the Negro voter in national elections. While an increasing number of Negroes were being aligned with dominant Democratic machines in northern cities, the bulk of the race, having little other choice, held firm to their Republican allegiance in both local and national elections.

In 1920 Negro voters were glad of the opportunity to take part in casting out the Democratic administration which, under President Wilson, had introduced Jim Crow in federal departments. The suppressed and cryptic stories about Warren G. Harding's antecedents also gave them hope that he would have a better understanding of and sympathy for their problems. James Weldon Johnson, the urbane and erudite Negro poet, then secretary of the NAACP, headed a delegation which urged Candidate Harding to appoint a national biracial commission to study and make recommendations on race relations in this country. Harding was elected with Negro support. This recommendation was embodied in a presidential message to Congress, but nothing ever came of it. Indeed, in Birmingham, President Harding, resurrecting Booker T. Washington's Atlanta Compromise, affirmed the "fundamental, eternal, and inescapable difference" of race which would forever keep black and white apart. The hope which Negroes reposed in him went unfulfilled even though he would "let the black man vote when he is fit to vote." Neither President Harding nor his successor, Calvin Coolidge, did anything to undo the evil which Wilson had wrought. Jim Crow remained the practice in most government bureaus. They made the usual political appointments and paid lip service to the constitutional rights of the Negro, but did little more.

During President Wilson's first administration, on November 14, 1915, Booker T. Washington died. He was succeeded as principal of Tuskegee Institute the following year by a huge black man who claimed unadulterated African descent. Robert R. Moton, the new head of Tuskegee, did not fall heir to Mr. Washington's mantle of race leadership. Indeed, the day of one-man leadership had passed. Meanwhile the growing militancy of the Negro had challenged and seriously impaired Mr. Washington's conciliatory program. While facing the necessity of getting along in the deep South, Dr. Moton realized also the inevitability of the Negro's taking a more affirmative position in his struggle for the ballot. Negroes were no longer willing to accept any leadership which condoned curtailment of their civic and political rights.

Recognizing the end of the strategy of retreat, Dr. Moton affirmed the Negro's stake in voting. "The Negro has property and other interests also at stake in this matter of the ballot," he said. "At bottom the reason for the neglect of the Negro section of the city by public officials is the pressure that is brought to bear by other elements of the community that have the ballot wherewith to influence the distribution of public funds. Bond issues for civic improvements, education, recreational facilities, and the like, are authorized by the vote of the citizens. Those who vote have their interests provided for in the provisions of the act; those who do not vote have no one to speak for them. It is wholly consistent with the processes of a republican form of government that the voteless element should find its interests uncared for."[2]

Dr. Moton's most significant political role was his support of the candidacy of Herbert Hoover. Following protest by the NAACP and other Negro groups, Dr. Moton had been named head of an advisory committee to assist Mr. Hoover in the readjustment and relocation of families displaced by the Mississippi flood of 1927. There had been bitter complaints that the American Red Cross and the Flood Control Commission under direction of Mr. Hoover had discriminated against Negro displaced persons. Dr. Moton's committee was named to ameliorate these conditions. This association with the plump Californian led the Negro leader to look upon the future President as a man both liberal and efficient. By religion Hoover was a Quaker, a sect long in the forefront of the fight for equal rights. He had spent years working as an engineer in South Africa and in the Orient—an experience which should have given him a world perspective on the color problem. Convinced of the liberality and competence of Mr. Hoover, Dr. Moton dispatched his genial secretary, Albon L. Holsey, to Kansas City to drum up votes for the candidate among the Negro delegates attending the Republican National Convention meeting there in 1928. Mr. Hoover won the nomination and the election in November.

Despite Dr. Moton's undercover support of Mr. Hoover, the

[2]Robert R. Moton, *What the Negro Thinks* (New York: Doubleday, Doran & Co., 1929), p. 136.

Democrats made deeper inroads on the Republicanism of Negro voters than in any previous national election. In part this was due to the virulence of the southern attack upon the Democratic nominee, Alfred E. Smith, a Tammany Hall Catholic, the son of Irish immigrants. An influential section of the Negro press, which in the years since World War I had achieved a new maturity and large circulations, supported the Democratic candidate. The Chicago *Defender,* the Baltimore *Afro-American,* the Boston *Guardian,* the Norfolk *Journal and Guide,* and the Louisville *News* were among the Negro publications which advocated the election of the New York governor. A Negro division was established in the National Democratic Campaign Committee to work among Negro voters. Negro voters' clubs supporting Governor Smith were organized in Arkansas, Georgia, Florida, Kentucky, Maryland, Missouri, North Carolina, Oklahoma, Tennessee, Massachusetts, Connecticut, New York, Ohio, Indiana, Illinois, Nebraska, Kansas, New Jersey, Pennsylvania, Minnesota, Colorado, and Arizona. In Texas, "Goose-neck Bill" McDonald, a former Republican national committeeman, openly supported Smith.

The campaign marked the revival of the Negro as a burning issue in southern politics. Anti-Catholicism in that region was fanned to a white heat. Governor Smith was depicted not only as an agent of the Pope and a tool of Tammany, but also as a friend of the Negro. In the South this latter attack proved to be even more damaging than the religious issue. Photographs of Ferdinand Q. Morton, Negro civil service commissioner in New York City and a Tammany appointee, with his white secretary were published and widely circulated in the South as an example of the kind of interracial relationships Smith would introduce in the federal service. In the press, from the platform, and over the radio this deadly propaganda was spread. Throughout the campaign, day after day, the fires of racial and religious bigotry were kindled. All other issues were eliminated. The split within the ranks of the white voters in the South enhanced the value of the small Negro vote in that region, for which undercover bids were made by Democrats, Republicans, and Hoovercrats, as Hoover's southern Democratic supporters were designated.

The attack became so base and incendiary that a group of forty-six southern liberals felt compelled to make a public appeal to halt the ever-mounting flow of anti-Negro propaganda. They branded this propaganda as "both irrelevant and dangerous" and expressed the hope that no voter would allow it "to inflame his mind with antagonism toward our Negro neighbors, who too long have been pawns in the game of politics." They called upon "the leadership of the South—the pulpit, the press, the platform—and upon every right-thinking man and woman among us to disclaim, discourage, and discontinue such appeals to prejudice and fear, to the end that the gains of recent years in interracial good will and understanding may not be sacrificed to the passing interest of a political campaign." Signatories to the appeal included some of the leading churchmen and educators of the South.

Negro leadership, naturally, was distressed by the attention focused on the false issue of race. This distress and resentment were expressed in an "Appeal to America" over the signatures of thirty-four leading Negro citizens of both parties. Pinning the major responsibility upon the politicians, this statement (whose signatories included Dr. Moton, Dr. Du Bois, Mrs. Mary McLeod Bethune, C. C. Spaulding, James Weldon Johnson, Walter White, Channing H. Tobias, Eugene Kinckle Jones, Carl Murphy, Claude Barnett, Reverend L. K. Williams, and Bishop Reverdy C. Ransom among others) accused "the political leaders of this campaign of permitting without protest, public and repeated assertions on the platform, in the press, and by word of mouth, that color and race constitute in themselves an imputation of guilt and crime." This propaganda, the statement continued, had "been received by the nation and the adherents of these and other parties in almost complete silence. A few persons have deprecated this gratuitous lugging in of the race problem, but for the most part, this astonishing campaign of public insult toward one-tenth of the nation has evoked no word of protest from the leading party candidates or from their official spokesmen; and from few religious ministers, Protestant or Catholic, or Jewish and from no leading social reformer." Protesting any ambition for political domination on the part of the Negro, the statement avowed "it is too late for us to submit to political slavery and we most earnestly protest against the unchallenged assumption that every American Negro is dishonest and incompetent and that color itself is a crime. . . . We are asking, therefore, in this appeal for public repudiation of this campaign of racial hatred."

The campaign of racial and religious hate was effective. Mr. Hoover carried forty states. What was more significant was the large-scale breaking of the Solid South for the first time since Reconstruction. When the final vote was counted Florida, North Carolina, Tennessee, Texas, and Virginia as well as Kentucky and West

Virginia were in the Republican column. Alabama remained Democratic by the narrow margin of 7000 votes out of a total of a quarter of a million. Arkansas, Louisiana, Mississippi, Georgia, and South Carolina stood safely by the party of white supremacy.

President Hoover's victory in the South apparently engendered hope that that region could be brought back to the two-party system. The new President seemed unable to comprehend that bigotry was the basis of all political activity dominating the South. It was racial bigotry upon which the one-party system had been founded. Religious bigotry was the rock upon which the system floundered. Hoover moved to consolidate his gains in the former Confederate states. His first step was to ignore the Negro nationally and to eliminate him as a factor in the Republican party in the South. Departing from precedent set by other Republican presidents, he made no mention of the Negro or the problems of the race in his inaugural address. He proceeded then to clean up the last vestiges of Negro leadership in the party and to encourage the lily-whites in a desperate and futile attempt to build a Republican party acceptable to the southern whites. All federal patronage was taken out of the hands of the leaders of the black-and-tan state delegations. Ben Davis, the national committeeman for Georgia, was deprived of patronage, dismissed from the inner councils of the party, and forced to resign. Perry Howard, the Mississippi committeeman, was eased out of his position in the United States Department of Justice, denied the privilege of handing out jobs, and indicted for exacting fees from federal job holders in his state. Of the Negro leaders of Republicanism in the South, only Robert R. Church of Memphis and Walter L. Cohen of New Orleans retained positions of power and influence.

The President's open drive to make his party a lily-white organization in the South alarmed the Democratic leaders in that region. This was not what they wanted. Lily-white Republicanism, once firmly established, would offer competition and threaten the control held by the Democratic leaders. The black-and-tan outfits offered no such competition and held no such threat. The campaign of 1928 indicated the plausibility of developing the lily-white organizations. Moreover, the white-supremacy advocates of the Democratic party had very good working arrangements with the black-and-tan Republican leaders, who obligingly designated Democrats (white, of course) for the principal federal jobs in the South. The lily-whites would demand these jobs for themselves. Mindful of these considerations, an all-white jury of Mississippians cleared Mr. Howard of the charges brought against him in the federal indictment, charges that were believed to be "watertight and foolproof."[3] The President could look for no assistance from white-supremacy Democrats in building his lily-white party.

Plunging grimly ahead in his blind determination to whitewash southern Republicanism, President Hoover offered the bait of a seat on the United States Supreme Court bench to a leader of the lily-whites. This step proved his undoing and brought about the complete collapse of the gleaming white edifice he was industriously trying to erect. On March 21, 1930, he sent to the Senate the name of John Johnson Parker, a judge of the United States Circuit Court, for confirmation as an associate justice of the United States Supreme Court. An examination of the record quickly revealed Judge Parker's ideological unfitness for the position. He had offended organized labor by a decision upholding the constitutionality of the so-called "yellow-dog" contract, under terms of which the individual worker was compelled to waive his right to join a union for collective bargaining. Accepting the Republican nomination for governor of North Carolina in 1920, he had declared: ". . . the participation of the Negro in politics is a source of evil and danger to both races and is not desired by the wise men in either race or by the Republican party of North Carolina."

The American Federation of Labor immediately protested the nomination. The National Association for the Advancement of Colored People queried the nominee upon the statement attributed to him. Upon receiving no reply, the Association requested the President to withdraw the nomination, citing as a precedent President Taft's immediate withdrawal of the nomination of Judge Hook of Kansas, who, like Parker, had expressed himself as opposed to Negro voting. Defying both organized labor and the Negro, President Hoover refused to reconsider the nomination. The NAACP then took the fight to the people. It was the most important struggle in which the organization had yet engaged and was a test of its effectiveness and strength.

The Negro protest was at first ignored as insignificant by Judge Parker, President Hoover, and the country at large. But as the Association focused all of its efforts on the defeat of the nominee, it met with encouraging response. Soon the NAACP drive overshadowed that of the AFL and of the unorganized white liberals

[3]Lewinson, op. cit., p. 181.

who also opposed the Parker nomination. It was a dramatic, efficiently co-ordinated, and swiftly moving fight packed into six tense weeks. Spurred by the national office, the branches throughout the country swung into action, bringing pressure upon their respective senators for rejection of the recalcitrant appointee. "An avalanche of telegrams, telephone messages and letters began to descend upon Senators from the North, and even from southern states, and Senator after Senator hastened to assure the NAACP that he would oppose the confirmation of Judge Parker," the Association recorded in its *Twenty-first Annual Report.*

The Greensboro (N.C.) *Daily News,* which on April 19, 1920, had published Parker's slur upon Negro voters, at first denied that the nominee had ever made such a statement or that it had been published in that paper. Within twenty-four hours the Association placed photostatic copies of the clipping in the hands of the President, each of the senators and the Washington correspondents. The denial was dropped. The Association continued to rally support not only from its branches but also from church, fraternal, and civic organizations and from prominent individuals and political leaders, particularly state and local Republicans. It had the unanimous support of the Negro press and wide support among metropolitan dailies and liberal publications. The Society of Friends, Hoover's own church, joined the fight against Parker.

The battle raged across the country, reverberating to the far corners. The South, at first stunned and unbelieving, became alarmed and furious. The audacity of these blacks attempting to tell the country who shall not sit on the Supreme Court bench! What colossal impudence! The Norfolk (Va.) *Ledger-Dispatch* cried out in pained indignation: "Justice and fair treatment for the Negroes? Yes—a thousand times, yes. Let the Negroes decide who shall and who shall not sit on the bench of the Supreme Court? No! A million times, no! If any southern Senator is fool enough to oppose confirmation of Judge Parker in order to embarrass the President of the United States, or because he is afraid of any organization of and for Negroes, then let him perish in his folly!"

The attitude in the North varied. The New York *Times* saw "no principle . . . at stake. Only a political self-interest is driving on these Republican Senators. . . . Compared to them the Negro agitators, hot on their trail, are straightforward and honorable." To the liberal New York *World* opposition to Judge Parker's nomination was neither "capricious" nor "political except in the sense that politicians are sometimes required to consult the temper of their constituents." The Negroes, as the *News* of Springfield, Massachusetts, saw it, "made a brave fight and their victory is a handsome one." The Chicago *News* held that "the rejection of Judge Parker has advanced the colored race politically throughout the country."

A month from the day the nomination was submitted, the Senate Judiciary Committee, by a vote of 10 to 6, reported adversely on confirmation. Bringing all the prestige, pressure, and power of his office to bear, the President intensified his effort to have his nominee confirmed. The White House telephoned to Dr. Moton at Tuskegee, seeking his endorsement of Judge Parker. The disillusioned educator, while not joining openly in the fight against Parker, wisely refused to lend his name to the drive for confirmation. In North Carolina, despite pressure and threats, only two Negroes of any prominence could be found to say even a mild word in support of the nominee. Indeed, it was a North Carolina Negro who first brought to the attention of the Association the Parker record and supplied the incriminating evidence in the form of a clipping from the Greensboro *Daily News*. The threats against Negro citizens in North Carolina were immediately exposed by the Association, which publicly called upon the governor of the state to give protection to these citizens.

On May 7 the Senate voted 41 to 39 against confirmation. To the unyielding President it was a humiliating defeat; to the Negro it was an indication of his political maturity and a demonstration of the value of organization. Although the influence of the Negro protest was generally recognized, only Senator Robert F. Wagner deigned to mention this factor on the floor of the Senate. "I see a deep and fundamental consistency between Judge Parker's views of labor relations and his reported attitude toward the colored people of the United States," the New York senator said. "They both spring from a single trait of character. Judged by the available record, he is obviously incapable of viewing with sympathy the aspirations of those who are aiming for a higher and better place in the world. His sympathies naturally flow out to those who are already on top, and he has used the authority of his office and the influence of his opinion to keep them on top and to restrain the strivings of the others, whether they be an exploited economic group or a minority racial group."

To Heywood Broun the defeat of Judge Parker seemed ironic retribution. "Judge Parker had declared himself against Negro participation in politics," he wrote in *The Nation*, "and as a result, the American Negro became politically effective for the first time and barred the way to Mr. Hoover's appointee. And there was drama in the manner of the conflict. The President, as has been pointed out on many occasions, is a great organizer. With prestige and patronage at his command, he could exert terrific pressure for the confirmation of Judge Parker. . . . And so it is exciting to know that the man in the White House was checkmated largely through the efforts of a short and slight mulatto in a five-room Harlem flat. Walter White did the field work for the National Association and on the strength of his recent triumph he may become one of the most powerful forces in American politics."

This successful fight marked the emergence of Mr. White, then the Association's acting secretary, as a dynamic leader. With tireless energy he organized and directed the drive which aroused the whole of Negro America, as never before, and rallied the support of the leading white liberals. His triumph demonstrated that the new generation had mastered the technique of mass organization and sustained protest and had acquired skill in effective propaganda and legislative lobbying. He was later named secretary of the Association, which under his leadership continued to flourish and expand.

"That there were other elements in the defeat of Judge Parker is manifest," Dr. Du Bois wrote in reviewing the fight. "There was, for instance, the opposition of organized labor; there was the fear of Southern Democrats that this nomination would tend further to disrupt the Solid South; and there was the determination of the West to liberalize the Supreme Court. All these motives had influence. And yet, it was the Negro influence which curiously enough in the end solidified the opposition."[4]

The defeat of Parker, however, did not end the fight. There was follow-up work to do. The lesson had to be driven home at the ballot box. Those senators whose allegiance to the President was greater than to their constituents and the Constitution had to be reminded of the error of their ways. They were. The Association's field agents worked tirelessly to bring about their defeat. By the end of 1934, *The Crisis* records, "all the senators who voted for Parker and who could be reached by colored voters had been defeated. Of course, the colored voters alone could not have accomplished this feat, but they added their strength to others who voted against the senators. The list of those actually defeated in battle (exclusive

[4]Du Bois, "The Defeat of Parker," *The Crisis,* July 1930.

of those who died or withdrew) is an impressive one: Shortridge of California; Allen of Kansas; Patterson of Missouri; Watson of Indiana; Fess and McCulloch of Ohio; Reed of Pennsylvania; Hatfield of West Virginia; Kean and Baird of New Jersey; Walcott of Connecticut; and Hebert of Rhode Island. Hastings of Delaware and one or two senators from far north New England states escaped."

Mr. Hoover's administration hobbled along in the deepening gloom of depression. The President tried to hasten the prosperity which he kept seeing "just around the corner" by advancing huge sums of federal money to Big Business on the theory that such investments would ultimately trickle down to the little people in the street. The unemployed veterans marched on Washington, demanding a bonus. They were met by the military and dispersed by bullets. Meanwhile, President Hoover, defeated in his attempt to make Republicanism respectable among southern whites, avoided Negroes like a jungle plague. Meanwhile, Oscar De Priest, a Republican politician of Chicago, had been elected to Congress, the first Negro from the North to sit in the Capitol and the first of his race in twenty-eight years.

Near the end of his administration, on October 1, 1932, when he was vainly looking forward to re-election, President Hoover received a delegation of two hundred Negroes. Roscoe Conkling Simmons, a professional speechmaker and politician, was spokesman for the delegation. Invoking the memory of the Great Emancipator, he turned to Mr. Hoover and implored:

"Speak, Mr. President, and tell us Lincoln is not dead!" Rising to his usual empty eloquence, the famed orator went on:

"Speak and say that there is no higher theme than liberty. Tell us again that our President loves justice and will do it. Rededicate today in the trumphet tones of sincere phrase our great party of eternal truth."

The President responded. He would do all that was within his power to see that the rights of all the people were maintained. He assured them that the Republican party "would not abandon or depart from its traditional duty toward the American Negro." That was all. With these words he dismissed them and sent them out to rally the despised Negro vote. But it was the eleventh hour and later than he thought. The next month he was overwhelmingly defeated by the Democratic candidate. Mr. Hoover, who four years previously had carried forty states, in 1932 won only six states with fifty-nine electoral votes. The chastened white voters of the Solid South had returned en masse to the party of their fathers.

The counterattack against disfranchisement launched by the National Association for the Advancement of Colored People moved steadily forward. Having dealt a fatal blow to the "grandfather clause," and having demonstrated its political sagacity and power in the Parker case, the Association renewed its offensive upon the most stubborn citadel of political white supremacy—the Democratic "white primary." The opening gun was fired in Texas, where the state legislature, in 1923, had enacted a law forbidding Negro participation in the Democratic primaries. Prior to the passage of this law there were a number of counties in the state which permitted Negroes to vote freely in the Democratic primaries despite a state rule of the party excluding them. Dr. L. A. Nixon of El Paso, who as a regular Democrat had voted for many years in the primary, presented himself at the polls following enactment of this law. Denied the right to vote, he appealed to the courts. His case was taken up by the NAACP and carried to the Supreme Court, which on March 7, 1927, handed down a favorable decision. The opinion, written by Justice Oliver Wendell Holmes, declared that "it is too clear for extended argument that color cannot be made the basis of a statutory classification affecting the right set up in this case."

The effect of this decision was to ban exclusion by legislative enactment. Seeking a way out, the Texas legislature promptly passed a law empowering the State Democratic Committee to define the qualifications for admission to its primary elections. The party's state executive committee then passed a resolution "that all white Democrats who are qualified under the Constitution and laws of Texas . . . and none others be allowed to participate in the primary elections." On the basis of this ruling Dr. Nixon was again refused the right to vote. He again took his case to the courts, with the assistance of the National Association. Reaffirming its former position, the Supreme Court held in a decision handed down on May 2, 1932, that the state could not delegate to others powers declared unconstitutional for the state to exercise. Expressing the majority opinion, Justice Benjamin N. Cardozo wrote: "Delegates of the State's power have discharged their official functions in such a way as to discriminate invidiously between white citizens and black. The Fourteenth Amendment, adopted as it was with special solicitude for the equal protection of the members of the Negro race, lays a duty upon the court to level by its judgment these barriers of color."

The final storming of the bastion of the "white primary" was yet to come. The Supreme Court had merely affirmed that the state could not legislate exclusion of the Negro nor delegate that power to any agency. It had not held that a political party on its own could not designate race as a qualification for membership and participation in its primaries. There were eight southern states in which the Democratic party had so ruled. The Association abided its time, waiting for the precise case and the opportune time to take it to the Supreme Court. Meanwhile a group of interested citizens in Houston, Texas, carried the third case to the Supreme Court. R. R. Grovey, a Negro political and labor leader of Houston, had been denied the right to vote under the new party rule adopted by the Democratic party of Texas. The Supreme Court, in 1935, held that this action did not violate the Constitution.

It was not until six years later that the perfect case and the right time were conjoined. In 1941 the Court had ruled propitiously in U.S. *v.* Classic, a case involving the refusal of primary election officials in Louisiana to count the ballots of certain white voters. The Court ruled that where the primary is an integral part of the election machinery or where the primary determines the final election, such a primary is within the prohibitions of the Constitution. Using the Classic decision as a basis, NAACP lawyers filed a case in Federal Court on behalf of Dr. Lonnie E. Smith of Houston. The case was carried to the Supreme Court, which, on April 3, 1944, reversed its former decision in the Grovey case and upheld the right of qualified Negroes to vote in Democratic primaries in Texas. In a historic opinion which sounded the death knell for the "white primary," Justice Stanley F. Reed affirmed: "The United States is a constitutional democracy. Its organic law grants to all citizens a right to participate in the choice of elected officials without restriction by any state because of race. This grant to the people of the opportunity for choice is not to be nullified by a state through casting its electoral process in a form which permits a private organization to practice racial discrimination in the election. Constitutional rights would be of little value if they could be thus indirectly denied."

The organized Negro protest, spearheaded by the National Association, was making headway. Under impact of this sustained and brilliant counterattack, the Solid South was receding from its all-out opposition to Negro voting. Southern die-hards continued to fight back in South Carolina, Georgia, Mississippi, and Alabama. But it was they who were now fighting a hopeless rear-guard action. More enlightened Southerners settled down to the realization that Negro voting had returned to stay.

The political role of the Association has become increasingly a matter of controversy among the membership. There are those who believe that the organization should pursue a completely hands-off policy. There are others who demand a more affirmative policy with open endorsement of progressive candidates. Officially the NAACP has repeatedly and wisely affirmed a non-partisan policy. But the very character of the organization and the nature of the struggle in which it is engaged inescapably thrust upon it a vital role in shaping the political destiny of the Negro in America. Politically its task has been one of clearing away the legal debris which has impeded progress and of drawing the issues and articulating the demands upon which to rally the Negro vote in national elections. Save for the important issue of fair employment practices, the Association has initiated and sponsored practically every other national legislative fight in behalf of Negro interests. The FEPC issue was largely the creation of A. Philip Randolph of the AFL Brotherhood of Sleeping Car Porters and his march-on-Washington movement. And in this fight he had from the beginning the support of the Association.

The Association's principal legislative fight has been its long campaign for enactment of a federal anti-lynching law. In 1920, Congressman L. C. Dyer, at the behest of the Association, introduced such a bill which, passed by the House, was subsequently killed by a Senate filibuster. Both parties have been able to push similar legislation through the House but have been unable or unwilling to break the southern filibuster in the Senate. Although Congress has refused to pass such a measure, work in its behalf has by no means been futile. The campaign has been of immeasurable educational value and has placed the lynch states on guard. When the Dyer bill was introduced in 1920 there were fifty-seven lynchings. Over the twenty-seven-year period the lynching rate has declined, reaching a low of one in 1945, but rising the following year to six. In 1947 there was only one recorded lynching.

Inevitably the Association has assumed national leadership in the Negro's political fight. In this it is way out in front of the professional Negro politicians. Its non-partisan position enables it to draw the issues sharply and uncompromisingly. Tied to no political party, it does not face the need of trimming its demands to meet the exigencies of partisanship. It can be truly representative of the Negro's political aspirations. The leadership of the Association is wooed and listened to by the leaders of both the Democratic and Republican parties as well as by those who would launch a third party. Based on the Association's record and influence, John Gunther prudently includes Walter White, the organization's chief executive, among the sixty-four men of America who contribute importantly to the political shape of things developed in the nation.

In local elections, except in the South, the influence of the Association has not been strong. Here the politicians who are able to deliver votes exert far greater influence. However, the new voters in the South naturally turn for guidance to the organization through which they gained the ballot. Save in such cities as Memphis, Chattanooga, and San Antonio, where Negroes have long voted, the political leadership is frequently identical with the leadership of the local branch of the NAACP. It is this organization which, along with the Southern Conference for Human Welfare, the Congress of Industrial Organizations' Political Action Committee, and other groups, conducts poll-tax-paying and registration drives within the various Negro communities in southern cities. To maintain the non-partisan front of the organization, the branch leadership often sponsors the formation of a Suffrage Committee, or a Civic Council, or a Good Government League, to carry on an aggressive campaign in behalf of approved candidates. Through such efforts the Association has been perhaps the most important factor in the political development of the southern Negro. This local influence will probably wane as political leadership is developed in the South and as the Negro becomes integrated into the dominant political machinery.

In the thirty-eight years since the Association launched its counterattack against political exclusiveness, the political status of the Negro has been vastly improved. While the Association has made a major contribution to this advance, social and economic factors have been equally important. The impact of the New Deal created a political climate in which the pace could be accelerated. The increasing strength and independence of Negro voters in the North were important factors in retaining the New Deal and in the gaining of a liberal majority in the Supreme Court. The industrialization of the South and the development of a progressive labor movement helped immeasurably. The NAACP fight for political equality rallied the support of the increasingly influential Negro press, the church,

the fraternal organizations, and other societies. The Association afforded the medium through which all these groups could make
their demands effective. The mantle of leadership which had once
been Frederick Douglass's and later Booker T. Washington's is now
shared by the group which shapes the policies of the National Association for the Advancement of Colored People, and of which Walter
White is the chief spokesman.

CHAPTER VII

Greener Pastures?

CONSIDERED OBJECTIVELY, THE POSITION OF THE NEGRO IN America is such as would seem to make him ready to embrace any radical doctrine. All the conditions fostering discontent with the social and economic order are present. There is the oppression of the landless black farm population and the super-exploitation of the urban proletariat. There is economic and social discrimination in every phase of American life. There is a vast, vicious, and crushing system of Jim Crow, sanctified by law and hallowed by custom. There is denial of equal opportunity for work, for education, for health, and for the release of the race's creative abilities. There is cruel, systematic, and sadistic inhumanity paralleled in the modern world only by the Nazi persecution of the Jews and the brutal oppression of the colored population by the white colonists in the Union of South Africa. These, surely, are fertile fields in which to sow the seeds of revolution.

A pariah in the land of his nativity, the Negro appears to have little or nothing to lose by a fundamental change in our social order. In a vast section of the country he is robbed of his basic citizenship rights and thwarted in his development by a rigid caste system. His Americanism, as old as that of any of his countrymen of European descent, derives from the blood and labor and spiritual qualities he has contributed to the building of this nation and the development of its culture. He is in America and really of America, yet the dominant forces in this country choose to ignore his essential Americanism.

Recognizing this paradox, the Communist party sees in the Negro an important potential ally in the struggle for a revolutionary upheaval and a redistribution of wealth and power. Accordingly,

Communists have devoted more attention and energy to work among
colored citizens than any other non-Negro group seeking basic reform since the heyday of the Garrisonian Abolitionists. No other
political party, no branch of the Christian church, no labor organization, no other reform or revolutionary movement has devoted as
great a share of its resources to gaining adherents and spreading its
influence among Negroes as has the Communist party.

Yet with all their untiring efforts—their dramatic fight for the
freedom of the Scottsboro boys, their triumph in the Angelo Herndon case, their struggle for equal social, political, and economic
rights, as well as their day-to-day efforts along a far-flung front—
with all of this, the Communists have failed to gain and hold any
considerable number of Negroes in the party membership.

The influence of the party on Negro life, however, cannot be
measured in terms of membership alone. Communist activity has
been an important factor in sharpening the Negro's fight for equal
rights and in fostering his recognition in the labor movement, in
the arts, and in the civic affairs of the community. Through their
international connections the Communists have widely publicized
the plight of the Negro in democratic America, to the painful embarrassment of American travelers in Europe, Asia, and Latin
America.

Many of the Negro intellectuals and writers have at one time or
another been influenced by Communist philosophy. One of the
earliest Negro writers to be associated with the then new movement
was Claude McKay, poet and novelist. Mr. McKay, an editor of
the old *Liberator,* was in the vanguard of Negro intellectuals who
made the pilgrimage to Moscow. There, in 1922, he was tumul-
tuously received as the representative of an oppressed minority.
More than a decade later he returned to America after a long so-
journ in western Europe and northern Africa, repudiating the
Stalinist regime and rejecting international Marxism. Richard
Wright, Langston Hughes, Paul Robeson, and other writers and
artists have, at one time or another, espoused Communist movements. And W. E. B. Du Bois, returning from a Russian tour in
1928, exclaimed that if what he had observed was Bolshevism: "I'm
a Bolshevik!" Since then, as before, he has often been in controversy
with the party tactics and objectives. Later he became an editor
of *The New Masses,* the Communist cultural organ.

The Communists, of course, have their Negro critics, some whose
hatred of the party rivals that of Congressman Rankin or Westbrook

Pegler. But these censorious critics are not truly representative. With them Red baiting is largely an intellectual diversion with which the masses are apparently unconcerned. The latter, while not flocking to the Red banner, have refused to be stampeded into an anti-Communist bloc. Politicians seeking Negro support need more than the Red bogey to garner this vote.

Communism is not regarded as the enemy. The black folk of America know the enemy, the *real* enemy. They have looked into his hard white face. It is the fiendish face of reaction. The face of death—death to the spirit as well as to the body. This is the deadly enemy they know firsthand. They have met him face to face in the villages of South Carolina, in the swamps of Florida, on the banks of the Potomac, on the plains of Texas and Kansas, and in the dark ghettos of Detroit, Chicago, and New York. After such dread encounters they are not easily aroused by the reputed devilry of Communism in the Valley of the Danube.

In Harlem they have demonstrated their indifference to the Red label by twice electing to the City Council Benjamin J. Davis, a known member of the party's national board. Mr. Davis was not elected by Communists, but by Negro voters of all parties with the support of certain white liberals and Communists. He was elected neither because nor in spite of his membership in the Communist party. Rather he was elected because his constituents believed he would represent them ably and militantly. Believing this, they would have voted as readily for him had he been a Republican, Democratic, or American Labor party candidate. His election was a personal triumph rather than a victory for the party. It was also a tribute to the Negro voter's basic sense of values.

In their efforts to gain Negro support the Communists have employed the same tactics they have used with labor and other groups. These tactics have shifted in accordance with the frequent and unpredictable changes and reversals in the party line. Each shift has occasioned loss in membership and following, but others have been recruited to replace the delinquents.

The movement for active enlistment of Negro support developed early in the history of the party. In their Negro policy the Communists differed with the Socialist party, from which they split following the Russian Revolution and the establishment of the Third International. The Socialist party had formulated a program professedly appealing for the support of all workers and vaguely indicating the inclusion of Negroes. Little, however, was done to implement this declaration. The only serious bid the Socialists ever made for Negro support was during the period following World War I, when Socialist-led trade unions contributed to the support of *The Messenger,* a magazine of "scientific radicalism," edited by A. Philip Randolph and Chandler Owen. Associated with the editors were Frank R. Crosswaith, George S. Schuyler, Richard B. Moore, W. A. Domingo, and others who repudiated capitalism as a hopeless, decadent, and hypocritical system. The split in the left wing which gave birth to the Communist party naturally divided the thin ranks of the Negro comrades; some like Crosswaith remained with the Socialists, others like Moore cast their lot with the newly formed organization, and still others drifted into trade unionism, racial isolationism, or cynicism.

Boring from within was the party tactic of the early period. Negro comrades were delegated to the task of seeking converts within existing organizations with a view to capturing these for party purposes. The back-to-Africa movement of Marcus Garvey, then at its height, was the focal point of infiltration. The Garvey following was composed largely of working-class elements who believed that the frustrations encountered in this country could be alleviated through migration to Africa and the establishment there of a strong Negro nation developed along capitalist lines. The movement was not captured, but the Communist tactics contributed to its disruption. Today only shattered remnants of Garvey's Universal Negro Improvement Association remain. Similar efforts in the National Association for the Advancement of Colored People, the Brotherhood of Sleeping Car Porters, and other organizations failed to win wide support among the members of these organizations.

Failure in these endeavors led to the organization of the American Negro Labor Congress in 1925 under the leadership of Lovett Forte-Whiteman. This short-lived body, the forerunner of the National Negro Congress, appealed primarily to organizations of Negro workers and farmers, who were to be united "for the abolition of all discrimination, persecution, and exploitation of the Negro race and working people generally" and "to bring the Negro working people into the trade unions and the general labor movement with the white workers." Meeting with scant support from the Negro workers and even less from white workers, the congress lacked the vitality to survive.

The period of non-collaboration with persons and organizations not fully committed to the new party line followed. It was during this period that dual unionism was advocated and the Communists established the Trade Union Unity League in an effort to induce workers to abandon the American Federation of Labor and join the rival Communist unions. The National Miners Union, the National Textile Workers, and other unions were organized to rival the existing AFL internationals. Efforts were made to bring Negro workers into these unions and particularly into the National Miners Union, which had claimed jurisdiction over a field in which thousands of Negroes were employed and where they were active members of the United Mine Workers of America.

The tactics of discrediting labor leaders, liberals, and non-conforming radicals through violent verbal attacks were extended also to the leaders of Negro organizations. Walter White, the executive secretary of the National Association for the Advancement of Colored People; A. Philip Randolph, president of the Brotherhood of Sleeping Car Porters; the officers of the National Urban League; the clergy; the politicians, and others in positions of leadership within the race were victims of these attacks.

It was during this period, in the spring of 1931, that nine young colored lads, ranging in age from thirteen to nineteen years, were arrested in Alabama and charged with the rape of two nondescript white girls. The defense of these boys was first undertaken by the NAACP. But the Communists, through the International Labor Defense, captured the defense of the imprisoned youths and conducted a vigorous, leather-lunged campaign that echoed and re-echoed throughout the world. The Scottsboro boys were lifted from obscurity to a place among the immortals—with Mooney and Billings, Sacco and Vanzetti, fellow victims of bias in American courts.

It was a sorry spectacle—the scramble of the Communists to wrest the defense of the hapless boys from the control of the NAACP. To accomplish this end the whole propaganda machinery of the party was turned loose in a campaign to discredit the Association's leadership. Stunned by the violence of this attack, not only upon the principles and policies of their organization, but also upon their personal integrity, the leaders of the NAACP were bewildered and in the end relinquished the defense to the ILD. The Communists maintained that legal defense had to be supplemented by international propaganda. American consulates, legations, and embassies were picketed and stoned in many parts of the world. Mass meetings of protest were held in the capitals of Europe and Latin America at which resolutions demanding the freedom of the Scottsboro boys were passed. Letters, telegrams, and cablegrams poured in upon the President of the United States, the governor of Alabama, the presiding judge, and other state officials, demanding the immediate release of the boys. This propaganda was effective in exposing the hypocrisy of American justice, but it did not gain the freedom of the boys. Only after it had ceased was a compromise effected which resulted in the release of four of the accused.

Meanwhile the ILD had obtained the services of Samuel Leibowitz, New York's successful criminal lawyer. His defense was thorough, brilliant, and unanswerable. He proved conclusively the innocence of all the defendants. Eloquently and sincerely he pleaded for justice. All this, however, meant nothing to the insensitive Alabama backwoodsmen who composed the juries in Decatur, where the trials were held. They returned verdicts of "guilty."

During these years when the defense of the Scottsboro boys was second only to the defense of the Soviet Union on the party agenda, the Communists attained their widest influence among American Negroes. There were, of course, those who questioned the motives of the comrades and feared that their methods, antagonizing the southern whites, endanged the lives of the boys whose defense they were conducting. Caution was counseled by those who believed that more effective results might be obtained by an appeal to the "better elements" in the South rather than by challenging their deep-seated prejudices. But the black masses seemed intrigued by this bold, forthright, and dramatic defiance. Offering no quarter, the Communists put the South on the defensive in the eyes of the whole civilized world. They stirred the imagination of Negroes and inspired the hope of ultimate justice. In churches, in conventions, in union halls, in street-corner meetings, Negroes were clamorous in expressing approval of this campaign.

To the Communists, however, the whole campaign was much more than a defense of nine unfortunate lads. It was an attack on the system which had exploited them, fostered the poverty and ignorance in which they were reared, and finally victimized them by legal proceedings which were a mockery of justice. It was a case made to order for the Communists and well worth the scramble they made for the privilege of representing the defendants. They made the most of it. Presenting the case at Negro meetings and in the Negro press, they exposed "capitalist justice" and worked assiduously to undermine whatever faith the Negro may have had not only in the local courts but also in the Supreme Court, and in

democracy as a system of government. Nor did they fail to give
assurance that no such thing could happen in the Soviet Union,
where there was neither class exploitation nor racial prejudice.

With the development of the popular front after the rise of Hitler,
the Communists joined with non-Communist groups, including the
NAACP, to organize the National Scottsboro Defense Committee
headed by Dr. Allan Knight Chalmers, a distinguished New York
clergyman. All of the spectacular tactics which had featured the
earlier defense were abandoned. Working without fanfare, the
new committee obtained the release of four of the boys and an
agreement from Alabama state officials that the others would be
released within a specified period. The state of Alabama welshed
on this agreement and as late as February 1948 was still holding in
prison two of the remaining five, now grown to young manhood.

The popular front was a complete reversal of the non-collaboration policy. The front was so broad that it embraced not only working-class elements but practically all groups, excluding only the
dissident Communists, the outspoken Fascists, and the Liberty
Leaguers. A new spirit of conciliation replaced the violent attacks
upon liberals that had characterized the preceding period. The party
sought and made friends among middle-class elements who previously had been looked upon with disdain. Communism was trans-
formed into "twentieth-century Americanism." Now, under the
united-front program, the American people were all "one big happy
family."

In the Negro world the hatchet was buried and the bitter word
forgotten. The comrades began to speak with courtesy of Walter
White, with affection of A. Philip Randolph, with respect of Lester
B. Granger, and with restraint of the uncompromising Crosswaith.
The clergy was wooed and emissaries were sent to seek converts
among the black petty bourgeoisie. The invective which previously
had been heaped upon all these was reserved for Trotsky, Hitler,
Mussolini, and the Liberty League. Unquestionably these efforts of
the Communists, coming in a time of depression, broadened the
social horizon of a considerable section of the smug Negro middle
class, developed an awareness of the economic basis of race prejudice,
and stimulated interest in labor organization.

In the midst of this "happy-family" era, Negro support was
severely jolted by Soviet policies in regard to the Italian rape of
Ethiopia. While Maxim Litvinoff, then Soviet Commissar of Foreign
Affairs, was making an eloquent, albeit eleventh-hour, plea in Ge-

neva for the independence of Ethiopia, the Soviet government was shipping oil, manganese, and wheat for Mussolini's war machine. The comrades were embarrassed. They sought first to deny it, then to explain it as fulfillment of treaty obligations. Finally they forgot it, choosing only to remember the challenging words of the now discredited Litvinoff.

Later, when the Soviet government was actively aiding the Spanish democracy, there were many to recall bitterly that it was this same government which had given lip service to defend Ethiopia and war materials to aid Italy. Nevertheless, the Communists, then the advocates of internationalism and collective security, were successful in arousing a measure of interest among Negroes for the support of the anti-Fascists in the Spanish Civil War. They organized a Negro committee to aid Spanish democracy, raised funds for medical supplies and for the support of war refugees. They facilitated the recruiting of Negroes for military service for the defense of democracy in Spain, proclaiming that the fate of Spain was importantly related to the welfare of the Negro in America.

All this changed overnight. The Soviet-Nazi pact of 1939 brought an abrupt end to that era. The very voices which yesteryear were raised in lusty defense of democracy abroad now decried the "imperialist war" and shouted that "the battle for democracy lies at home." Yesterday they were urging Americans of all races to fight for democracy in Spain. The next day they made plausible mockery of the idea of a black man fighting to defend democracy in Europe when he had none in his native land. "What democracy do we have to spare?" the Communists sneered. It was a telling argument, but it left unanswered the question: Was there more democracy—enough to spare—in Mississippi and Alabama in 1936 than in 1940? Democracy in America, the Negro long ago concluded, is too scarce an item for the export trade.

To spread the gospel of the united front, the Communists initiated the National Negro Congress as a successor to the defunct American Negro Labor Congress. In accordance with the new party line, the call proposed a more inclusive organization than the earlier congress. The appeal was made "to all Negroes, native and foreign born. To all Negro organizations, churches, labor unions, farm and sharecroppers' organizations. To all fraternal, civic, professional and political groups. To all organizations and persons of whatever race, who are willing to fight for economic and social justice for Negroes."

Organized in Chicago in February 1936, the National Negro Congress proposed to unify all Negro groups and sympathetic whites on a basis of minimum demands. The congress was to be a co-ordinating body not duplicating the work of any existing organization. Disclaiming any political affiliation, the organizers asserted that it embraced all political, social, and economic creeds, seeking to obtain equal rights for the Negro in America. A. Philip Randolph was chosen president and John P. Davis executive secretary.

Although at one time suspected of being inspired by the Republicans, it soon became clear that the motivating force behind the congress was the Communist party. That the influence of the party remained dominant was indicated at the third congress held in Washington in April 1940. There was strict adherence to the party line as developed since the Soviet-Nazi pact. There were the high praise of the Soviet regime and the declaration of the executive secretary of his firm conviction "that the American Negro people will refuse to join American or world imperialism in any attack against the Soviet people." So pronounced was the pro-Communist sentiment expressed at the congress that Randolph refused to stand for re-election as president.

In the House of Representatives the conference was denounced as a "Red" meeting. And many Negro publications deplored the Communist trend, more obvious at the Washington meeting than at any time previous. The congress, according to the retiring president, had accepted funds from the Communist party and from other outside sources. This he characterized as "an unhealthy condition." The defection of Randolph and others, however, did not lead to a disintegration of the congress, which continued to follow the ever-changing party line until 1947, when it lost its identity through merger with another organization.

It is a matter of record that the Communists have generally fought for full recognition of Negro rights. They have carried on this fight through their own organizations and through those organizations in which they exert influence. They have pushed the Negro to the forefront in party work. They have consistently nominated him for office on the party ticket. They have dramatized his problem. They have risked social ostracism and physical violence in his behalf. They have challenged American hypocrisy with the zeal, if not the high principle, of the Abolitionists. In all this they have performed a vital function as an irritant to the American conscience.

Yet during the years of World War II these zealots tempered their militant fight for Negro rights. They abandoned all work in the

South. They abstained from the fight to end segregation in the
armed services. They did not, of course, approve military Jim Crow.
Indeed, they deplored it. But they did not mobilize their forces to
fight this most iniquitous of all Jim Crow practices. They left that
struggle to be carried on by Negro organizations and by the Socialists. They justified their new hush-hush policy by the naïve assumption that the war was a struggle against fascism, to which all other
considerations had to be subordinated. But the Negro masses, as well
as the leadership, knowing full well our moral unpreparedness for
an all-out fight against fascism, were completely cynical about our
professed war aims. They knew that Hitler's racist doctrine continued to be held in high esteem in some parts of the United States
and throughout most of the British Empire. They correctly recognized the war as a fight to the finish against the military might of
Germany and Japan but, unlike the Communists, were completely
skeptical about our pretensions to be fighting a war against fascism.

With the close of the war and the steadily deteriorating American-
Soviet relations, the Communists have rebounded to their former
militancy. The Negro is again their symbol of capitalist oppression.
Their wartime dereliction is a thing of the past. They have returned
to their pre-war championship of the Negro's cause. They are re-
building their record. In view of this record, why has the Negro
failed to rally to the party? Mr. Randolph, in his valedictory at the
third National Negro Congress, gave one answer. "Negroes," he said,
"do not reject the Communist party because it is revolutionary or
radical, or because of its alleged extremism. They reject the Communist party because it is controlled and dominated by a foreign
state whose policy may, or may not, be in the interest of the United
States, or the Negro people."

The complete subordination of the party to Soviet interest is made
evident by every shift of the party line in conformance with the demands of the Kremlin. There is no reason to believe that if expediency demanded alignment of the Communist party with the Ku-
Klux Klan the American party would balk. Individuals, of course,
would repudiate such a step and withdraw from the party, as hap-
pens with each change in policy. Others would seek to justify it with
involved dialectics. It is clear that the Communists are concerned
primarily with the interests of the Kremlin. Their eyes may be fixed
on the stars, but their sodden feet are mired in the muck of power
politics.

Only subservience to policies formulated in Moscow without

regard to conditions on the American scene could explain the Communist concept of the Negro in America as a "nation" and the slogan of self-determination in the black belt for that "nation."[1] Nothing so completely reveals the utter lack of understanding by Moscow of the Negro problem in this country as this fantastic proposal. Such a pattern may have validity in Russia, where many peoples are differentiated from one another by language, customs, traditions, religion, territory, culture, and aspirations, as well as by physical distinctions. Through centuries these peoples have retained their national character and under the Soviet regime have been encouraged in the development of their respective cultures through their own schools, press, and other non-political institutions.

This is the exact opposite of what has developed in this country. Negro Americans are essentially a part of the national culture, differentiated from other Americans only by physical characteristics. They speak the same language, follow the same customs, are joint heirs to the American tradition, live in the same territory, worship the same God in the same manner, are nourished by the same diet, pledge allegiance to the same government, and entertain similar aspirations. Moreover, the black belt, comprising those counties in the South where Negroes are in the majority, has been steadily shrinking since 1880. Instead of seeking separation in schools and other institutions, the basic Negro demand has been and continues to be for integration as the only means of attaining equality. Where separation prevails it has been either superimposed by the dominant race or accepted as an expedient in the hope of ultimate justice. There is far less justification for considering Negroes of the South as a "nation" than the Jews of the Bronx or the Minnesota Swedes. Negroes in this country do not even have a common tribal origin, and today they largely represent an amalgam of African, European, and Amer-Indian stocks. The concept is historically and psychologically inacceptable.

When this concept of the Negro as a nation was first broached, practically all of the Negro comrades are reported to have opposed it. But Moscow had so ordained and there was nothing to do but accept it or withdraw from the party ranks. The Negro members of the party knew full well that the race which had striven long and earnestly to gain recognition of its basic Americanism would reject

[1]For a fuller discussion of this proposal see Joseph Stalin, *Marxism and the National and Colonial Question* (New York: International Publishers), and William Z. Foster, Benjamin J. Davis, et al., *The Communist Position on the Negro Question* (New York: New Century Publishers, 1947).

this Russian proposal. Similar movements had time and time again been rejected by Negroes. Acceptance of such a separatist movement would be defeatism—the acceptance by the Negro of his inability to compete on equal terms in the American civilization. All that the Negro asks in the black belt, as elsewhere in America, is full equality in opportunity, rights, privileges, and responsibilities under a truly democratic system.

An equally important factor in the Communist failure to enroll large numbers of Negroes is the lack of understanding of the psychological reactions of the Negro masses. First, there is a certain contempt in which many Negroes hold poor whites, and Communists ordinarily are not wealthy persons. There is a widespread conviction among Negroes that the only reason why any white person in this country should be poor or ignorant is due solely to that person's indolence and lack of character. Further, he is convinced that if the Negro had half the poor white man's opportunities he would far outstrip the latter. Moreover, the costly and unrelenting efforts of the South to keep the Negro "in his place" is convincing evidence to him that the whites also believe this.

And then there is the natural suspicion of a white person suddenly offering him the warm hand of fellowship. Long and bitter experience has fostered this suspicion. It is a case of fearing the Greeks "even bearing gifts." There must be some trick, he generally reacts. Something the white man wants from him, something valuable to the white man. Better look the gift horse in the mouth.

There has been no evidence in the general approach of the Communists to indicate that they are aware of these important psychological factors. Richard Wright, himself a onetime Communist, reveals this basic failing in *Native Son*, that grim and unforgettable tale of murder, race and class conflict. His character, Bigger Thomas, resented the friendly overtures of the white Communist and his philanthropic fellow traveler. ". . . he did not understand them; he distrusted them, really hated them. He was puzzled as to why they were treating him this way." No more did his would-be white friends understand Bigger. They saw him as a problem which they were eager to solve rather than as a personality warped by environment.

The difficulties which the Communists have encountered in building membership among Negroes stem principally from the same source: the alien character of the movement, its domination from abroad by persons ignorant of the varied facets of race relations in this country, the lack of understanding by its American agents of the true nature of the Negro problem in America.

But the Negro need not reject all that the Communists advocate. While co-operating with the party in the fight against lynching, terrorism, disfranchisement, unemployment, and the whole damnable Jim Crow system, Negroes have the responsibility to retain control of their organizations and institutions created to carry on this struggle. Aid should be welcomed, but outside control, whether by Communists or other cliques, must be rejected if the organizations are to hew to the line of their original purposes.

On the other hand, there is every reason why Negroes should oppose any attempt to purge the Communists from American life. If the abrogation of the civil rights of this minority political group can be justified, what is to prevent the complete nullification of the rights of racial minorities? Conscious of this deadly parallel, a notable group of Negroes publicly protested the proposed suppression of the Communist party in the spring of 1947.

The Negro must act to protect, preserve, and expand such rights as he enjoys in his native land. Foremost among these are the democratic rights to organize, agitate, protest, resort to the courts, and vote for improvement in his status, for full recognition as an American. Once these most elemental rights are abrogated, all is lost.

CHAPTER VIII

Labor as an Ally

PREDOMINANTLY A RACE OF WAGE EARNERS, THE NEGRO masses share the basic problems, interests, and destiny of all workers. Recognition of this common economic and political interest has dawned but slowly and painfully upon the American worker, Negro and white alike. Even today, with approximately 1,000,000 Negroes among the nation's 15,000,000 organized workers, a number of unions, notably the railroad brotherhoods and certain affiliates of the American Federation of Labor, either exclude or restrict Negro workers. In former years, black workers, usually with the support of the Negro community, often responded to these Jim Crow practices by accepting every opportunity to break strikes of lily-white trade unionists. Today the Negro worker is turning increasingly to political action as a means by which to attain equal job opportunity. And in this effort he has the support of all the truly progressive elements in the labor movement.

Executive and legislative measures to combat discrimination in employment preceded the Roosevelt era. In 1932, Ogden Mills, then Secretary of the Treasury, issued an order to construction engineers on government projects banning race discrimination in employment.[1] And seven states—Colorado, Illinois, Indiana, New Jersey, New York, Ohio, and Pennsylvania—had passed laws forbidding job discrimination in the construction of public works. These laws set forth a general policy providing for non-discrimination. Although penalties were indicated, the laws usually were vague about ways of determining discrimination and have rarely been invoked.

It was the New Deal labor legislation, however, together with

[1]Robert C. Weaver, *Negro Labor, a National Problem* (New York: Harcourt, Brace & Co., 1946), p. 10.

President Roosevelt's executive order establishing the Fair Employment Practices Committee, which gave new impetus and added significance to the political aspects of the fight against economic discrimination. The job-equality program was further implemented by administrative action by such New Deal agencies as the Public Works Administration and the United States Housing Authority. These agencies established minimum quotas for the employment of Negro skilled, semi-skilled, and unskilled workers in the construction of government-financed projects. The National Labor Relations Act and other legislation lifted the level of labor all along the line, facilitated the movement for the organization of the unorganized, stimulated the moribund AFL, and expedited the formation of the Committee for Industrial Organization, later to become the powerful Congress of Industrial Organizations.

A working-class people, Negroes naturally shared in the benefits of this legislation. A marginal worker in American industry, the Negro has been an important factor chiefly in times of industrial crises—strikes, lockouts, and wartime labor shortages. When workers in an industry demanded higher wages and better working conditions, there were always employers who sent labor scouts scurrying through the Negro community to recruit heretofore neglected black labor. Let a serious man-power shortage develop, and industry rediscovers the black reservoir in the deep South.

That, in large measure, has been the tragic story of black labor in American industry—in coal mining, steel, meat packing, automobiles, the needle trades, the water front, the railroad shops. It was a story made possible by adroit and selfish manipulation of longstanding patterns of racial prejudice. On the one hand, there had been a lack of understanding of trade unionism on the part of Negro workers; and on the other, an incredible shortsightedness on the part of large and important segments of the American labor movement which permitted the exclusion of the Negro worker or discriminated against him within the union. The employers have been the beneficiaries of this obtuseness.

That, in the main, has been the story. Fortunately it is changing with the growth of the Negro's political strength and with the development of more progressive ideas in the trade-union movement, particularly under the impact of the non-discrimination policies of the CIO. With freer participation within the unions, black workers have gained greater understanding of the meaning and objectives of the labor movement. In the nationwide strikes of 1946 in steel, coal, auto, packing house, and electrical equipment there was no racial break in the solid front which white and black workers presented in their demands for substantial wage increases. Even in the deep South, in the steel and textile and tobacco towns, Negro and white trade unionists, both CIO and AFL, have often worked together for trade-union objectives in the face of a continuing and vicious barrage of divisive racial propaganda.

In its first triumphant sweep across the country the CIO enrolled Negroes in the mass-production industries along with the white unorganized workers. Thousands in steel, automobile, transit, and food processing joined the militant new organization. Naturally there were some who hesitated and remained aloof. In the Little Steel strike of 1937, Negro workers were found on both sides of the fence. The Memorial Day massacre that year in Chicago had its Negro martyr, even as the massacre on Boston Common in 1770.

Fortunately the unions which gave guidance to the lusty CIO drive were relatively free of racial discrimination and recognized the role of the Negro in industry. Moreover, they had had experience in the organization of black workers and were well aware of the special problems involved. They had opened their own union doors on equal terms to all workers within their respective jurisdictions regardless of race, color, creed, or national origin. They had discovered that the Negro, accepted on equal terms with other workers, made a good union man. This experience stood them in good stead in the initial CIO drive. Negro organizers were employed to work among the black steel, maritime, and auto workers. Support was sought in the Negro community. Effort was made to surmount the racial barriers which tended to divide the workers. Recognition was given to Negroes within the union.

When the CIO was permanently organized as the Congress of Industrial Organizations at its Pittsburgh convention in 1938, a clause was incorporated in its constitution forbidding discrimination by member unions against any worker within their jurisdictions because of race, color, or creed. Certainly this was not because of any "love" for Negroes. Rather it was because the realistic leadership of the CIO recognized the black worker as an important element in American industry. To implement this constitutional provision, the CIO later established its Committee to Abolish Racial Discrimination, under the chairmanship of Secretary-Treasurer James B. Carey and with George L-P. Weaver as director.

By its very nature the industrial union cannot abide racial discrimination any more than it can recognize the overlordship of the crafts to the detriment of the semi-skilled and unskilled mass of workers. Whatever the motivation, the CIO is introducing a greater measure of democracy into the labor movement by maintaining low initiation fees, by opening its doors to all workers in an industry, by affording opportunity for representatives of minority groups to develop leadership and hold responsible office within unions, by educating the members to the need of political action to supplement activities on the economic front, and by broadening their social horizon.

In sharp contrast is the selfishness and snobbery of many of the AFL craft unions which not only bar the Negro worker but also exclude the bulk of all workers through prohibitive initiation fees and indifference to the plight of the unskilled. More than a dozen of these organizations openly raise the color bar. Others admit Negroes only into Jim Crow locals or auxiliaries, or accept their membership, fees, and dues only to discriminate against them within the union. A few others have recognized in the Negro a fellow worker entitled to membership in, and full protection of, the union.

Some of the lily-white unions, during the war and the post-war years, have been cracked. Competition with non-discriminating unions has compelled some to abandon their former exclusionist policies. A few yielded to the pressure of the FEPC in a period of wartime man-power shortages. Others, threatened with the loss of bargaining rights by court decisions, opened their membership to non-white workers. But the most effective instrument in breaking down the color bar has been legislation, the ultimate expression of political action. Seven states—New York, New Jersey, Massachusetts, Connecticut, Indiana, Wisconsin, and Oregon—have enacted legislation against job discrimination by employers or trade unions. These laws have contributed importantly to the breakdown of Jim Crow practices in the labor movement. Significantly, both the CIO and the AFL have supported this legislation.

The Negro's demand for job opportunity was dramatically projected upon the national consciousness in the spring of 1941 when A. Philip Randolph, the onetime Socialist who organized and became president of the Brotherhood of Sleeping Car Porters, AFL, threatened to mobilize 50,000 Negroes for a grim march on Washington. The demand was for jobs in the booming defense industries, many of which, although faced with serious labor shortages, refused to employ or upgrade Negro workers. The White House regarded the political implications of such a demonstration as grave, not only on the domestic front but also in international relations, particularly as Mr. Roosevelt was then earnestly striving to establish the moral ascendancy of the United States as a defender of democracy. Alarmed by the prospect of thousands of unwanted black men and women milling about the Capitol, the President summoned Mr. Randolph and his committee to the White House. With his attention increasingly focused on problems of defense and foreign affairs, Roosevelt was inclined to look upon the Randolph complaint as a matter of secondary importance.

It was a tense conference. The President tried to prevail upon Randolph to call off the projected march on Washington. The labor leader refused. Negroes had too long been given the run-around by government and by industry. Something had to be done. It was up to the government to take the lead. The march-on-Washington movement was ready to call for a showdown, Randolph insisted. In the end the President agreed to take administrative steps to end discrimination in employment in defense industries and government. Mr. Randolph agreed to hold his movement in abeyance. He did not commit himself to calling the march off. As a result of this conference the President issued the now-famous Executive Order 8802 on June 25, 1941, five and a half months before Pearl Harbor.

In this order, regarded by many as a sort of second Emancipation Proclamation, the President reaffirmed "the policy of the United States that there shall be no discrimination in the employment of workers in defense industries or government because of race, creed, color or national origin, and I do hereby declare that it is the duty of employers and of labor organizations, in furtherance of said policy and of this order, to provide for the full and equitable participation of all workers in defense industries, without discrimination because of race, creed, color or national origin." The order set up a Fair Employment Practice Committee charged with the responsibility of carrying out its provisions. Five years later the FEPC was permitted to die by failure of Congress to appropriate funds or to pass legislation establishing it as a permanent federal agency. While the FEPC by no means solved all the problems of job discrimination confronting minority groups, it proved helpful in enlarging the opportunities for many disadvantaged workers. It was a triumph for Randolph's uncompromising pertinacity.

In addition to Randolph, the labor movement has developed other able, militant, and honest leaders on the national level as well as in scores of local communities throughout the country. Willard S. Townsend, president of the United Transport Service Employees, CIO, continues to grow in stature and influence. A member of the General Executive Board of the CIO, he has three times been designated by President Philip Murray as a CIO representative abroad—in Cuba, Mexico, Korea, and Japan. He also was a member of the CIO delegation participating in President Truman's labor-management conference in 1945. Others prominent in the new labor leadership include Philip Weightman, vice-president of the United Packing House Workers, CIO; William Oliver, co-director of the Fair Practices Department, United Automobile Workers, CIO; Noah C. A. Walter, New York State Industrial Commissioner and former official of the Amalgamated Clothing Workers of America; and Richard Carter, member, General Executive Board, International Union of Marine and Shipbuilding Workers of America.

This new leadership has brought added prestige of the labor movement in the Negro community. The professional and business classes realize more and more that they have a definite stake in the black workers' role in trade unions. Confined, as they generally are, to a Negro clientele, the earnings of these classes are dependent upon the wages and welfare of the black masses. They are learning that the trade unions are instruments for increasing and stabilizing the income of their customers, tenants, patients, clients, and parishioners. Unemployment and depressed wages for Negro workers mean curtailment of income for the black middle class which during the war years enjoyed an unprecedented affluence.

Likewise the Negro press has become more receptive to labor news and editorially more sympathetic to labor's cause. When the Brotherhood of Sleeping Car Porters was organized in 1925 not more than half a dozen of the nation's two hundred Negro publications supported the organization. Today it would be difficult to find six Negro papers opposed to the brotherhood. However, even those publications which have been most vocal in support of trade unionism have been skittish about the organization of their own workers. Attempts of the American Newspaper Guild to organize employees of the Negro press have generally been discouraged by the publishers.

Historically the American labor movement has eschewed partisan political action. Samual Gompers, the long-time president of the AFL, advocated "pure and simple" trade unionism, discounting community interest and political action. This was during a period when European labor was embarking on a course of independent political action. Marxism ultimately became the dominant political philosophy of trade unionists in practically all countries except the United States. Meanwhile the AFL adopted a non-partisan political policy expressed in the Gompers slogan: "Reward your friends and punish your enemies." Significantly, the National Association for the Advancement of Colored People, the largest and most effective secular organization among Negroes, has adopted essentially the same policy of political opportunism. With rare deviations, notably in the 1924 presidential election, when organized labor helped in the formation of the new Progressive party and supported the candidacy of the elder Robert M. La Follette, the AFL has continued to adhere to the Gompers dictum. Certainly in America there are merits as well as inadequacies in such a program. An expanding economy has fostered the two-party system and convinced the American workers that, through collective bargaining, they can obtain their objectives of higher wages, shorter hours, and better working conditions within the framework of the American system of free enterprise. Negroes generally believe that enforcement of the Constitution would afford them the equalities which are their basic demands. They have hoped to attain this goal through the election of responsive candidates under the banners of the old parties.

Faced now with the restrictions of the Taft-Hartley law, the AFL has given evidence of a reawakened interest in political action. At its 1947 convention in San Francisco, the federation set up Labor's Educational and Political League through which to channel the political activities of its affiliated unions and their memberships. Prior to enactment of the law, the federation conducted an intelligent, though futile, nationwide campaign to halt passage of the legislation. Like the CIO, it has expressed the intention of mobilizing all its resources to defeat, wherever possible, the congressional supporters of the bill and to elect a Congress in 1948 that will remove this act from the federal statutes. The federation, however, still stands aloof, having rejected President Murray's proposal for joint action of all organized labor for the purpose of invalidating the Taft-Hartley law, which they all find crippling and objectionable.

The working people of the country have from time to time attempted to exercise political influence through movements which have had within them the seeds of mature political development and which generally offered programs to meet the needs of the Negro masses. In the 1890s the Populists gained enough strength among farmers and workers of the South and Midwest to alarm the politicians of the old parties. The party, which was initially built in the South on Negro-white political unity, was finally destroyed by a successful appeal to the racial prejudices of the white workers and farmers. Time was, too, when the Socialists polled nearly a million votes in a national election. And of course there have been such regional and state movements as the Non-Partisan League in the Dakotas, the Farmer-Labor party in Minnesota, the American Labor party and the new Liberal party in New York State, and the Progressive party in Wisconsin. While most of these movements have been ephemeral, they generated ideas which endured. Although third-party talk persists within segments of the labor movement and among certain liberals, American labor has, on the whole, sought political expression through the two-party system. The efforts of the supporters of Henry Wallace to gain support of organized labor in 1948 were rejected by the American Federation of Labor, the railroad brotherhoods, and the majority of the Congress of Industrial Organizations' affiliates. By a vote of 33 to 11, the General Executive Board of the CIO rejected the third-party bid. Support for the third party within the CIO came only from those unions commonly designated as left wing and in varying degrees under influence of Communist elements.

The advent of the New Deal gave added impetus to labor participation in politics. At the same time the Roosevelt program stimulated wider voting by Negroes and succeeded in alienating the majority of these voters from their traditional Republican moorings. The New Deal made possible the rapid expansion of trade unions and encouraged the development of industrial unionism which, by its very nature, was more democratic and inclusive than the craft or horizontal organization predominating in the AFL. Millions of workers, both black and white, joined these unions and through their participation developed greater political consciousness. New Deal programs had opened the way for disfranchised Negro farmers and workers to vote on economic issues. Participation in voting on political issues and candidates was the natural and logical sequence.

Following the expansion of trade-union membership, organized labor, under the leadership of John L. Lewis, established Labor's Non-Partisan League in 1936. The league was organized primarily to assure the re-election of President Roosevelt and the election of a progressive Congress. After haphazard existence it was finally dissipated. In 1943 the CIO, under the leadership of Philip Murray,

Sidney Hillman, R. J. Thomas, and others, organized the Political Action Committee with Mr. Hillman as chairman. After reviewing the casualties sustained by the progressives in the 1942 elections, these leaders were convinced that the setback was largely due to the failure of workers and liberals to go to the polls on election day. It was their idea to provide an organization through which labor could effectively support its friends.

Like the AFL, the newly organized CIO-PAC adhered to a non-partisan policy in the hope of exerting influence through the election of progressive candidates of the two major parties. But the CIO leaders differed from the old AFL approach. First, they realized that endorsement of candidates was not enough. There was need for political education and political action to implement the endorsements. The issues of the campaign had to be clarified and the records of the candidates made known to the voters—the non-labor electorate as well as to the union membership. Then there was need for developing the machinery—the ward and precinct organization —to get the voters registered and to the polls on election day. The AFL rarely went beyond endorsing candidates and, on occasion, contributing to campaign funds. The CIO leaders realized that effective political action required a year-round program.

There was this further difference: The CIO evaluated a candidate not merely on his labor record but also on his position with regard to international and domestic issues affecting the welfare of the whole people. Labor legislation was only a phase of the PAC's comprehensive program. Thus in 1944, when Senator Gerald P. Nye of North Dakota was a candidate for re-election, he was opposed by the CIO and, in line with its policy, supported by the AFL. His labor record had been fair. CIO opposed him as an isolationist whose program was regarded as dangerous to the successful prosecution of the war and to the establishment of a stable world peace.

In 1944 the PAC conducted a vigorous campaign contributing importantly to the re-election of President Roosevelt. This campaign was also instrumental in the elimination from Congress of some of the worst labor-hating and race-baiting members, including Joe Starnes of Alabama, Martin Dies of Texas, John M. Costello of California, "Cotton Ed" Smith of South Carolina, and Hamilton Fish of New York. From the beginning the PAC realized that the Negro was a vital factor in any progressive political movement. The committee sought and received the support of Negro voters in all the large industrial cities. These voters, numbering more than a million, were reached not only through their trade unions but also through the established avenues of communication long existing within the Negro community—the political and civic organizations, the church, the press, and the fraternal orders. While it is impossible for any one segment of the electorate to claim the sole responsibility for the election or defeat of a candidate, it was apparent in 1944 that Negro and labor votes were important and even decisive factors in the re-election of the President. Certainly Mr. Roosevelt could not have been returned to the White House without the combined support of these voters. The Democratic party can afford to sacrifice the entire 127 electoral college votes of the Solid South and win. It cannot, however, hope for success in a presidential election without the Negro and organized labor.

Nothing so fully demonstrates the political maturity of the masses of Negro voters as their high consistency in support of progressive candidates. Despite pressures and blandishments, the Negro voter, since the advent of the New Deal at any rate, has usually been found on the side of those candidates who not only advocate fuller opportunity for colored citizens but who also stand for progressive labor and social legislation. Even among the new voters in the South, this propensity is evident. Time was when the politician believed that he could buy the Negro vote with money or liquor or false promises. This certainly is no longer true in the over-all picture. Even those Negroes attached to political machines and, like other low-income groups, subject to pressures of ward heelers no longer are satisfied with empty gestures. Their demands now are higher, varying from community to community and conditioned by their political status in the particular locality. In one place it may be for recognition in appointments to positions of responsibility; elsewhere it may be for better schools, adequate recreational facilities, improved housing conditions, or for so ordinary a thing as regular removal of garbage or the cleaning and paving of streets in a Negro neighborhood. And everywhere there is a pressure and demand for job equality.

Obviously organized labor and the vast majority of Negro voters have common interests and common objectives. Twenty years ago Scott Nearing wrote: "To be black in America is to be proletarian." This observation is equally true today and is more widely recognized by both the Negro leadership and the Negro masses. The PAC legislative program is certainly a program to meet the needs of the workingmen and -women of this country, of whom the Negroes are an integral part. The immediate and prime objectives are repeal of the restrictive Taft-Hartley labor bill and enactment of legislation to implement President Roosevelt's Economic Bill of Rights. This program, as outlined by the late President, seeks to guarantee:

The right to a useful and remunerative job in the industries, or shops or farms, or mines of the nation.

The right to earn enough to provide adequate food and clothing and recreation.

The right of every farmer to raise and sell his products at a return which will give him and his family a decent living.

The right of every businessman, large and small, to trade in an atmosphere of freedom from unfair competition and domination by monopolies at home or abroad.

The right of every family to a decent home.

The right to adequate medical care and the opportunity to achieve and enjoy good health.

The right to a good education and

The right to adequate protection from the economic fears of old age, sickness, accident, and unemployment.

Congress has had before it bills to implement this program—proposals for a higher minimum wage, for full employment, for a permanent Fair Employment Practices Commission, for federal aid to education, for raising health standards through the provision of adequate health and hospital facilities, for adequate housing, for continued price control, and for expansion of the coverage of the Social Security Act. Spearheaded by an anti-labor and anti-Negro coalition, Congress has killed the FEPC bill, emasculated the full-employment measure, prevented passage of the minimum wage bill, blocked enactment of the national health bill, eliminated price control, abandoned the veterans' housing program, and passed punitive labor legislation. Not only FEPC, but such other measures as minimum wage, health, education, housing, and price control are relatively of greater importance to colored people, with their generally low income, than to other segments of the population.

It was Sidney Hillman's conviction that the basic interests of organized workers and the Negro masses were essentially the same. Conscious of this natural alignment, he sought to fuse the two into a strong political movement to carry on the fight for a truly great America with freedom, justice, equality, and security for all without regard to race, color, creed, or national origin. Not only did he succeed in integrating Negro workers into the political structure of CIO, but he also reached beyond the ranks of labor to obtain the support of Negro leadership through participation in the National Citizens PAC which he set up in 1944 to supplement labor's efforts to establish a progressive political movement.

"All that the Negro demands and is justly entitled to as an American citizen and as a worker are encompassed in the immediate and long term objectives of the progressive movement," Mr. Hillman wrote. "These objectives the PAC has spelled out in its *Peoples Program for 1944*. Victory and peace, employment, security, housing, health and education for all our people are among the PAC objectives."[2]

In the crucial elections of 1944, a declaration by Negro voters, sponsored by the National Association for the Advancement of Colored People and signed by the leaders of twenty-five church, civic, fraternal, labor, and political organizations, closely paralleled the program supported by the CIO-PAC. The declaration not only demanded enactment of anti-poll-tax and anti-lynching legislation and the establishment of a permanent FEPC, but also asserted: "In evaluating the merits of parties and candidates we must include all issues—those touching the life of Negroes as a group as well as those affecting the entire country. The party or candidate who refuses to help control prices, or fails to support the extension of social security, or refuses to support a progressive public program for full post-war employment, or opposes an enlarged and unsegregated program of government-financed housing, or seeks to destroy organized labor, is as much the enemy of Negroes as is he who would prevent Negroes from voting."

In order to achieve a closer working relationship with organized labor, the NAACP in 1946 appointed a secretary of labor and named Philip Murray, CIO president, to its board of directors. The Association actively opposed the Taft-Hartley anti-labor bill of 1947.

The Hillman policy now being directed by his successor, Jack Kroll, continues to bear fruit. Not only was a high degree of political co-ordination between Negro groups and organized labor achieved in the 1944 elections, but in numerous subsequent local elections, in the South as well as in the North, the two groups have worked together effectively. Spearheaded by the Political Action Committee of the CIO Tobacco Workers, Negro and white voters elected two members to the City Council of Winston-Salem, North Carolina, in

[2]Sidney Hillman, "Should Negroes Vote for Roosevelt or Dewey?", *Negro Digest*, II, October 1944, p. 50.

the spring of 1947. One of the successful candidates was a Negro clergyman, the first of his race to be elected to city or state office in the deep South (save in all-Negro communities) in longer than a generation. In Richmond, Virginia, leaders of organized labor, AFL and railroad brotherhoods as well as CIO, approved the candidacy of a capable Negro lawyer for the lower house of the Virginia legislature in an effort to get Negro votes for a labor candidate. The coalition succeeded in nominating the labor candidate in the Democratic primaries. The Negro candidate failed by the narrow margin of 190 votes. In Dayton, Detroit, Buffalo, New York, Atlanta, and many other cities Negro and labor voters have participated in joint political action.

The continued success of this coalition depends upon the degree to which colored citizens are integrated into the fabric of the movement. This requires not only a consideration of whatever special conditions may confront Negro voters, but also active participation on their part in the shaping of the program and in the determination of the candidates to be supported. There have been instances in which candidates have had good records on labor and social legislation but have fallen down completely on legislation designed to equalize the political and economic status of the Negro. This has been particularly true in the South, where certain supporters of good labor legislation have engaged in filibusters against the FEPC and the anti-poll-tax bill. However, with the growing power of the Negro vote in the South, we may anticipate more consistent records from southern liberals.

The dilemma in American life which is symbolized by the so-called Negro problem is recognized by the CIO. In its effort to rally the support of Negro voters for progressive candidates in 1944, the CIO-PAC utilized the services of a small staff of active Negro organizers and published and distributed 4,600,000 pieces of literature—pamphlets, leaflets, stickers, and posters—appealing directly to this segment of the electorate. In recognition of the contradiction in American life, the widely distributed PAC pamphlet, entitled *The Negro in 1944,* concluded with the following words:

The CIO Political Action Committee, speaking for itself as well as all the progressive minded people in the United States who resent discrimination against any of its loyal citizens, regrets the need of this pamphlet.

Quite clearly it is addressed to Negroes. Quite as clearly it implies a separate appeal to citizens and workers because of color. But that situation is not of our making. If we had our way, that situation would soon be resolved.

We hope that some day soon, pamphlets such as these will not be necessary.

We hope that some day soon, Negroes will be addressed in general along with all general groups of the population.

But, hoping alone will not do that for us.

We must join hands now and gain equality for all our people.

CHAPTER IX

Grass-roots Political Action

IMPORTANT POLITICAL POLICIES AND ISSUES MAY BE DE-
bated, developed, and formulated on the national level, but in
America they are settled only in the community—back home in the
neighborhoods, precincts, and wards where the people live. It is here
that the people, by their votes, ultimately determine the shape and
direction of political policy. Even though issues of national importance may be subordinated to local considerations, the real political
behavior of the American voter may be studied only in his community. For the purpose of obtaining a close-up view of the Negro
as a voter and as an issue, the story of his participation in local campaigns in three representative American cities is cited in the following accounts. Detroit, the industrial boom town of the Midwest;
Richmond, the capital of the late Confederacy, and New York, the
cosmopolitan world capital, each affords opportunity for the study
of the Negro's political behavior in his home precincts.

In Detroit the new Negro population had to face hard economic
and political competition with the white newcomers who brought to
the city all their ancient prejudices. The struggle for political recognition was further impeded by the lack of cohesion within the Negro
community and the character of the municipal elections which,
under the city charter, are non-partisan and conducted on a city-
wide basis, obliterating ward lines and retarding the development of
neighborhood political organizations. The neglect and antipathy of
the city administration finally drove the Negro population into a
common political fight against the incumbent mayor and councilmen. In 1943 and 1945 this fight was carried out in collaboration
with the local affiliates of the Congress of Industrial Organizations.

The old and stable Negro community in Richmond was confronted with a somewhat different political situation. The Negro

leaders in that city were faced with the problem of overcoming the political apathy which a long period of disfranchisement had engendered. Unlike Detroit, race was not a prime issue in the 1947 elections, when members of the state legislature were chosen. Although Richmond is a southern city adhering to the regional pattern, there was no open hostility on the part of white electors to Negro participation in the campaign. Without experience in the political arena and without tutelage, the Negro leaders undertook the task of mobilizing the race's potential voting strength for effective political action. While not achieving their goal in 1947, they demonstrated their capacity for political organization and laid the groundwork for a triumph which cannot long escape their pursuit.

New York City represents still another cultural background and political pattern. Since the dawn of the twentieth century there has been a substantial Negro population in the city. The development and expansion of Harlem during the 1920s made New York the site of the largest Negro community in the world. Here in this capital of the Negro world the race attained a certain cultural sophistication and a political maturity seldom matched in any other colored community. Integrated into the dominant political machine, the power of which is rooted in district organizations, Negro voters have played an important and effective role in determining the outcome of crucial elections. Both major parties and the new left-wing political organizations actively compete for the Negro vote in New York City.

THE DETROIT FORMULA

Detroit is a city of paradox. Renowned as the arsenal of democracy, it has long been the refuge for native fascist elements. The symbol of America's great technological pre-eminence, the city is perhaps the country's most dismal failure in the field of social engineering. The nation's fourth largest city, with nearly 2,000,000 inhabitants, it is in many respects as provincial as a backwoods county seat. The home of the world's largest trade union, the lusty CIO United Automobile Workers, it is also the sanctuary of the most vicious forces in the political underworld, flourishing within the very shadow of the giant industrial corporations which dominate the city.

The city suffers from growing pains, never quite able to adjust its municipal attire to its expanding size. Overgrown and underdeveloped, it staggers from one dizzy climax to another. A vast, sprawling, overcrowded community of more than forty different racial and nationality groups, Detroit is in a constant state of tension engendered by a mad competition for jobs and living space. Even in the midst of the war, at a time of acute man-power shortages, the workers, both black and white, were haunted by the fear of in-security. The tensions, economic in origin, were carefully nurtured by groups which made a profitable business of setting race against race. Thriving on the inflated ethnocentrism of a large section of the white population, clerical fascists and other demagogues sowed the wild seeds of race hate and reaped the bitter fruit of riot.

The disastrous race riot of 1943 surprised no one. It was as if it had arrived on a delayed schedule. The thirty-four men and women who were killed during that hot June week of jungle fury were fated for death. They were the victims not only of economic forces and hate propaganda but also, and more importantly, of the weakness, timidity, and inefficiency of the city administration under Mayor Edward J. Jeffries. "The whole community, white and black, knew for a matter of years that a tinder box was in the making," William H. Baldwin, president of the National Urban League, asserted, "but, although surveys and reports were made and handed around, no responsible individuals or agencies—public or private—provided any persistent and effective follow-through. It was pretty much a 'business as usual' psychology on the part of all concerned."[1]

Of the racial and national minorities in Detroit, the Poles and their American-born progeny are the largest, numbering nearly 300,000. The Negro minority, next in size, numbers about 220,000. Like most of Detroit's 2,000,000 inhabitants, the Negroes are largely newcomers attracted to the city by opportunities for employment in the huge automobile industry. In 1916, during World War I, there were only about 10,000 colored persons in the city. Within ten years this figure had risen to 80,000. By that time the city was very con-scious of its Negro population. The tensions, the causes, and the results were the same then as in 1943. The attempt of a Negro physician to escape the confines of the overcrowded black belt by moving into a so-called white neighborhood precipitated a riot in 1925. Nevertheless, the Negro population continued to swell until by 1940 it reached 150,000. The man-power demands for wartime production brought in an additional 65,000 by 1945.

[1]Quoted by Alfred McCluny Lee and Norman D. Humphrey in *Race Riot* (New York: Dryden Press, 1943), p. 120.

The steady inflow of Negro migrants, chiefly from the South, was synchronized with the in-migration of tens of thousands of poor whites from the hills and backwoods of Kentucky, Tennessee, Arkansas, Oklahoma, and other southern states. Their mores and attitudes were such that a social worker classed them among the "foreign elements" of the city. They not only brought with them their traditional prejudices, but also sought to impose their bias upon the patterns of Detroit, which in the years before this influx, prior to World War I, had been justly celebrated as a city of liberal racial attitudes. With them came loudmouthed, ignorant preachers of race hate, fomenters of conflict, advocates of segregation. The confluence of these two streams of migration, one black and the other white, was a continuing source of friction in the highly competitive climate of Detroit.

The Negro community in Detroit affords greater contrasts than any similar group in an American city. During the boom years of full employment and high wages, the upper crust of business and professional men, battening on the income of the black workers, attained a glittering affluence. Their ranks were augmented by the sportsmen-racketeers, whose take from the policy game ran into the millions. Like the white robber barons of the nineteenth century who ruthlessly fleeced the people, the policy kings of Detroit turned to legitimate business and moved into respectable circles. Their comfortable, and sometimes palatial, homes and living standards contrast sharply with the ancient and dilapidated slums of the ghetto, incongruously known as Paradise Valley, in which the great bulk of Negroes are compelled to live, even in a period of good wages. These are among the worst slums in the country. The Negro's long struggle to escape from this neglected and overcrowded ghetto has met with the flinty resistance of the real estate interests to which the city administration long ago surrendered. As a consequence, only 3000 of the 43,200 new homes built in Detroit between 1940 and 1945 were made available to Negro families. An official administration policy refuses approval for Negro housing except in predominantly Negro districts. As these districts are already overbuilt, the city policy means, in effect, no new housing for Negroes.

The hemmed-in Negro community, bursting at its seams, was ready in 1945, as it had been in 1943, to express at the polls its resentment against this slow strangulation. In the mayoralty campaign that year Mayor Jeffries was opposed by Richard T. Frankensteen, then a vice-president of the UAW. The Negro group as a whole naturally supported the CIO candidate, not only because of their dissatisfaction with Jeffries, but also because Frankensteen offered a program to make more housing available as a means of lessening racial tensions. In the primary these voters were responsible for 25 per cent of the total cast for the labor leader. They cast 69.8 per cent of their votes for Frankensteen as compared to 9.1 per cent for Jeffries. The remainder of the vote was scattered among other contestants. In the August primaries Frankensteen received a total vote of 83,887, leading Jeffries by 14,402. In the November general election the incumbent mayor won with 274,000 votes to 217,000 for his opponent.

How did this reversal come about in the three-month period between August and November? How did so colorless, humdrum, and unimaginative a candidate as Mayor Jeffries defeat Frankensteen, a dynamic campaigner and a progressive labor leader? Jeffries was in no way a popular candidate. Even his friends were only lukewarm. He had none of the popular appeal of a man like Fiorello La Guardia of New York. Following his previous election, the Detroit *Free Press* had sneered at him as "a village wisecracker" who had "failed in the hour of crisis." Yet in 1945 this newspaper supported him for re-election. Why? By trading on the race issue, in true Bilbo style, Mayor Jeffries was able to consolidate the support of the bulk of the white population in spite of his widely publicized weaknesses. The just resentment of the Negro voters was turned into an asset to rally support for Jeffries as a defender of "white supremacy."

Contributing to the mayor's victory were many factors, most of them false and irrelevant to the basic issue of replacing an ineffectual municipal administration. Jeffries's failures had been as dismal as they were obvious. Under his administration transportation deteriorated, recreational facilities remained inadequate, sanitation was neglected, the public school system suffered, and the desperately needed housing program was completely stymied by race prejudice. Nor had the administration developed any adequate program to stimulate post-war employment. These were the real issues on which Frankensteen based his campaign. Backed by the Wayne County Political Action Committee of the CIO and endorsed by the Democratic party, the Michigan Citizens Committee, and other organizations, he conducted a vigorous, clean, and honest campaign attacking Jeffries's failures and promising a program of action. There was, however, the opposition of the principal body of the organized workers in the American Federation of Labor. Moreover, the factionalism within the UAW left some CIO members lukewarm in their support of Frankensteen, whom they accused of being a "self-starter," having entered the race without first clearing with the PAC, which could not help endorsing him once he had filed for the office.

Subordinating the real issues, the Jeffries supporters countered with a campaign designed to confuse and divide. They accused Frankensteen of trying to seize City Hall in order to turn the local government over to organized labor. They depicted PAC as an alien organization engaged in a sinister conspiracy to enthrall the free citizens of Detroit as a prelude to the subjugation of the nation. Although known to be a Democrat, the PAC candidate was branded, by their propaganda, a Communist. Holding membership in the Episcopal Church in which he was reared, Frankensteen was misrepresented among anti-Semites as a Jew, and among Jews as a Coughlinite.

All these false charges undoubtedly influenced gullible voters. But the decisive factor, overshadowing every other issue, real or phony, was the direct and devastating anti-Negro appeal. When this line was laid down there were few fence-sitters. The deadly hate campaign waged by Jeffries and his supporters not only consolidated the upper- and middle-class whites, but also split the ranks of labor, despite the avowed support of CIO leadership. In a city which for years had been tense with ill-concealed racial antagonisms, Jeffries and his supporters, risking a possible riot, used every avenue of communication—newspapers, radio, illustrations, leaflets, word-of-mouth rumors—to foment fear and hatred of Negroes.

As a result of this fierce campaign of hate Frankensteen was defeated by a 57,000 majority along with Charles Hill, progressive Negro clergyman, and Tracy M. Doll, secretary of the Wayne County CIO-PAC. Hill, Doll, and the Texas-born liberal, George Edwards, were the PAC candidates for the nine-man Common Council. Edwards, an incumbent, was re-elected, leading the entire field to become president of the Council.

Under the Detroit City Charter, municipal elections are "nonpartisan." In reality there were two unformalized but active parties. The first of these, the majority party, was the well-financed white-supremacy organization which backed Jeffries and of which he was spokesman and symbol. Opposing the lily-whites was a mixed party spearheaded by the CIO and including the vast bulk of the Negro population and all the genuine liberals in the city. Supporting the Jeffries party were all the Negro haters, all the labor baiters, all the anti-Semites, and all the followers of Gerald L. K. Smith, of whatever origin. Nor did Jeffries repudiate this support. Opposing him were all the genuine liberals and real progressives in the city. There was no middle ground.

Realizing that he had earned the antipathy of Negro citizens, Jeffries made only one overt bid for their support. This was an advertisement published in the Negro press during the primary campaign warning Negro voters: "Don't Be Caught out on a Limb Again." For the final election an anonymous green leaflet was circulated in Negro districts proclaiming that *Frankensteen has not proved himself a true friend of the Negro race.* The circular attacked Frankensteen but disdained to make an appeal in behalf of Jeffries to a people among whom his name was already anathema. Like his Mississippi counterpart, Jeffries did, however, assert that he "had tried to be fair to Negroes."

The so-called non-partisan election simplified the organization of the hate campaign. Neither Republicans nor Democrats could afford to conduct such a campaign in any large northern city. Although certain Republican leaders announced their support of Jeffries, formal endorsement was withheld not only because of the City Charter but, more important, because of the kind of campaign Jeffries conducted. With the national party trying to woo Negro voters for 1946 and 1948, the local Republican leaders could ill afford to share responsibility for the Jeffries hate campaign. One leaflet, illustrated with thuggish-looking photographs of Frankensteen and Hill and calling "For Equality in the City Hall," was circulated in *white* neighborhoods under pretense that it was Frankensteen literature intended for distribution to Negroes. Another trick was the distribution, again among whites, of a card announcing: "Negroes can live anywhere, in any area—any section of Detroit— with Frankensteen mayor. Negroes—do your duty Nov. 6."

That the race issue was decisive is indicated by the post-election statements of both candidates. Piously Mayor Jeffries remarked: "This has been the most vicious, nasty campaign that I have ever witnessed. Many charges and countercharges were hurled. Racial and religious issues have been raised. . . . I have never subscribed to this type of campaign and I want to say here and now that I intend to be representative of all the people and that I am a zealous disciple of tolerance, not only in theory but in practice. America's best characteristic is that we have only one type of citizen and that is an American citizen whose color, religion, and accent make no distinction."

This was the ex post facto declaration of a man who had refused to sign a pre-election pledge against the introduction of racial issues. He had invoked and benefited by the issues which he vainly decried in the post-election statement.

Frankensteen realized that he had been victimized by these forces and issues. "For better or for worse," he said, "we must all live together, black and white, Jew and Gentile, labor and capital. Only by facing this fact, and facing it frankly, will we be able to retain what is best for our democracy. The closing and decisive days of the campaign were marked by the injection of racial and religious and class fears which had no relationship to the actual issues involved. . . . It is this, far more than the fact that I have been defeated, which concerns me most."

He added hopefully: "Progressive forces do not look upon the election results as a defeat. We have polled the largest vote ever given a progressive candidate, even a winning candidate. This can mean but one thing: That despite the injection into this campaign of issues having no place in a democratic election—despite this, more thinking voters than ever have seen through the haze of race and class hatreds to the basic truth that the aims of progressive forces are the ultimate aims of the American people."

All the principal avenues of communication were on the side of Jeffries: the three daily papers, the radio stations, the community press. Frankensteen had the support of the CIO press, the local Democratic organ, and the Negro press. The weekly community press was flagrant in its race baiting, the daily papers more subtle. The Detroit *News*, which conducted a pre-election poll, isolated only the Negro voters from the other myriad groups which comprise the city of Detroit. According to this poll, taken a few days before the election, Negroes would vote 96.4 per cent for Frankensteen as compared with a city-wide 55.7-per-cent majority for Jeffries. There were no similar breakdowns for Poles, Italians, Hungarians, Jews, or other groups. The racial breakdown was for the purpose of frightening white voters into support of the mayor by demonstrating that the colored citizens were united in their opposition to him.

Actually an analysis of the ballots cast in 172 predominantly Negro precincts reveals that Frankensteen received 83.3 per cent of the votes—60,321 to 12,110 for Jeffries. The white vote in these precincts may vary from zero to as high as 20 per cent. In the precinct comprising the all-Negro Sojourner Truth Housing Project the vote was Frankensteen 276, Jeffries 3. Ward 3, consisting of 24 pre-

cincts with a 90- to 98-per-cent Negro population, gave Frankensteen 92 per cent of the votes cast or 9,035 to 794. A sampling of the
balloting in other selected precincts, 90 per cent or more Negro,
showed the following votes for Frankensteen and Jeffries respectively: 323–27; 452–9; 432–17; 411–12; 343–14.

Had the white working class voted as consistently as the Negro
workers, the results might have been different. Some of the districts
which, because many trade unionists lived in them, had been expected to give Frankensteen heavy majorities went for Jeffries, and
others gave the CIO candidate only slim margins. The "silk-stock-
ing" districts went overwhelmingly for the mayor, as anticipated.
Throughout the city 62 per cent of those registered voted. The percentage was higher in wealthier districts but fell to 60 in Negro
precincts.

Racial tensions in Detroit have developed along four fronts:
employment, transportation, recreation, and housing. It is just in
these areas that the administration had failed most dismally, particularly in the field of housing, which has remained the core of the
Negro question in Detroit. The housing shortage is city-wide but
is distressingly acute in Negro districts, the population of which has
increased by more than 30 per cent since 1940. Two days before the
election Mayor Jeffries smugly asserted: "I have always tried to be
fair with Negroes, but when certain Negro leaders tried to push me
into a program that would promote Negro housing projects in established white neighborhoods, I simply would not be pushed into
changing the racial characteristics of the residential districts."

This was the most dishonest and dangerous statement of the entire campaign—dishonest in that it misrepresented the real issue,
which was simply one of making adequate housing available to all
in-migrant war workers; dangerous in that the mayor cannot keep
his promise to confide the Negro population within its present areas.
Many white persons who voted for him on the basis of this promise
are doomed to disappointment and accordingly will react resentfully
when Negroes inevitably move into their now lily-white neighborhoods.

Because it is physically impossible to keep the Negro population
imprisoned in its present warren, the city will find itself confronted
with an expansion—possibly violent—of the Negro ghetto. Indeed,
while most of the Negroes are concentrated in segregated areas, the
overflow has already started. According to the 1940 United States
Census, Negroes lived in each of the city's twenty-two wards. Within

some of the wards, however, there were many blocks, census tracts, and precincts in which no Negroes lived. This overflow will continue with accelerated pace as white families move out to the suburbs once more housing comes on the market. A wise city administration could give guidance to this development and avert violence.

Propagandized by real estate interests and encouraged by Mayor Jeffries, the white population, including large sections of the working class and the foreign-born, had come to believe it has a vested, exclusive, and permanent "right" to certain districts. During the campaign this issue was revived and intensified. The attempt was made to make every white person believe that a vote for Frankensteen was a vote to have a Negro living next door. The headlines, stories, and advertisements in the community press and the leaflets were frantic appeals to "protect" their homes against the dreaded black contamination. Spurred by this propaganda, the majority of the white citizens voted to retain the Jim Crow pattern. This pattern had been sanctioned ten years ago by the public housing program which established separate "white" and "Negro" projects. Jeffries, throughout his administration, upheld this Jim Crow pattern, with the result that eligible Negro families in need have been denied housing even when there were vacancies in "white" projects developed with federal funds.

With full knowledge that the housing problem is a continuing source of friction and violence, the Jeffries administration took no step to meet this situation rationally. Indeed, there were two proposals—one for the development of a medical center and the other for construction of a super highway through the heart of the Negro district—which would require the dislocation of some 4000 Negroes. To carry out these proposals with no provision for the housing of the displaced persons would be to pour oil on a smoldering fire. While taking no step to avert a repetition of the riot of 1943, the Jeffries administration instead prepared to handle another riot more efficiently. That is, the police were equipped and prepared.

Frankensteen's proposal for a solution of the housing problem was an expanded public housing program and a stimulation of private development to increase the supply of housing for all the people, thereby relieving the sharp competition for living space. By spurning public housing and insisting upon keeping Negroes within their present confines, Jeffries rejected this solution.

After the election an organization calling itself the Midwestern

Political Survey Institute gleefully pointed out that a new pattern had been established. "The Detroit election portends a very decided change in political currents which is likely to show itself in most large northern cities," a release from the institute stated. "If the Detroit formula could be reproduced in other large cities, which is not at all doubtful, it would rescue both parties from the bulldozing domination of political racketeers who have fattened themselves on the Negro vote by making it appear to be the balance of power. . . . The Detroit election has proved that the PAC cannot deliver the vote of the CIO. It has proved that Negroes are not the balance of power. . . . The impression is rapidly developing that the PAC is dominated by Jews and Communists."

In the northern city of Detroit, Negroes had to face the active hostility of the majority of the white citizens with whom race was the prime issue. In the southern city of Richmond, the Negro leaders, amateurs in politics, were confronted with the poll tax and the long-standing political apathy of the Negro masses. Theirs was a job of pioneering in an unfamiliar field.

REVIVAL IN RICHMOND

Save for Tennessee, where Boss Ed Crump makes his own rules, Virginia was the first southern state in which Negroes breached the Democratic white primary on a state-wide basis. Previously they had been permitted to vote by county or city Democratic committees in certain localities in North Carolina and Texas. Even in Tennessee there were a few black-belt counties where the color ban stood. The Virginia break came in 1930, following a United States District Court decision in 1929. In that decision Judge D. Lawrence Groner held that the Virginia primary law, which delegated to the party the right to exclude Negroes, was in conflict with the federal Constitution. His decision was upheld by the United States Circuit Court of Appeals in a ruling handed down on June 30, 1930. In the fall of that year election officials in Richmond were instructed to "vote Negroes who satisfy officials that they are Democrats under the same condition applying to white voters."

The abolition of the white primary left only one important barrier to mass voting—the poll tax. Virginia is one of the seven remaining states which require payment of a poll tax as a prerequisite for voting. This tax of $1.50 per year is cumulative for three years. It must be paid for the three preceding years not less than six months prior to the general elections in November. The decisive Democratic primaries are held in August. In May of 1947, Dr. Luther P. Jackson of the Virginia Voters League estimated that 56,000 Negroes in the state had met the poll-tax requirement. Registration, in addition to payment of poll taxes, is also required. Almost half of those who pay their poll taxes fail to register. This is particularly true of persons living in rural areas. "Only a few years ago the presence of thousands of unregistered, poll tax paying Negroes in Virginia would have been explained on the grounds of racial discrimination so common to registrars in the days of old," Jackson asserts in his seventh annual report on the voting status of Negroes in Virginia. "But whereas formerly most registrars refused registration to colored people, today the overwhelming majority draw no color line. Instead of obstructing them, the registrars in all of the cities and in nearly all of the counties extend Negroes every courtesy." However, according to the Virginia State CIO, it is occasionally necessary to remind a registrar that in attempting to discriminate against Negro citizens he is exceeding his authority.

When the white primary ban was lifted in 1930 there were fewer than 1000 Negro poll-tax payers in the city of Richmond. The ranks of qualified Negro voters had been slashed as a result of the disfranchising convention of 1902 which, under the whiplash of Carter Glass and other Bourbons, imposed the poll tax and other restrictions upon the suffrage rights of Virginians. Under the new Constitution the Negro's voting strength was all but depleted. The first year only 760 Negro citizens in Richmond out of a potential 8000 qualified to vote.[2] The Negro vote remained in the neighborhood of that figure. Even after the 1930 decision the increase was painfully slow. In 1943 only 2097 colored citizens had paid the qualifying poll tax. In the presidential year of 1944 the number reached 2561. For the congressional elections of 1946 there were 3800. Against this background of political futility the campaign and near victory of Oliver W. Hill for the House of Delegates in the Democratic primaries of 1947 takes on real significance for the future of Negro suffrage in the South.

Determined to arouse the Negro community to the need for political action, leaders in Richmond decided late in 1946 to organize a concerted drive for poll-tax payment and registration. The Richmond Civic Council, a delegate body composed of representatives of eighty church, civic, fraternal, labor, business, educational, and

[2]*The Negro in Virginia* (New York: Hastings House, 1940), p. 240.

social organizations, undertook this task and assigned the responsibility to its suffrage committee under the able leadership of Dr. J. M.
Tinsley. President of the Richmond branch of the National Association for the Advancement of Colored People and chairman of the
Virginia State NAACP Conference, the wiry little dentist worked
tirelessly and selflessly to expand the Negro vote. Associated with
him were the president of the Council, the Reverend W. L. Ransome,
and a devoted group of civic, church, and labor leaders.

With the objective of doubling the Negro vote in the city, the
committee employed a full-time worker whose job was to organize
the community on a ward, precinct, and block basis. Effective
organization of the type is rare among either race in the South.
Amos Clark, to whom this task was assigned, went about his job
methodically. Negroes live in each of the four wards of Richmond,
constituting about 50 per cent of the total in Jefferson and Madison
Wards, 20 per cent in Lee, and 17 per cent in Clay. They are slightly
less than a third of the city's total population. The socioeconomic
composition of the Negro community consists of a small and substantial class of business- and professional men and women, a larger
group of trained and skilled workers steadily employed, and a great
mass of poorly paid and irregularly employed unskilled workers and
domestic servants. In the job of organizing for political action there
were no class lines. Clark's task was to get all these groups moving,
to reach them in their offices, stores, shops, and organizations, and
especially in their homes. To do this he obtained volunteers, both
men and women, to work in the blocks, precincts, and wards in
which they lived. It was their job to see that every potential voter in
their respective neighborhoods was contacted at least once and urged
to pay his poll tax and to register. There were in Richmond nearly
40,000 Negroes of voting age. While not every prospect was reached,
the framework of the machinery for getting into every home was
set up. Meanwhile the committee members were carrying the message into meetings of practically all the organizations.

Having set up the machinery for qualifying voters, the committee
needed to give the Negro community an incentive. The opportunity
to choose among equally hostile or indifferent white candidates had
seemed, to a large number of colored citizens, a privilege hardly
worth paying for. Recognizing the importance of a living symbol
around which to rally support, the leaders decided to enter a Negro
candidate in the Democratic primaries for the House of Delegates,
the lower branch of the Virginia state legislature. Colored men had

run for office in Virginia before, but none had served in the legislature since 1889–90, and none had campaigned with any hope of being elected since the late Senator Glass pushed through his disfranchising measure in 1902. This time it was not as a mere gesture that the committee decided to support a candidate. This time there was the intent, the possibility, and the hope of winning. The committee agreed upon the candidacy of Oliver W. Hill. It was a most fortunate choice. The candidate, a well-known young lawyer and veteran of World War II, was not only highly regarded in the Negro community but had also won the respect of the legal profession by the competency with which he had handled his cases before the Virginia bar. A poised, balanced, and intelligent person, he was militant without being offensively aggressive, courteous without being obsequious.

The organization was now set up and the candidate chosen; there remained the campaign for the widest possible support. There was no intention on the part of the Committee or Hill to campaign as a candidate concerned merely with the problems of the Negro. His platform called for repeal of the poll-tax requirement, revision of the child labor act, minimum wage and hour legislation, tenure and minimum salaries of $2400 a year for public-school teachers, increased appropriations for hospitals and public health programs, and establishment of a state department of race relations to collect and disseminate factual information on the activities and contributions of Negroes and the effect of racial relations on the economic, sociological, and political development of Virginia. All in all, it was a progressive platform which should have had wide appeal.

In the hope of gaining additional votes for Hill, a tentative coalition was entered into with organized labor. This was no little achievement in the South in view of the traditional fear and distrust between the Negro group on the one hand and the white workers on the other. While there was agreement among the leaders, there was hesitation among the rank and file on both sides. Fortunately Charles C. Webber, president of the Virginia State CIO Council and director of PAC activities in that state, was well known to and highly regarded by the Negro leaders. They trusted him because of his consistent and uncompromising fight against discrimination in the trade-union movement. Largely through his efforts the Negro leaders and the officers of the United Labor Political Action Committee, composed of representatives of CIO, AFL, and the railroad brotherhoods, agreed upon joint support of Hill and W. H. C. Murray, president of the Richmond Central Trades and Labor Council, AFL. Murray, although known to Negro trade unionists as a progressive leader, was not known to the colored community as was Webber. It was an uneasy alliance, with each side apprehensive lest the followers of the other group fail to go down the line for the joint ticket—the Negroes skeptical about the ability of the labor leaders to get white workers to vote for a colored candidate; the trade unionists fearful that the Negroes would vote only for Oliver W. Hill. It was, however, a coalition essential to the success of either or both candidates.

When the books for poll-tax payment were closed early in May there were 6230 colored citizens on the rolls. The committee had failed in meeting its goal of doubling the previous year's figure but had expanded the number of Negro poll-tax payments by 67 per cent. The best estimate of the number of trade unionists who had paid up did not exceed 2500. And this figure included a sizable proportion of organized Negro workers. Negro support was thus more vital to the trade-union candidate than labor support to the colored candidate. The drive for registration continued after the deadline for poll-tax payment. A special effort was made to register recently discharged veterans and the twenty-one-year-olds, both of whom were exempt from the poll-tax requirement. Accurate figures on registration by race are not obtainable, but the committee estimated that at least 6750 colored people were qualified to vote in the August primary. A total vote for the city of less than 20,000 was anticipated.

The unprecedented Negro registration attracted the attention of the community at large, but it occasioned no public expression of hostility or resentment. Unlike campaigns in Georgia, Mississippi, and Detroit, the race issue was not raised publicly. There were, as far as could be discovered, no surreptitious distributions of anti-Negro literature and no organized whispering or telephone campaigns against Hill. The daily papers began to speculate on his chances of winning the nomination. If they were distressed by this possibility they did not express it in their editorial or news columns. One columnist, listing the strong contenders, predicted that "Hill is going to get a lot of white votes" in addition to those from "an unprecedented backlog of well-organized Negro voters."[3] Hill's committee not only sought Negro and labor support but made an appeal to white liberals and schoolteachers on the basis of his platform.

[3]Charles Houston in Richmond *News-Leader,* August 1, 1947.

As the strength of the Negro vote became apparent, white candidates came to the Negro leaders seeking their support and contending against "single-shot" voting for Hill or the double shot for Hill and Murray. While not required, each voter could cast a ballot for seven of the eighteen candidates. The single openly untoward incident in the campaign was the failure of the Young Democrats to invite Hill along with all the other candidates to participate in a political rally. He was, however, invited to address trade-union groups and other meetings attended by white voters. Near the end of the campaign there was a rumor current that, should either Hill or Murray be nominated, the dominant Democratic machine would seek to replace them by undercover support of Republican candidates in the November general election. In Richmond, as in most southern communities, nomination in the Democratic primaries is generally tantamount to election.

A well-organized effective campaign was conducted—the best that had been organized for a Negro candidate in a contemporary Virginia election. Every church, every Negro organization was contacted in this drive. To get out the vote on election day there were 150 volunteers and a score of cars. Hopes were high in the Negro community. Victory seemed within reach. The symbolic significance of such an eventuality was not missed by the colored citizens of the city. The turnout on election day, while not 100 per cent, was encouraging. When the final count had been completed, Hill, with a total of 6313 votes, placed eighth and missed the nomination by the narrow margin of 187. Murray, the labor candidate, was nominated as the seventh and last man on the slate with a total of 6500. An analysis of the balloting by precincts indicated that at least 40 per cent of Murray's total was cast by Negro voters, without which he could not have been nominated. Estimates of the size of the white vote for Hill ranged from 800, according to the Richmond *News-Leader,* to 1500, according to the United Labor Political Action Committee. The Negro committee arrived at the figure of 1200. Hill received some votes in each of the city's 55 precincts, in several of which no Negroes were registered. It is impossible to determine what share of this vote came from white trade unionists, but, judging from the character of the precincts, it appears that the major portion of Hill's white vote came from middle-class liberals.

Disappointment in the Negro community was keen. A few persons bitterly assailed the labor movement for failure to live up to the bargain made by the trade-union leaders. These expressed regret that all Negro voters had not voted for Hill alone. There was talk of running an independent Negro candidate in the general elections on the basis of single-shot voting. Both Dr. Tinsley, chairman of the suffrage committee of the Richmond Civic Council, and Mr. Hill repudiated this move and urged continued support of Mr. Murray in the general election. "I think it will be unwise to discontinue our friendly relationship with labor at this time because we need the support of white as well as colored people if we hope to win in the next election," Dr. Tinsley asserted.[4] Defending the coalition, Mr. Hill characterized it as an effort "to produce a common understanding among the working people of this city irrespective of race."[5]

The city, for the most part, took the election returns in stride. "The surprise of the Democratic primary in Richmond was, of course, the size of the Negro vote," commented the Richmond *News-Leader*. "Probably 5500 Negroes responded and cast their ballots for their candidate, Oliver W. Hill. . . . If Mr. Hill had been nominated and had been elected—what then? It would have been the first instance since 1889–90 in which a Negro would have been elected to the House of Delegates, and the first instance on record of the election of a Negro Democrat. Speaking generally, the decision of Negroes to participate in the Democratic primary will give them, in the end, some representation in Southern legislative bodies. It now is logical for them to enter the primary, which is the equivalent of the general election."[6]

Mrs. Daisy Lester Avery, publicity chairman of the League of Women Voters, expressed herself as being "very proud of the Negroes, whose vote yesterday indicated that they are really interested in the elections."[7] The league's legislative chairman, Mrs. Jacob Cohn, was "simply delighted to see the wonderful vote Mr. Hill received. Many white votes were cast for him and no voters could say anything against him."[8]

The Richmond *Times-Dispatch* concluded "that the Negro vote will be an important factor in future Democratic primaries." Editorially it asserted: "Since Virginia and Richmond are almost one-third colored, there is nothing revolutionary in the idea that Negro citizens of the city and State desire to have representation in the Legislature by their own people. It should be competent and honest representa-

---

[4] Quoted in Richmond *Afro-American*, August 16, 1947.
[5] Letter published in Norfolk *Journal and Guide*, August 30, 1947.
[6] Richmond *News-Leader*, August 6, 1947.
[7] Ibid.
[8] Ibid.

tion, of course. Richmonders who are familiar with the record of Oliver Hill . . . are aware that he is qualified by character and training for such a responsibility. . . . We do have a democratic tradition which holds that American citizens are entitled to vote and to hold office. It is natural, then, that our Negro citizens should hope to exercise that right. Furthermore, it seems inevitable that as they rise higher in the educational and cultural scale, they will succeed in doing so. . . . So we may as well accustom ourselves to the thought that the Negro citizens of the Old Dominion may send one of their number to the General Assembly before many years are past."[9]

To Dr. Luther P. Jackson, who for many years has been striving to broaden the base of Negro suffrage in Virginia, nothing in "Negro political life in America during the year 1947 . . . has been more gratifying than the candidacy of Oliver W. Hill. . . . I interpret his candidacy as representing the most significant advance in the citizenship aspirations of southern Negroes by way of the ballot box that we have had in the past half century. . . . Although the attorney lost this time, I have reason to believe that he or some other good candidate will win next time. Indeed, it appears that the winning of this office and other elective offices in Virginia is an event just around the corner."[10]

The near nomination of Hill brought from Charles H. Phillips, a successful candidate for renomination, a threat to introduce a bill in the General Assembly to outlaw "single-shot" bloc voting. Phillips expressed concern that none of the candidates for the House of Delegates received a majority of the votes cast in the primaries. He was disturbed also, he admitted, by the concentration of Negro voters behind the Hill candidacy, which he viewed as a "disservice" to themselves. "Instead of trying to elect representatives who would represent the best interests of all the voters, they let themselves be talked into playing politics," he said. In one precinct where the city's most influential and best-educated Negroes lived, he complained, he received only 20 of 500 votes cast. To prevent a recurrence of such bloc voting, he proposed an amendment to the election laws requiring each voter to cast ballots for as many candidates as are to be nominated and elected.[11] Delegate Phillips's proposal was not only resented by Negroes, but also by many whites. The Norfolk *Virginian-Pilot* suggested that "the best thing Mr. Phillips can do

<hr />

[9]Richmond *Times-Dispatch,* August 7, 1947.
[10]Norfolk *Journal and Guide,* August 16, 1947.
[11]Richmond *Times-Dispatch,* August 17, 1947.

about his proposed outlawing of single-shot or fractional ticket voting, is to junk it."[12]

The disappointment which many Negroes felt because of the failure to nominate Mr. Hill was in large measure assuaged by the first official acts of Delegate Murray. Following the opening of the legislative session, Mr. Murray introduced five bills to repeal existing statutes requiring segregation of the races in public carriers and places of assembly. These bills represented what was perhaps the first serious attempt to repeal Jim Crow legislation in a state south of the Potomac River. At a public hearing held on the bills on February 20, 1948, eight persons testified for repeal of the segregation laws. No one testified against the Murray bills. Seven of the witnesses were white men and women, prominent in the religious, educational, and social-welfare activities in the state. The Richmond Council of Churches approved the measures. What had at first appeared to be a hopeless gesture gained strength and support, and progressives began to entertain the hope that at least the bill eliminating Jim Crow on public carriers would be passed. However, this hope was banished following a second hearing in which there was further testimony in favor of repeal. The bills were then arbitrarily discarded by the House committee.

There was a strong undercurrent of opposition to the bills. Murray's own local of the International Typographical Union disavowed "any actions, past and present, that [he] has taken as a legislator." He was dropped as a delegate to the Richmond Central Trades and Labor Council of which he had been president. He was also replaced as a delegate to the Allied Printing Trades Council. Elsewhere within the ranks of the labor movement, both CIO and AFL, there was resistance to this effort to remove the color bar in travel and assembly.

The Richmond campaign, while not a complete success, set the pattern for a revival of Negro-labor political unity. If such unity could have been firmly established during the period of the Populist movement, the South may well have eliminated the one-party system which fosters political apathy and concentrates governmental control in the hands of the few. The development of such unity will not be looked upon with favor by the most influential elements in the South. The Richmond *News-Leader*, which saw no cause for alarm in Mr. Hill's near success, believes that "in the State as a

[12]Norfolk *Virginian-Pilot*, August 20, 1947.

whole, the prospect of a Negro-CIO coalition is dim" and "must remain local, not to say temporary or casual."[13]

The campaign demonstrated that Negroes, even under the leadership of middle-class business- and professional men, are more advanced politically and more aware of the essential need for such unity than the bulk of organized white trade unionists. As the strength of the Negro vote increases, as it surely will at an accelerating pace throughout the South, white politicians, who are more realistic than the general run of workers, will seek out the leaders in an effort to make deals for the Negro vote. The degree to which the professional politicians will be successful depends in large measure upon the response of rank-and-file white workers to the imperative need for Negro-labor political co-operation. Unlike the trade unionists, the politicians will not hesitate to make deals with anyone who can deliver the vote, prejudice notwithstanding.

Unlike the Negroes in Richmond who, on their own initiative, were re-entering the political arena after a long period of forced inactivity, the colored voters of New York were being eagerly sought by all political factions. Through long years of experience, able machine-wise politicians had been developed in Harlem. By the time of the municipal elections of 1945 they were old and skilled hands in the political game.

NEW FACES IN HARLEM

New York was the first city in which the Democratic party developed a sizable and regular following among Negro voters. Tammany Hall, always in eager search of additional voters, made overtures to New York Negroes as early as the 1870s. The party's feeble gestures met with indifferent success until the 1920s, when more substantial inducements were offered the black electorate. Negroes were appointed to responsible public office, the time-honored means of stimulating and rewarding political support. Chief among these appointees was Ferdinand Q. Morton, one of three New York City civil service commissioners. Morton headed the United Colored Democracy and was designated by Tammany as its unofficial representative in Harlem. The official representatives, the ones with real authority, were the white district leaders who clung to their positions of power and influence long after Harlem had become predominantly Negro.

[13]Richmond *News-Leader,* August 18, 1947.

Until 1930 Harlem was one of the few districts in New York City which regularly sent Republicans to the state Assembly. Since that time, beginning with the election of James E. Stephens, the area has been consistently represented in Albany by Democrats, with William T. Andrews as the community's veteran legislator. It has, however, occasionally gone Republican in gubernatorial and local races. The election in 1930 of two Negro Democrats—James S. Watson and Charles E. Toney—as municipal judges in the newly created judicial district comprising the Harlem area strengthened Tammany's hold. Nevertheless, colored Democrats grew increasingly restive under the district leadership of white men often domiciled in other sections of the city. The demand for representative black leadership was intensified. The Republicans had already yielded to this pressure, but as they were perennially out of office, the position of Republican district leader was little more than an empty honor. The gravy was on the Democratic table, and Negroes were becoming ever more insistent in their demand for a taste of it.

District leadership is achieved by organizing a following among party members in an area and getting delegates elected to the county committee, who in turn select the leader. As a rule, the leader so chosen becomes a member of Tammany, although occasionally the majority choice has been rejected by the Hall. Abortive efforts had been made in Harlem to depose the white leadership and replace it with black men representative of the community. The white leaders naturally resisted this attack upon their positions. They were able to retain leadership, however, only through vote of the county committeemen, the majority of whom were Negro district workers and persons who held minor city jobs by grace of the district leader. The job was to dislodge these committeemen and replace them with delegates pledged to support a Negro candidate. Not until 1935 were the colored Democrats of Harlem successful in electing one of their own as a district leader. Herbert L. Bruce, rugged, independent, and tough-minded, became the race's first member of Tammany Hall. He held this post for ten turbulent years, beholden to no white man and fighting the Tammany chiefs for equal and unrestricted recognition and a full share of patronage.

Bruce's uncompromising position irked the Tammany chiefs, who threw their influence to insurgent candidates seeking to unseat him. In 1945 he was deposed. Meanwhile, the remaining predominantly Negro districts in Harlem came under Negro leadership. With the ousting of Bruce, J. Raymond Jones emerged pre-eminent among the Harlem district leaders. His position was made secure when Mayor William O'Dwyer appointed him deputy commissioner of housing and buildings with the admonition "to surround himself with the best thinking people of his community" and to act as a liaison between City Hall and Harlem. Jones, more adept than Bruce in the give and take of political maneuvering, had established an effective machine in his district and had won the respect of diverse elements within the community.

While Republican organizations declined in Harlem after 1930 with the increasing strength of Tammany under Negro district leadership, the community did not become a mere appendage to the Democratic party. After voting strongly for Franklin D. Roosevelt in the presidential election of 1932, the voters of Harlem the following year gave generous support to Fiorello H. La Guardia, the reform candidate for Mayor. This support, Mayor La Guardia, a maverick Republican-Fusionist, retained in his two succeeding elections. In 1938 Negro voters were an important factor in the slim margin of victory by which Governor Herbert L. Lehman was returned to office over his Republican opponent, the crusading Thomas E. Dewey. Four years later, in his successful bid for the governorship, Dewey carried Harlem, only to lose it in the presidential race of 1944 and again when he ran for governor in 1946. Meanwhile Harlem supported Francis E. Rivers for city judge on a Republican-ALP ticket and had twice voted overwhelmingly for Benjamin J. Davis, Communist candidate for City Council. The vote in Harlem was by no means in the bag for any political party. It had to be contended for.

The La Guardia regime was one of the best things that ever happened to New York City and one of the few reform administrations that ever showed any concern for the welfare of the Negro population. While disclaiming any political motivation, Mayor La Guardia appointed Negroes to posts in the city administration for which Tammany had never seriously considered them. He retained Morton in his position as civil service commissioner, appointed a Negro tax commissioner, and named three to judicial posts. He encouraged the development of public housing projects for low-income families. He named Negroes to important municipal boards like the Housing Authority and the Emergency Relief Board. He insisted upon the merit system in the appointments and promotions in the municipal civil service. He handled the so-called race riots in Harlem with a tact and skill which kept these disturbances from exploding in the disastrous manner of the Detroit tragedy. Only in one crucial test did the "Little Flower" let his Negro followers down. That was in his acquiescence in the Jim Crow policy of the Metropolitan Life Insurance Company's semi-public urban redevelopment project, Stuyvesant Town. In this his record was better than President Roosevelt's, but likewise his milieu was more favorable. On the whole, he earned the appreciation and gratitude of the people of New York, including those who made their homes in Harlem.

In the meantime a colorful new figure enlivened the political scene in Harlem. Adam Clayton Powell, young, handsome, and eloquent, the pastor of the huge Abyssinian Baptist Church, hurtled into the political arena to the well-timed blare of trumpets. Elected to the City Council in 1941 as an independent, he began laying the groundwork for the congressional race of 1944. Election of a Negro had been assured by the redistricting that had consolidated the Harlem area, formerly split among three congressional districts. With his large congregation as a base, he reached out to gain the support of other elements in the community. First among these were the left-wingers. The fanfare which accompanied his every political activity created an impression of invincibility. Many opportunistically hastened to join the band wagon. Politicians couldn't afford to be caught short. Others, who had quite definite reservations about the egocentric and ambitious young cleric, hesitated to oppose him. He stormed Tammany Hall and, over the head of his district leader Bruce, obtained Democratic endorsement for the congressional race. He had already the endorsement of the American Labor party. Only the Republicans halfheartedly entered a candidate against him. He swept all three primaries and, unopposed in the general election in 1944, became New York's first Negro congressman. Two years later the Reverend Mr. Powell was re-elected, but much of the reluctant support he had previously enjoyed refused to go along with him. He lost the Republican primary to Grant Reynolds, another young and handsome cleric. He retained his Democratic and American Labor party support, though there were evidences of a lack of enthusiasm in the ranks of both organizations.

On notable occasions the compact, well-organized district machines in Harlem have simply refused to deliver on demand of Tammany Hall, particularly when the leaders realized that the party candidates or program met with little response in Harlem. This tactic was most obvious in the special election in the Twenty-first Congressional District in March 1944. The Democratic-American Labor party candidate was a man denounced by La Guardia as a "Tammany ward heeler" with no qualifications for the post. The candidate was elected by the narrow margin of 1571 votes, but he lost the Negro areas in the district, comprising about 35 per cent of the vote. In one election district the Democratic candidate did not receive a single vote, which clearly indicated that even the Democratic precinct workers failed to vote for him.

Again when pressure by General William O'Dwyer, then the candidate for mayor, compelled Tammany Hall to withdraw the name of Ben Davis from its list of designated candidates for City Council, the Harlem district leaders tacitly continued to support the Communist candidate, who was the popular choice in Harlem, regardless of party. Two years later, in 1947, when both the Democrats and Republicans were fighting for repeal of proportional representation, two assembly districts in Harlem were among the few in the city which voted to retain PR. The Harlem voters had demonstrated their ability to elect a member of the City Council under PR, while there was grave doubt that they would be able to do so under the new plan of electing Council members from senatorial districts. The flexibility of the Harlem voter has, on occasion, been abetted by his district leaders.

The real test of the strength of the Democratic organization in Harlem came in the 1945 city elections. In this campaign there were three candidates for the office of mayor: Judge Jonah J. Goldstein, an anti-Tammany Democrat running on the Republican ticket and endorsed also by the Liberal party; Newbold Morris, president of the City Council, a Republican, nominated by La Guardia's newly created No Deal reform party; and General William O'Dwyer, nominated by the Democrats and endorsed by the American Labor party. Two of the candidates, Goldstein and Morris, were favorably known in the Harlem community. Goldstein, through his work on the bench, his sponsorship of Negro admissions to the Grand Street Boys Club, and his frequent appearances at public gatherings in Harlem, was widely known. Morris, a blue blood, was a member of the Board of Trustees of Hampton Institute, a Negro college in Virginia, and was known to advocate "genuine racial equality in local affairs, with particular attention to the problems of Negroes." He had openly opposed and, as a member of the Board of Estimate, voted against the city's signing a contract with the Metropolitan Life Insurance Company for the development of Stuyvesant Town unless the ban against Negro occupancy were removed. This was a vote that La Guardia had ducked. Mr. Morris, however, was not believed to have a real chance of winning the election.

About General O'Dwyer the Negro community knew little—almost nothing. He had been a policeman—and to most Negroes, cops are, with just cause, among the least admired public servants. He had been a city magistrate and district attorney in Brooklyn. In 1941 he had run unsuccessfully for mayor against La Guardia. He was brass in the Army, and the Army is Jim Crow. Among Brooklyn Negroes he was somewhat better known than in Harlem. In a letter to Oliver D. Williams, Brooklyn Negro lawyer, he had expressed the conviction that crime and juvenile delinquency in colored neighborhoods "grow out of the injustices and the frustration the Negro is forced to endure by the communities in which he lives, such as inadequate housing, discrimination, unemployment, high prices and other evils of which the Negro is not the creator but the victim."[14] This position, however, was not widely known in Harlem.

To supplement the work of the district clubs, a citizens' committee, under co-chairmanship of Congressman Adam C. Powell and Dr. Channing H. Tobias, was set up to rally support for O'Dwyer in the Harlem-Riverside area. A recently returned veteran, Lieutenant Colonel Vernon C. Riddick, was chosen as executive director to coordinate the work. Riddick was selected for the post not only because of his experience and ability, but also because his years in the service had removed him from the bickering and strife that seriously threatened unity among the various clubs in the Harlem area. He was acceptable to and well thought of by all factions, who knew him familiarly as "Hank," a good lawyer and a regular Democrat. Though conservative in manner, he was a progressive without being a leftist. The job of this committee was to overcome the handicap under which their candidate entered the race, to promote his candidacy among a people who knew too little about him.

The campaign had hardly got started before it ran into a serious snag. Ray Jones, after first wavering, joined other district leaders in obtaining Tammany endorsement of the Communist City Council candidate, Ben Davis. Davis had wide support in the community and Jones had agreed, even when earlier he was suggesting another candidate, that "he has made a very good record."[15] Two of the three Harlem weeklies had endorsed Davis, the leftist *People's Voice* and the Republican New York *Age*. Terming him "a brilliant and

[14]Quoted by Julius J. Adams in the New York *Amsterdam News,* July 28, 1945.
[15]Quoted in the New York *Herald Tribune,* February 9, 1945.

forceful Councilman," the *Age* maintained that "on his record alone Councilman Davis deserves re-election. . . . Not even his most severe critic can ever accuse Mr. Davis of ever having espoused any cause in the City Council except the cause of American democracy, which is more than can be said of some other Councilmen elected on major party tickets." For mayor, the *Age* was supporting Newbold Morris. The *People's Voice* supported Davis as "an uncompromising fighter for the rights of Negroes and the masses of all other people." Various non-Communist leaders in the community endorsed him: Dr. Tobias of the National YMCA, Edward S. Lewis, executive secretary of the Greater New York Urban League; James E. Allen, president of the New York branch of the National Association for the Advancement of Colored People, and many others. Davis, however, was not without opposition in Harlem. The Republicans, with the Liberal party, entered a candidate against him. A. Philip Randolph, the respected labor leader, urging the defeat of Davis, denounced him as "a member of a party which takes its orders from an alien government, whether those orders are in the interests of Americans or not." The *Amsterdam News,* the Dewey organ in Harlem, charged that Davis had "changed fronts" and accordingly was no longer able to serve the community.

In the face of this all but unanimous support for Davis in Harlem, Tammany, upon insistence of O'Dwyer and other powerful anti-Communist forces, rescinded its endorsement. This inevitable development should have surprised only the most politically naïve person. The astonishing thing was that the Hall should ever have made the endorsement and that it should have been sought by an avowed Communist. Time was when no Communist would have permitted his name to be linked with Tammany. But the needless endorsement was made—needless because the smart thing would have been to work quietly for Davis without any endorsement. After the Hall's designation with withdrawn this was precisely what the Harlem leaders did, except that they had to go through the gesture of naming a candidate with no radical taint. "Now that Mr. Davis has been dropped from the Tammany ticket," commented Earl Brown, the political analyst for the *Amsterdam News,* "it would have been far better if he had not been put on it. He and Jones of the 13th A.D. could have cooked up an off the record you-help-me-and-I'll-help-you deal . . . and in all probability it would have worked without anybody getting his political backsides burned."[16]

[16]The Amsterdam *News,* August 4, 1945.

While *l'affaire* Davis created an embarrassing situation, it did not halt the work of the committee. Meanwhile, the situation was somewhat eased when the *People's Voice,* then the principal organ of the Davis forces in Harlem, announced its continued support of O'Dwyer. Despite his repudiation of Davis, the *Voice* said, "William O'Dwyer is admirably well qualified by experience to head our City Government; he is thoroughly committed to a city-state-federal governmental program for economic security and genuine democracy. . . . We urge his election as Mayor." The left-wingers were not easily deterred.

After the fuss and fury had blown over, Colonel Riddick's committee settled down to its task of winning Harlem for an unknown Democrat. The clubhouse boys were ready to go. Davis had been sacrificed, but that was no skin off their backs. For the first time since the districts had come under Negro leadership there was a chance to win a mayoralty election. There had been no real pickings for the boys during the La Guardia regime. They had to be satisfed with the slim offerings at the disposal of county officers and occasional crumbs of federal patronage. The lush city jobs were closed to them. Now they hoped (though they were not too sure about how "regular" O'Dwyer would be) for a return of the good old days of political preferment in jobs. They were willing to work, and they did work to turn out the vote.

"At the outset we realized that our candidate was unknown in Harlem," Riddick later recalled. "But we thought we could turn that very fact into an asset in view of the absence of any anti-Negro record in the career of General O'Dwyer. Our program was to get across to the voters his record as a sound, capable administrator and an honest man who was just in his dealings with all people. No one could point to any injustice he had ever done to any Negro in any of his varied activities. Moreover, he was committed to the Roosevelt program and had the active backing of Mrs. Roosevelt and Henry Wallace."[17]

The campaign was carried on through the district clubs, supplemented by the work of the citizens' committee. It was the responsibility of the clubs to conduct the door-to-door canvass of all registered voters in the blocks and election districts under their respective jurisdictions. The thoroughness of this job was perhaps the most important factor in getting out the vote and winning the election. The citizens' committee made contacts with the churches

---

[17] Personal interview, November 11, 1947.

and other community organizations. Sound trucks were stationed at important intersections and at points where large numbers of citizens gathered or passed. The American Labor party prepared and distributed thousands of attractively designed leaflets setting forth the candidate's program of "Equality, Jobs and Security for all." O'Dwyer himself came to Harlem only once during the campaign. He addressed no mass meeting in the area. Two nights before election he visited each of the five Democratic clubs in Harlem for a brief meeting with the leaders and election day workers.

General O'Dwyer was overwhelmingly elected, obtaining 57.31 per cent of the city-wide vote. In the four Harlem Assembly Districts, where he was little known, 64.39 per cent of the vote went to the Democratic-ALP candidate. Colonel Riddick was able to boast: "We carried every election district in the area." Riddick, who had been in charge of the over-all campaign operations in the Harlem area, was subsequently appointed magistrate by the new mayor. Ray Jones, Tammany's leader in the Thirteenth Assembly District, became, as the *Herald Tribune* put it, "the mayor's man in Harlem." However, other demands were raised, particularly for the appointment of a Negro to the Board of Education. Harlem waited to see if the new mayor would equal the record of Fiorello La Guardia. In the meantime Mr. Davis was returned to the City Council without benefit of Tammany endorsement.

CHAPTER X

Dixie in Transition

So long as the vast majority of negroes continue to reside in the South, that region will hold the key to the political destiny of the race. Negro voters in northern states have been of immeasurable aid to their southern brothers in the struggle to attain full suffrage for the race throughout the country, but the brunt of this struggle must continue to be borne by the southern Negro himself. The ultimate outcome of this drive for equal suffrage rights will be determined by the militancy of the southern Negro, the receptiveness of the advance elements of the white South, the political sagacity and adroitness of the Negro's national leadership, and the fidelity of the federal government to its constitutional responsibility under the Fourteenth and Fifteenth Amendments.

Although the Negro had ceased to be a decisive or even important factor in southern politics by the opening years of the twentieth century, his vote was never completely eradicated in the South. The southern reactionaries did not succeed in turning the clock all the way back to 1860. Throughout the period of the Great Blackout some Negroes continued to vote despite discrimination, fraud, intimidation, and a growing sense of futility. Voting was spotty and ineffectual, but it continued. Its extent depended largely upon two factors: the degree of insistence upon the part of the Negro voter, and the willingness of local officials to admit a select few Negroes to the ballot box in order to maintain the fiction that there was no discrimination. These exceptions enabled the sensitive Southerner to voice a 10-per-cent truth and say that the Negro was not barred from voting, that if he qualified and wanted to vote he could do so freely. The number of Negroes voting was nowhere representative and was practically nil in small towns and in rural areas. Voting was almost entirely confined to the larger cities and to certain university towns in which a feeble tolerance was acceptable.

The principal bar to Negro voting in the South was the "white primary" which excluded colored persons from participating in the nomination of Democratic candidates. As these nominations were almost invariably ratified by the general elections, exclusion from the Democratic primary was effectual disfranchisement. The poll tax, of course, excluded the great mass of Negro citizens along with millions of poor whites. But throughout the South there was an ever-increasing number of colored persons who could well afford to pay the poll tax. These were generally the persons best able to meet the literacy and "understanding" tests imposed by the disfranchising conventions in the southern states between 1890 and 1908. However, neither their economic standing nor their cultural level enabled them to meet the color test of the "white primary." Doubtlessly the number of Negroes who qualified for voting could have been enlarged had colored citizens believed it worth while risking the hazards and going through the futile gesture of casting a ballot in the general election, the result of which had already been determined by the Democratic primary. Even among those who could qualify there was a widespread conviction that it was hardly worth while.

The slow revival of Negro voting in the South was first stimulated by the opportunity to participate in non-partisan local elections in which there were no closed primaries. These contests were subject only to the laws governing general elections and, accordingly, were not restricted by party regulations. Likewise, voting in special elections and on city bond issues for public improvements was open to all qualified voters. In such balloting the small Negro vote was often sought by candidates for office or by advocates of certain public programs. In a region in which the suffrage is highly restricted, a few hundred votes assume great importance. There were in 1930, Lewinson reports, 115 southern cities with the city-manager and commission form of government usually elected in non-partisan contests.[1] Some of these, as Jackson, Mississippi, nominated the candidates in an all-white primary. But in most the commissioners were chosen in an open election.

By intelligent and concerted use of the ballot, Negro citizens were able in a number of instances to gain certain concrete benefits such as new school buildings and equipment, parks and recreational facilities, paved streets and improved sanitation. The most celebrated in-

[1]Lewinson, op. cit., p. 147.

stance was probably the effective use of the Negro vote in an Atlanta referendum on a school bond issue in 1921. The city administration was sponsoring a four-million-dollar school-expansion program. There was the usual opposition by the real estate interests. Negroes also voted against it, but for different reasons. They saw that its provisions did not adequately meet their needs. After having been twice defeated at the polls, the sponsors of the program reached an agreement with the Negro leadership. Negro voters then responded and the bond issue was approved. As a result, colored citizens got their first public high school in the city and new equipment for other schools. Elsewhere in the South the small Negro vote has been helpful in bringing to the colored community certain public benefits and other improvements.

In a score or more southern cities Negro voting continued: in Memphis, Nashville, Chattanooga, and Knoxville, Tennessee; in Roanoke, Richmond, Norfolk, Portsmouth, and Newport News, Virginia; in Raleigh, Durham, and Greensboro, North Carolina; in Atlanta and Savannah, Georgia; in Birmingham, Alabama; in Jacksonville, Florida; in Houston, Galveston, Dallas, Fort Worth, and San Antonio, Texas, and in other cities in almost every state of the South. The largest Negro vote was reported from Memphis, where about 5000 colored citizens have for a number of years been participating in the Democratic primaries through a deal between the Democratic boss, Edward Crump, and the onetime Negro Republican leader, Robert R. Church. In Atlanta the vote varied from 1800 to 3000. Elsewhere this vote was much smaller, seldom numbering more than a few hundred. In some of these cities the Negro vote was actively sought by competing candidates who were willing to pay off in support of public improvements needed and desired by the Negro community.

Clinging precariously to their enfeebled right to vote, southern Negroes began an attack upon the restrictive white primary in the late 1920s. Suits were filed in the courts of Texas, Florida, Virginia, and Arkansas. Unable to obtain satisfaction in the state courts, the fight to crash the white primary was carried through the various federal courts to the Supreme Court, which did not render a conclusive decision until 1944. Meanwhile the New Deal had given new impetus to the struggle for the ballot in the South. President Roosevelt's efforts to develop liberal southern support gave added encouragement to Negro voting throughout the South. Whereas Lewinson, who gathered data from miscellaneous sources, was able to account for no more than 70,000 registered Negro voters in eleven southern states between 1920 and 1930, a study by the *Virginia Spectator,* University of Virginia publication, estimated that the Negro vote in the same states totaled nearly 200,000 in 1938, five years after the advent of the New Deal.

In Virginia, Tennessee, and North Carolina, states in which the white primary was breached more than a decade before the Supreme Court decision, Negroes were actively participating in the Democratic primaries and, in some instances, were again approaching a balance-of-power position between contending candidates and factions of the party. Also they were beginning to run candidates of their own for minor local offices. In 1936 they elected Negro justices of the peace in Durham and Raleigh, North Carolina. The small Negro vote in the Second Virginia Congressional District was credited with the victory of a New Deal candidate over an organization man in Democratic primaries of 1936.[2] In eastern Tennessee, where the Republicans remained the dominant party, the Negro was a continuing and important factor, strong enough to influence the two Republican congressmen from that area to vote for anti-lynching legislation.

Here and there in the South the Negro began to establish tentative bridgeheads as election officials in some communities relaxed the discriminations which previously had been harshly applied. There was in some instances less distortion of the legal restrictions when qualified Negroes applied for registration. Bunche cites the following incident as gleaned from an interview with a member of the Board of Registrars in Saluda County, South Carolina:

"We had half-a-dozen 'niggers' come in," he said. They were asked to read a portion of the Constitution and write it out, and to answer certain questions about it which the clerk had given to the registrars. None of the Negroes was turned down, which the registrar thought was due to the fact that the Negro community had sent "the best ones in here first. When they found out what they had to do, they went out and told the rest," so that now "Negroes don't come in here unless they can pass." He admitted frankly that white applicants were never tested by the registrar because "we were never asked to."[3] While whites were being accorded preferential treatment, Negro applicants were being required to meet the law.

In Alabama, however, the old pattern continued. Emory O. Jackson, editor of the Birmingham *World,* reported that a Negro school-

---

[2]*Virginia Spectator,* University of Virginia, November 1938.
[3]Ralph J. Bunche, op. cit.

teacher had been refused registration because she could not explain to the satisfaction of the board the meaning of the phrase "domestic tranquillity." Complained the editor: "Such a question has absolutely nothing to do with one's qualification for voting."[4] In Montgomery a Negro who had done graduate work at the University of Chicago was required to bring in two white sponsors before he was permitted to register. "I'll approve of him, but don't ever bring this class of person here again," the chairman of the board warned the sponsors.[5]

Many forces were at work in the South undermining in one way or another the political status quo. The whole New Deal philosophy, while resisted bitterly by the reactionaries, had an ameliorative impact upon southern attitudes. Increasing urbanization and industrialization contributed to less rigid enforcement of policies of political exclusion. The labor movement, and particularly the CIO, stimulated voting by its membership of both races. The development of a small group of advanced liberals in the colleges and universities, among the clergy and other professional groups, and in the publishing field was helpful. The cultural and economic advance of the Negro and the development of a more honest, aggressive, and articulate leadership in Negro communities throughout the South made possible greater participation in the electoral process. The sharpening of the issue as between conservatism and liberalism in the South tended to replace the traditional personal rivalries with the competition of ideas.

While all these factors contributed to the slow growth of the Negro vote in the South, the real impetus did not come until the Supreme Court decision of April 1944 invalidated the white primary. All the way from Virginia to Texas a new ferment stirred among the 9,000,-000 black Americans living in that region. For the first time in nearly half a century there was a concerted South-wide movement on the part of these long-disfranchised millions to participate actively in the selection of their local, state, and federal officials. Following hard upon the court decision, Negro voters' leagues mushroomed throughout the South, belying the old contention that the Negro was uninterested in the ballot. Within two years there was a spectacular expansion in the Negro vote. Thousands of new Negro voters were registered. The time had come to reassert themselves politically.

[4] Cited in *Report of 30th Annual Policy Conference on Democracy and the Constitution,* Montgomery, Ala., 1945.
[5] Ibid.

By the time of the primary elections in 1946, the southern Negro vote had more than tripled since 1938, passing the 600,000 mark. Texas and Georgia, each with intelligent and alert leadership, led the way in this drive for an expanded suffrage. In the Lone Star State, 175,000 Negroes paid their poll taxes, which in that state qualifies them for voting without further registration. In Georgia, where the poll tax had been removed and the voting age lowered to eighteen years, 150,000 Negro men and women got their names on the registration books, a greater number than the 110,000 who paid their poll taxes in 1904 before the enactment of the disfranchising measures.

Elsewhere there were significant increases in the number of qualified colored voters, with only Alabama, Louisiana, Mississippi, and South Carolina lagging behind. And even those states slightly enlarged their slim Negro vote. It was in the cities that the advances were most spectacular. During the year of 1946 alone, the registration of colored citizens jumped from 5000 to 25,000 in Atlanta; from 1200 to 20,000 in Savannah; from 2500 to 15,000 in Jacksonville; from a few hundred to 7100 in Augusta; and in city after city in Georgia, Florida, and Texas there were similar increases. This rapid expansion of the Negro vote also stimulated increased registration among the white population. The total voting strength in Texas reached 1,800,000 in 1946, exceeding by 350,000 the 1944 total. Registrations in Georgia, which never before exceeded 500,000, went over the 1,000,000 mark in 1946, with more than 350,000 new white voters being added to the lists. Many of these new voters were from the ranks of organized labor, which more and more was insisting that its members qualify for voting.

What was the South's reaction to the Supreme Court decision opening the way for Negro participation in southern politics? The response was as varied as are the different elements which compose the South. The Negroes indicated their reaction by the eagerness with which large numbers of them embraced the opportunity. The advance guard of southern liberalism welcomed the decision and saw in the new Negro vote an important potential ally. The professional "liberals" of the South were, as always, timorous, urging caution, and fearful of conflicts should Negroes push too hard in the exercise of their suffrage rights. Certain canny politicians, looking forward to tomorrow's vote, took it in stride as an inevitable development. But the still dominant elements in the South, aware that their privileged positions were imperiled by this new vote, reacted characteristically. They sought to evade, circumvent, or nullify the clear intent of the Court's decision. Nothing was to be allowed to upset the status quo.

Despite the die-hard opposition of reactionary elements, there was a substantial white minority prepared to go along with the idea of Negro participation in the Democratic primary. "There is, in fact, a powerful bloc in almost every southern state of those who believe that qualified Negroes should have the vote," observed the journalist, Stewart Alsop. "Sometimes this is a mere pious and public wish, but more often it is sincere. Yet all of these men are gradualists. They would work the Negroes slowly into the existing political system, in such a way that a bloc Negro vote, the nightmare of all white Southerners, would be avoided."[6] This gradualist approach was generally favored by the cautious liberals who affirm their conviction that the southern Negro will eventually attain political and economic equality if only he will remain patient and depend upon the good will of his white friends. Southern Negroes have grown increasingly impatient with this approach.

The development of a white leadership in the South willing to extend suffrage rights to Negroes is a significant indication of a new trend in that region. Indeed, the most hopeful aspect of the movement to re-enfranchise the Negro has been the encouragement which some recognized white leaders have given to colored citizens. Ellis G. Arnall, the progressive young governor of Georgia, flatly declared that the "white primary is dead," following the federal court's rejection of a Georgia test case. Defying the pressure of the die-hards, he refused to call a special session of the legislature to devise means to evade the law. "The Supreme Court of the United States says that everyone—Jews, Catholics, Baptists, Negroes—is allowed to vote, and so long as I am governor the opinion of the Court will be carried out," Arnall told the Georgia State Democratic Executive Committee.

In a state-wide radio broadcast, Dr. Homer P. Rainey, former president of the University of Texas and an unsuccessful candidate for governor of that state in 1946, sought to dispel the "popular misconception that if the Negro were given his civil rights he would become a political menace. . . . But such a fear would have to be based upon the assumption that Negroes feel and act as a solid body and that their interests would be different from those of the white population. This certainly would not be the case. I think it can be

⁶New York *Herald Tribune,* September 16, 1946.

fairly assumed that their political affiliations and their voting would follow very closely that of the general population."

Within a month after the Supreme Court handed down its historic decision, Governor Chauncey Sparks of Alabama told a gathering of colored churchmen in Birmingham: "The Negro should be given his civil rights, which includes the right to vote, when he is qualified, on the same basis as the white man. . . . I have expressed throughout this state, and in some instances urged, and will continue to urge Boards of Registrars to reappraise their situation and to place upon the voting lists those of all races qualified by education, by training, by intelligence, and by character to vote. More of our Negroes should be on our voting lists. Our Registrars should take a practical view of their obligations and duties, recognizing that one who meets a reasonable test is entitled to participate in his government."

In many communities less famous spokesmen for the South have urged acquiescence in the Supreme Court decision. S. Henry Harris, member of the Florida state legislature and a conservative Democratic politician, called upon his fellow Southerners to accept this decision without reservation. "As good citizens and also as good Democrats," he maintains, "we should make haste to accord the colored citizens of our state the rights which it appears we have failed to accord them in the past, and that without equivocation, evasion, or even effort at legal avoidance." Savannah politicians and officeholders, according to William H. Fields, writing in the Savannah *Morning News*, were unopposed to and "unperturbed by Negro registration and appear to accept the Negro vote as a matter of fact rather than something to be fought."

And in Alabama, Charles N. Feidelson, a Birmingham newspaper columnist, exhorted: "Let's do away with the poll tax, let's do away with other discriminatory laws directed at keeping the Negro in his place. Let's have registration laws that can be applied without making a mockery of fair play and democracy. Let's do everything in our power to abolish the shadow under which southern whites move and have their being. Let's wipe out a double standard which divides us against ourselves. Let's have a 'white supremacy' dependent upon the white man's superiority and not on doing violence to the rights and hopes of the Negro."

The encouragement which many Southerners now openly give to Negro suffrage stems from the New Deal policies of Franklin D. Roosevelt which created a political climate in which such ideas—

long taboo—could be openly expressed. Certainly there are entrenched interests and politicians in the South who hated the late
President, and Mrs. Roosevelt even more, for their broad humanitarianism. But the Roosevelts also had just as strong and devoted
admirers among southern whites as among any other race or region.
The New Deal introduced Negro farmers to voting under the AAA
and Negro workers in labor elections under the NLRB. They were
not only permitted to vote in these elections, but their votes were
eagerly sought by their fellow white farmers and workers. These
were steps toward a free vote on political issues.

Meanwhile southern reaction was preparing for a last-ditch stand
against Negro voting, for the control of a small electorate through
appeals to a specious doctrine of "white supremacy." The devices
for restricting the suffrage had run thin. The white primary was
doomed. Increasing demand in the South portended the elimination
of the poll tax. Educational tests, if fairly administered, could no
longer keep the majority of the colored citizens away from the polls.
Something had to be done. Some new expedient had to be found.
South Carolina led. The state legislature, summoned into special
session by Governor Olin D. Johnston, promptly removed from the
statutes all laws dealing with primary elections. In this way it was
hoped that the Democratic party would be established as a private,
voluntary association without any legal standing and with the right
to determine its membership on any basis it chose. It was a dangerous move which ultimately would place the control of the state in the
hands of an even smaller and more centralized clique than formerly.
It would facilitate gangster rule, political corruption, and double-
dealing. But if it got by the Supreme Court it would continue the
exclusion of Negroes from the politics of the state.

Other states contemplated the South Carolina formula. Georgia
took similar action on demand of the Talmadge forces, only to have
it vetoed by Acting Governor M. E. Thompson. Arkansas instituted
a dual system of primaries, one for federal offices and another for
local and state offices. In accordance with the Supreme Court decision, Negroes were to be allowed to vote in primaries for federal
offices while being barred from a voice in the selection of local and
state officials. Within a year this costly and cumbersome device had
to be abandoned. Alabama answered with the Boswell Amendment,
ratified by a state-wide referendum in 1946. This amendment established as a qualification for voting the ability to "read and write,
understand and explain any article of the Constitution of the United

States" to the satisfaction of the registrar. It further requires that voters be persons of "good character . . . who understand the duties and obligations of citizenship under a republican form of government." The Mississippi legislature enacted a law requiring primary voters to swear they are "in accord" with the party doctrines, including provisions which the framers of the law deemed unacceptable to Negroes, such as opposition to federal legislation on lynching, the poll tax, and fair employment practices. Efforts to enact restrictive legislation in Florida failed. Texas, accepting the decision, gave up the fight for further restricting the Negro vote.

Enactment of these discriminatory measures met with varying degrees of opposition in each of the states. Even in South Carolina there were those who questioned the wisdom of placing the primary outside of the law. A notable group of Georgians, including the widow of Confederate General James Longstreet, opposed the white primary bill in open legislative hearings. Mississippi was likewise warned by one of its elder statesmen, Chief Tax Commissioner Alfred Stone, against adoption of "any new hare-brained ideas" and urged to stick by the Constitution of 1890. There was strong opposition in Alabama, headed by Governor-elect James E. Folsom, against the Boswell Amendment, which was approved by a narrow margin of Alabama voters. Much of the opposition of the liberals to these measures was due to the realization that dissident whites, as well as Negroes, could be disfranchised by the clique in control of the party machinery.

The legal attack on the South Carolina plan bore first fruit. Two years after the plan had been adopted, George Elmore, a Negro citizen of Columbia, challenged the Democratic Executive Committee and the election officials of his home county for refusal to permit him and other Negroes to vote in the party primaries solely because of race. A battery of lawyers from the National Association for the Advancement of Colored People, competently headed by Thurgood Marshall, took the case to the Federal District Court. The suit contended that, although the primary laws had been abolished, the Democratic party, by holding primaries in South Carolina, still performed the same state function which it had prior to 1944 when the laws were repealed and, accordingly, remained a state agency and, as such, was prohibited by the Constitution from denying Negroes the right to vote.

In a far-reaching decision handed down on July 12, 1947, a native South Carolina jurist, Federal Judge J. Waties Waring, upheld the right of Elmore and other Negroes to participate in the Democratic primaries, "the only material and realistic elections" held in the state. Colored citizens "are entitled to be enrolled and to vote in the primaries conducted by the Democratic party of South Carolina, and the defendants and their successors in office will be enjoined from excluding qualified voters from enrollment and casting ballots by reason of their not being persons of the white race," Judge Waring said in his opinion. The unbiased South Carolinian went further. "For too many years the people of this country, and perhaps particularly of this state, have evaded realistic issues," he said. "In these days when this nation and the nations of the world are forced to face facts in a realistic manner, and when this country is taking the lead in maintaining the democratic process and attempting to show to the world that the American Government and the American way of life is the fairest and the best that has yet been suggested, it is time for us to take stock of our internal affairs. . . . It is time for South Carolina to rejoin the Union. It is time to fall in step with the other states and to adopt the American way of conducting elections. . . . Racial distinctions cannot exist in the machinery that selects the officers and lawmakers of the United States; and all citizens of this state and country are entitled to cast a free and untrammeled ballot in our elections, and if the only material and realistic elections are clothed with the name 'primary,' they are equally entitled to vote there."

Although there appeared to be substantial elements in South Carolina prepared to accept Judge Waring's decision with complete equanimity, the Democratic politicians persisted in carrying the case to the Federal Court of Appeals, reiterating their contention that "the Democratic party has as much right to give a ballot to whomever it pleases as does a women's sewing circle during its elections." Meanwhile, according to the Columbia (S.C.) *Record:* "It must have been a bit surprising to the South Carolina politicians to discover how calmly the press and people of South Carolina have taken the decision of Judge Waring allowing the Negroes to participate in South Carolina's primaries. . . . The politicians do not, of course, agree with this thinking. They have a vested interest in preserving the status quo and the admission of Negroes to the primaries . . . would inject an unknown element in elections for these politicians whose primary interest is in getting re-elected year after year. Some of them would have to rewrite their campaign speeches to eliminate appeals to race prejudice." Pointing out that "neither Texas nor

Georgia has apparently suffered any ill effects" from Negro voting, the Sumter (S.C.) *Item* concludes that there is no reason to believe that "South Carolina is going to the dogs just because Negroes are allowed to vote in our primaries, in spite of the doleful forebodings of professional politicians."

Judge Waring's decision was affirmed by the United States Circuit Court of Appeals in an opinion handed down on December 30, 1947. "No election machinery can be upheld if its purpose or effect is to deny to the Negro, on account of his race or color, any effective voice in the government of his country or the State or community in which he lives," the opinion held. "The use of the Democratic primary in connection with the general election in South Carolina provides . . . a two-step election machinery for that State; and the denial to the colored man of the right to participate in the primary denies him all effective voice in the government of his country. There can be no question that such denial amounts to the denial of the constitutional rights of the colored man; and we think it equally clear that those who participate in the denial are exercising State power to that end, since the primary is used in connection with the general election in the selection of State officers."

Ironically, this forthright opinion of the three-man court was written by Judge John Johnson Parker who, as Republican candidate for governor of North Carolina in 1920, declared: ". . . the participation of the Negro in politics is a source of evil and danger to both races." On the basis of this early declaration Negro voters successfully opposed his confirmation by the Senate for the Supreme Court after he had been nominated by President Hoover in 1930.

The Boswell Amendment in Alabama had been opposed not only by Governor-elect Folsom, but also by the Congress of Industrial Organizations, the Southern Conference for Human Welfare, the major newspapers, the state Republican organization, the Montgomery Junior Chamber of Commerce, and other groups, as well as by the various Negro organizations. The amendment, following ratification in 1946, was headed toward a constitutional test. Both the NAACP and the Southern Conference declared their intention to test the measure in federal courts. Meanwhile dissension developed among Alabama legislators. There were those who urged adoption of the South Carolina plan because "educated" Negroes could pass the stiff Boswell test and in some communities would become a balance-of-power factor. On the other hand, Gessner T. McCorvey of Mobile, chairman of the State Democratic Executive

Committee and an original supporter of the measure, expressed the opinion that the stipulation to "explain" the Constitution should be deleted inasmuch the other restrictions met "all necessary requirements." Previously he had urged ratification of the amendment as an "effective way of keeping Negroes from voting in the future."

Undismayed by the last-stand fight of the reactionaries to maintain suffrage as an exclusive white man's privilege, southern Negro citizens forged steadily ahead. Encouraged by the liberals and refusing to be intimidated, the advance guard of the race courageously continued to push for equal suffrage rights and to enlarge the group's voting strength. They were to be stayed neither by violence nor legal subterfuge. While efforts of the Ku-Klux Klan and other terrorists may retard the growth of the Negro vote in small cities and rural areas, it does not now seem that such activities will deter any great number in the larger cities.

The night before a non-partisan municipal election in Miami in 1939 the Klan, in full regalia, burned twenty-five crosses and paraded through the Negro section carrying black effigies strung up on poles bearing placards announcing: "This Nigger Tried to Vote." The result was that more than 1000 of the 1500 registered Negroes, protected by police, turned out to vote under the leadership of the intrepid Sam Solomon, Negro businessman. No one who witnessed the grim determination with which colored men and women in Atlanta waited patiently and orderly for five or six hours to register can doubt that they mean to vote. This new insistence upon exercising their constitutional rights has been stimulated by the total experience of the war years. Returning Negro veterans are psychologically prepared to struggle at home for the principles for which they fought abroad. Former war workers are not content to go back to the underpaid jobs of the pre-war period.

Within three days after the Democratic primaries in Georgia in 1946, which had been preceded by the late Eugene Talmadge's inflammatory campaign, five Negroes were lynched. One of them, Macio Snipes, a veteran, had been the only Negro to vote in Taylor County. The others were two men, one a veteran, and their wives who were executed near Monroe on July 20 by a mob of unmasked white men who were never apprehended. A hundred thousand Negro men and women had voted in that primary election. A year later Negro leaders in the state were making plans to double that vote in 1948. Throughout the South, Negro groups, sometimes in collaboration with labor and progressive organizations, sometimes alone, were setting up schools to instruct new voters in the intricacies of registration, marking the ballot, and manipulating the voting machine. They organized poll-tax payment and registration drives. They made plans for getting out the vote and, as in Georgia, anticipated a 100-per-cent increase in voting strength. A Negro vote of 1,000,000 in the eleven southern states comprising the late Confederacy is not only possible for 1948 but highly probable.

Even in Mississippi the Negro has given clear indication that he is no longer to be pushed around easily and unresistingly. The willingness, and even eagerness, with which Negro witnesses rallied to testify against Theodore G. Bilbo during the Senate committee investigation of the legality of his election served public notice that the psychology of terror could not be depended upon to keep them from demanding their political rights. Prior to the hearings which opened in Jackson on December 2, 1946, it had been predicted that few if any Negroes would dare appear to testify against the loudmouthed Mississippi demagogue. Nearly 150 black Mississippians crowded into the federal courtroom the first day of the hearing, prepared to tell how Bilbo's rabid anti-Negro campaign had aroused election officials and private citizens to defy the Constitution by using threats and violence to keep Negroes from voting in the Democratic primary. "More than a score of the Negro witnesses," reported Victor Bernstein in the newspaper *PM*, "dressed carefully in their Sunday best, dignified in manner but by no means servile, calmly laid bare some of the less appetizing aspects of American democracy, including the propensity for certain sections of our population to argue with whips where they could not intimidate with words." The testimony of these witnesses was undoubtedly an important factor in developing the Senate impasse which prevented the seating of the white-supremacy advocate who at that time was diseased in body as well as in mind.

The return of the Negro as a positive factor in southern politics was dramatically projected in Atlanta in February 1946. A special congressional election was held to fill the unexpired term of a congressman who had resigned. Seventeen candidates filed for the position. The outcome of this contest was uncertain until the ballots in the last precinct—a predominantly Negro district—were counted. The successful candidate, who had been running second by more than 100, was declared the winner by 770 votes when the ballots from the Negro precinct were counted. In order to forestall a recurrence of such a decisive vote, the entrenched politicians contrived to reintroduce the county unit system in the district's next primary election, thereby practically nullifying the entire vote, white as well as black, of populous Fulton County in which Atlanta is located. The unit votes of the two outlying rural counties, which with Fulton comprise the district, outweigh those of the urban center though their popular vote is much smaller. As a result of this stratagem the candidate who won the special election in February was defeated in the July primary and in the November general election.

Although Negroes had occasionally run for public office in the South during the period of the blackout it was merely as gesture to indicate that they had not given up the right to aspire to public office. It was not, however, until after the Supreme Court decision of April 1944 in the Texas primary case that Negro candidates undertook serious campaigns for local and state offices. There were candidates for the City Council in Nashville, Raleigh, Jacksonville, Winston-Salem, and Norfolk, and for other offices in Durham, Richmond, and Nansemond County. These efforts did not bear fruit until April 1947, when the Reverend Kenneth R. Williams, backed by Negro groups and the local CIO-PAC, won the nomination to the Board of Aldermen in Winston-Salem in the Democratic primaries. Ordinarily the winners of the primary are unopposed in the general election, but the Republicans, seeing an opportunity to capitalize on the nomination of a Negro, entered a full slate in the general election. The Reverend Mr. Williams, winning in the general election also, became the first Negro elected to public office in competition with white candidates in the South since the dawn of the twentieth century. The Winston-Salem victory was followed by the election of William Lawrence to the Board of Supervisors of Nansemond County, Virginia, by a two-vote margin in the general election. Running as an independent, Mr. Lawrence defeated the white Democratic candidate in the predominantly Negro Cypress District. Meanwhile in Richmond, a Negro lawyer narrowly missed being nominated for the Virginia House of Delegates in the Democratic primary. The pre-election fears that the success of a Negro candidate in the South would react harmfully failed to materialize. More and more Southerners, in the upper South at least, are prepared to accept the inevitable inclusion of Negroes in lawmaking bodies. The election of the Negro officeholders occasioned no vituperative outbreak; indeed there were editorial expressions of acceptance, if not of approval.

The new Negro vote in the South is perforce a liberal vote. Naturally the Negro electors are opposed to such mountebanks as the Bilbos, the Talmadges, and Rankins. But significantly Negro voters in Virginia are, by and large, opposed to the dominant machine of Senator Harry F. Byrd. The senator, whose record is as consistently conservative as Senator Robert A. Taft's, the Republican mentor from Ohio, has not engaged in the vicious and uncouth race baiting of the typical Dixie demagogue. Nevertheless, Negroes voted against him because they realized that in opposing New Deal measures he was opposing their best interests as a working-class people. They have sided with organized labor and the liberals against the entrenched Byrd machine. In Tennessee, Negro voters have been closely tied in with the Crump machine and its affiliates. The test of their independence and liberalism will come in 1948, when they will have the opportunity to choose between Congressman Estes Kefauver and a Crump-picked candidate for the Senate. Kefauver, one of the outstanding southern liberals in political life, is highly regarded by the Negro citizens of his home city, Chattanooga. Neither of the incumbent senators has made any real contribution to the advancement of the masses of Tennesseeans, either black or white. On the basis of Congressman Kefauver's record, the issue of liberalism versus reaction may be drawn clearly as it seldom is in the South.

William G. Carleton, a University of Florida professor, sees in this increasing Negro vote "a boon to liberals in their fight within the party to gain and keep party control." The political liberals, however, have too often been overcautious on any issue involving race. Claude Pepper, Lister Hill, and Ellis G. Arnall have all made obeisance to the sacred cow of southern politics: white supremacy. In Texas it was Homer P. Rainey, the liberal candidate for governor, who in 1946 suggested segregated polling places for Negro and white voters. This proposal so vexed Carter Wesley, publisher of a chain of newspapers in the Southwest and perhaps the most influential Negro in the state, that he withdrew editorial support from the former university president and advised Negroes to go fishing on election day. Acting Governor M. E. Thompson, whose "liberalism" consists chiefly of being anti-Talmadge, pushed through a measure providing for segregation in voting. Curiously enough, Negro leadership in Georgia has not challenged this proposal in the uncompromising manner of Mr. Wesley in Texas. "The southern political liberal, insofar as his attitude on the Negro question is concerned, must be judged only in terms of a less frequent and vigorous recourse to Negro baiting," Ralph Bunche concludes.[7] In the future,

[7]Op. cit.

as the Negro's voting strength increases this will not be enough to hold his vote. There will probably be a diminution of race baiting as a campaign technique. Already there are progressives in the South fighting desperately to bury the bogey of "Negro domination" which is perennially resurrected by the old-line demagogues. Once this specter is disposed of, the South may move forward to a consideration of real issues affecting the welfare of the people and to the election of candidates responsive to the needs of their constituencies.

The admission of Negroes to the ranks of the Democratic party also presages the return of the two-party system in the South. With the Democratic party no longer an exclusive white man's club, its snob appeal is lost. Republican-minded Southerners who have remained in the party because of tradition and its lily-white policies are now confronted with the choice of voting with Negroes in the Democratic primaries or voting their convictions in the ranks of the Republican party—also with Negroes. Or they may withdraw and form a third party of their own as the Texas Regulars did in 1944.

With the revival of Negro participation in politics, both parties may be compelled to engage in real campaigns in the South in the near future. Since the disfranchisement of colored citizens at the end of the nineteenth century, Southerners, both white and black, have been practically ignored in national campaigns. The Negroes were voteless and the whites committed. There was no need to seek votes among them or to appease either. Both, however, were important factors in the quadrennial national conventions—the Negroes in the Republican and the whites in Democratic meetings which selected the presidential and vice-presidential nominees. But by November both were forgotten. With the base of the franchise broadened and the prospects of real interparty contests, political activity in the South will be revitalized. In the future some of the energy now expended on garnering votes in the congested black ghettos of northern industrial centers will have to be directed to the South.

As significant as is the political development of the Negro in the South today, too much cannot be immediately expected by way of changing patterns. Realistic, level-headed Negro leaders are proceeding cautiously. No revolutionary demands are being made. Even the cumbersome Jim Crow system is not being consistently challenged. "The abolition of separate institutions is not our immediate objective," says John Wesley Dobbs, the graying, dynamic leader of the Georgia Civic-Political League. "We are after full political recognition. We want Negro public servants—police and firemen,

better schools with equalization of salaries and facilities, more adequate hospital facilities, decent homes and paved streets. Of course,
in the end, segregation must go, but we recognize that it will be a
slow process."

While there is increasing demand on the part of Negroes, and to
some extent on the part of the advance guard of southern liberalism,
particularly among the youth, for abolition of segregation in higher
education and, in Virginia at least, for an end of Jim Crow in transportation, there are many who believe that integration is unattain-
able in the near future. Indeed, such southern "liberals" as Mark
Ethridge and John Temple Graves assert that segregation will remain the pattern of the South for the next thousand years. Few
Negroes have such little faith in the capacity of the human race for
progress. But there are those who maintain with Carter Wesley, the
Texas publisher, that "we cannot get integration in the South
except that we can break segregation. While we all agree that
ultimately we are going to have to break segregation, those of us who
are practical accept the fact that we cannot break segregation now in
time to benefit any of our present students, so that on the lower levels
it is more efficacious and beneficial to force equality, which is within
our reach in the very constitutions and laws of the Southern states,
all of which provide that where there is separation, there must be
equality." Meanwhile the NAACP contention that there can be no
equality in separation was reaffirmed by the report of the President's
Committee on Civil Rights which bluntly states "that the time for
action is *now*." The Negro, however, has not yet been able to achieve
integration in public services and facilities in such states as Kentucky, Missouri, and West Virginia, where he has long been an important and uncontested political factor. The ballot has thus far
proved inadequate to meet this test.

The report of the President's committee brought immediate response in Virginia, where Negro leaders organized the Virginia Civil
Rights Organization with the avowed objective of repealing the
state's segregation laws. Efforts were initiated toward getting legislation introduced in the General Assembly to ban segregation in
public carriers throughout the state. During the war a leading Virginia newspaper had already openly advocated repeal of the obsolete
Jim Crow laws requiring segregation in the streetcars and busses of
Richmond. This proposal was at that time rejected. It has now been
renewed by leaders of the Negro suffrage movement in Virginia.

Although what may be termed "outside" interests paved the way for Negro voting in the South, the real drive to register and get out the vote is essentially a grass-roots movement with local Negro leadership. The National Association for the Advancement of Colored People, the Congress of Industrial Organizations through its Political Action Committee, the American Federation of Labor, the Southern Negro Youth Congress, the National Council of Negro Women, and the Southern Conference for Human Welfare have all contributed to the awakening of the southern Negro's political consciousness. However, the work has not been done by suave emissaries from New York and Washington, but rather by community groups sometimes affiliated with the national organizations and uniting locally to conduct registration and voting campaigns. Generally, although not always, these committees are non-partisan, wisely refraining from openly endorsing candidates.

The question of endorsements by Negro groups is still a delicate one in many southern communities. Avowed Negro support may prove a boomerang. Nevertheless, candidates quietly seek the Negro vote, meeting with a few leaders for off-the-record discussions and agreements. But the Negro's bargaining power is limited by the social environment. He seldom has much choice among the candidates for major offices. There is rarely more than one candidate whom the Negro voter can afford to support. In certain cities, such as San Antonio, Texas, where they have voted for many years, support may be more open and based on the same kind of considerations which prevail in any city where political machines are seeking power. With the increasing strength of the Negro vote, candidates in many cities and states are beginning to seek that vote openly and to make agreements with Negro leadership to meet the needs of the group.

The drive to increase the Negro's voting strength has developed new leadership and fused divergent groups within the race. All segments of the community, supported by an articulate and militant Negro press, have rallied to this crusade. Even in areas where differences as to party affiliation and to candidates may arise, there has usually been a united front in the registration campaign. Lacking the ordinary incentives of political favors and jobs, these groups are held together by the realization that only through political action will the race be able to make certain important gains.

In Atlanta scholarly professors from the Atlanta University system have forsaken their ivory tower and joined with students, trade unionists, clergymen, clubwomen, fraternal orders, social workers, professional and small businessmen and -women in promoting the

DIXIE IN TRANSITION 193

highly successful campaign in that city. Outstanding in the movement is A. T. Walden, the only Negro lawyer in the city, an officer
in World War I, and an astute politician. Head of the associated
Negro Democratic clubs in the state, he wields considerable influence in a quiet unobtrusive way. He is respected by the labor and
liberal movements in the state, with which he maintains cordial
relations.

Spearhead of the movement in Savannah is earnest John W.
McGlockten, young businessman and president of The Hub, a
luncheon club composed of Negro professional and businessmen. In
1945 the club, through its political action committee, launched the
drive which has expanded the Negro's voting strength in that city
more than tenfold. Supporting the younger group is eighty-year-old
Sol Johnson, veteran editor of the Savannah *Tribune,* one of the
oldest Negro newspapers in the country. With Mr. Johnson the important thing today is to improve the Negro's living conditions
through political action rather than an assault on the biracial system.

Of a different type is Elbert D. Koelman of Jacksonville. Originally from New York, he has now lived and worked in Jacksonville
for twenty-two years. Slim, bespectacled, and fast-talking, the ener-
getic Koelman is less deferential in his attitude toward whites than
the average Negro in the South. He moved into the political field following work as a CIO organizer, first with food-processing workers
and later with Jacksonville shipyard workers. Into his office in the
dingy and busy headquarters of the Cannery Workers Local came a
steady stream of eager new voters, during the 1946 campaign, seeking guidance and instruction. A competent young Negro woman
demonstrated the intricacies of the voting machine, showing which
levers to pull for particular candidates.

Others working to attain a registration of 150,000 Negro voters
in Florida in 1948 include Albert Bethune, state president of the
fraternal order of Elks; Milton Rooks, president of the Florida
Progressive Voters League; and Harry T. Moore, secretary of the
Florida conference of NAACP branches.

Down in New Orleans, where the vote remains small because of
the resistance of election officials and the exhaustive and complicated
registration forms, younger men and women have taken the lead,
including two CIO trade unionists, Ray Tillman and Ernest Wright;
Daniel E. Byrd, executive secretary of the New Orleans NAACP,
and Mrs. Edmonia White Grant, administrator of the Southern Conference for Human Welfare. In Chattanooga the veteran politician

and newspaper publisher, Walter Robinson, sits tight and runs his district with all the competence of a ward leader in Chicago or New York but with far less power to get recognition in the way of appointive jobs or public benefits for his constituents.

Easily the most outstanding and effective mentor in this South-wide drive has been the stouthearted Osceola McKaine, who returned to his native South Carolina in 1941 after living for twenty years in Europe. Appalled by the political decadence of his home state, he determined to do something to improve the status of his people. Joining with John H. McCray, newspaper editor, and other Negro leaders, he organized the Progressive Democratic party. Designated as his party's candidate for the United States Senate, he vainly sought official recognition for his delegates at the Democratic National Convention in Chicago in 1944. Running in the general election in November, he placed second in a field which included the successful candidate, former Governor Olin D. Johnston, and two other white aspirants. The official count gave him less than 4000 votes, but the party claims at least 15,000 South Carolinians cast their votes for him.

"We in the South—both Negro and white—are afraid of ghosts," McKaine insists. "Phantoms, I tell you. We are beset with fears which we have conjured up in our own imagination. Now is the time to cast off these fears, if we are going to make any progress down here."

During the 1946 campaign Mr. McKaine, working as a field representative of the Southern Conference, was invited by many local groups to assist in the organization of registration campaigns in various southern communities. He spent ten days in Augusta helping the local leaders in a well-organized drive which increased the number of registered Negro voters in Richmond county from a few hundred to 7100. In the subsequent primary, Roy V. Harris, speaker of the Georgia House, defender of the "white" primary, and bitter foe to Governor Arnall, was defeated by a combination of progressive white and Negro voters. Harris, who had been in the legislature for twenty-four years, attributed his defeat to Negro voters, even though it was demonstrated that he lost by a greater margin than the total number of ballots cast by colored citizens.

In the states where large numbers of Negroes are voting for the first time there has been a strong tendency toward bloc voting. In part this has been due to the new voters' unfamiliarity with the issues, the candidates, and the electoral processes. In need of guidance, they turn to leaders whom they can trust and who have studied the issues and agreed upon candidates to support. Moreover, colored voters are frequently forced into bloc voting by the record and campaigns of such candidates as Talmadge in Georgia and Bilbo in Mississippi. Following his election in the Democratic primary in 1946, the late Eugene Talmadge charged that 90 per cent of the Negro vote had gone to a single candidate, although there were five in the race. Talmadge, by his tactics, had created the bloc voting which he decried and cited as evidence of the Negro's unfitness for the ballot. The inescapable logic of the situation compelled the colored voters to support the candidate who they believed had the best chance of defeating an avowed enemy.

In Tennessee, Virginia, and North Carolina, where Negroes have been voting over a period of years, there is a greater tendency toward the development of factions within the group. Certain leaders, having acquired a personal interest in particular candidates, work for them among Negro voters, much as is done in New York, Philadelphia, or Chicago. In such communities issues are frequently of less importance to the Negro politicians than to the principled leaders in the states farther south, and differences in the communities are much sharper. They have grown accustomed to political competition. However, in Durham the effort is made to keep the Negro group united politically. Leadership has resided in the Durham Committee on Negro Affairs. Formerly this committee was completely dominated by the prosperous businessmen of the city whose industry and thrift have won for this small North Carolina city nationwide fame as the "Capital of the Black Bourgeoisie." Organized labor, the AFL Tobacco Workers, supported in part by younger professional men and the intellectuals of the faculty of the North Carolina College for Negroes, has exerted increasing influence within the committee.

Although the CIO early disclaimed any political objective in its southern organizing drive, the impact of this campaign, together with that of the AFL, will inevitably be reflected in political activity in the South. Both labor organizations are committed to equal suffrage rights for Negroes. The organization of Negro and white workers will more clearly demonstrate their common political as well as economic interests and will serve to overcome some of the fear and distrust that now exist between the races. In a number of southern states Negro trade unionists already are members and officers of local and state CIO political action committees. In Durham two

Negro tobacco workers were members of the joint CIO-AFL political steering committee in the congressional campaign of 1946.
Negro voters have come to realize that the candidates endorsed by
the CIO are less likely to be antagonistic to the Negro than other
candidates. Organized labor and Negro voters have in several instances united in the support of a particular candidate. The anti-
labor politicians in the South are invariably and bitterly anti-Negro.
Thus the expansion of the organized labor vote in the South points
the way to the further stimulation of the Negro vote and to a new
unity between white and black labor, without which there can be no
hope for a really progressive movement in that region.

Large-scale Negro voting has returned to the South to stay. Not
later than the presidential election of 1956, Negroes will be voting
in all the major southern cities as freely as they do in Boston or Detroit or San Francisco. The free vote in the small towns and rural
areas will be slower in coming both because intimidation can be
made more effective in those areas and because the people are not
as well prepared as in the cities. Only the complete failure of the
federal government to carry out its constitutional responsibility will
subvert the Negro struggle for the ballot in the South. That the Truman administration intends to uphold the Supreme Court decision of
April 1944 was made evident by the declaration of United States
Solicitor General J. Howard McGrath. "There is no doubt," Mc-
Grath said at a press conference in the spring of 1946, "that the
decision affects local as well as general primaries and elections in all
states. It will be the position of this department that any state or
party official who attempts to prevent a person from voting because
of color will be in violation of Section 18 of the Criminal Code."
This section provides fines and prison sentences or both for any
abridgment of the rights of citizens. The forthright demand of the
President's Committee on Civil Rights for a free and unrestricted
suffrage gives further indication that the administration means business. The committee's report was followed by the President's message
to Congress on February 2, 1948, asking for legislation to ban the
poll tax and for other measures to assure a free ballot.

CHAPTER XI

The Negro Vote in 1948

THE TIME-SERVING COALITION OF CONFLICTING ELEMENTS which sustained Franklin D. Roosevelt through four elections had already begun to crumble before his death in April 1945. The northern Negro voters who in the early days of the New Deal had been hopeful that the Roosevelt policies would bring about a regeneration of southern politics became increasingly distressed by the virulence with which Bilboism survived. The southern reactionaries, alarmed by the growing power and influence of the Negro vote, banded together in a last-ditch fight to maintain what they called white supremacy. They demanded that the Negro be deprived of any voice in Democratic party councils and resisted the spread of Negro voting in the deep South. Organized labor became restive under the wartime restrictions imposed to freeze wages while Big Business was piling up huge profits. The liberal reformers were dismayed by the virtual abandonment of the New Deal program. The process of disintegration which had begun during the third Roosevelt administration was accelerated after his passing. Within a year after Mr. Roosevelt had been interred in Hyde Park, his ancestral home, talk of third-party movements became prevalent; some of it inspired by disgruntled Communists reacting to international developments, but some of it springing from disillusioned grass-roots sources.

Against this background of political instability, the Negro citizen, possessed of the greatest ballot potential in his history, faces the presidential year of 1948. His full voting strength in the states beyond the borders of the old Confederacy amounted in 1940 to 2,450,000. This basic strength has been augmented by the migration of more than 700,000 Negro workers, mostly adults, seeking employment in war industries in the North and West. Of this number, 121,000 settled in five congested production areas in the West, the Census Bureau estimates. Another 83,000 crowded into the Detroit-Willow Run area of Michigan. The Chicago-Gary area absorbed 60,000; Baltimore, 40,000; Philadelphia, 36,000; Cleveland and St. Louis, 15,000 each, and Cincinnati and Indianapolis, 8000 each. Additional thousands sought jobs and refuge in New England cities, in the Buffalo-Niagara Falls area, and in the smaller industrial cities of the Midwest. An undetermined number continued to stream into New York City. While there was migration of white workers to these centers, many of them also from the South, the percentage increases owing to migration were much greater for the Negro populations. In the Portland-Vancouver and San Francisco areas the percentage increases of Negroes were 437 and 227, respectively. In the Detroit-Willow Run area the Negro increase was 60.2 compared to a 47-per-cent increase of the white population. While fewer in absolute numbers, the Negro migrants contributed a much greater percentage growth to the colored populations among whom they settled than did white migrants to the local white populations.

The Negro's political influence in national elections derives not so much from its numerical strength as from its strategic diffusion in the balance-of-power and marginal states whose electoral votes are generally considered vital to the winning candidate. In the 1944 elections there were twenty-eight states in which a shift of 5 per cent or less of the popular vote would have reversed the electoral votes cast by these states. In twelve of these, with a total of 228 electoral college votes, the potential Negro vote exceeds the number required to shift the states from one column to the other. Two of these marginal states—Ohio with 25 votes and Indiana with 13—went Republican. The ten remaining states—New York, New Jersey, Pennsylvania, Illinois, Michigan, Missouri, Delaware, Maryland, West Virginia and Kentucky—gave to Mr. Roosevelt 190 electoral college votes essential to his victory. The closeness of the popular vote in the marginal states accented the decisive potential of the Negro's ballot. While in the year of the great Roosevelt landslide, 1936, balance of power could be imputed to no particular segment of the American electorate, it may well be that we shall not soon see again any such overwhelming victory.

An alert, well-organized Negro electorate can be an effective factor in at least seventy-five congressional districts in eighteen northern and border states. Increasing political activity in the Democratic primaries in the South should result in the removal or silencing of some of the most rabidly anti-Negro politicians who have owed their seats in Congress to the suppression of the Negro vote and the elimination of a competitive political system. With the wartime migration, the expanded black ghettos in northern and western industrial towns have inevitably spilled over, consolidating Negro voting strength in additional congressional districts. Two Negroes, both Democrats, now hold seats in the House of Representatives: William L. Dawson, the Chicago politician and supporter of former Mayor Ed Kelly, who believes that quiet fighting within the party councils is the most effective method of getting results for racial advancement; and flamboyant Adam C. Powell, Harlem's outspoken clergyman, who wants the fight carried on out in the open with plenty of publicity focused upon his role. In addition to Representatives Dawson and Powell, there were Negro candidates for Congress in three other districts in 1946. Dawson and Powell ran against Negro candidates in predominantly Negro districts, whereas the others were in competition with white candidates in districts which are in a state of flux and which, if not gerrymandered, will be predominantly Negro within a few years. The defeated Negro candidates ran in Los Angeles (Fourteenth Congressional District, California); Philadelphia (Pennsylvania Fourth), and the Bronx, New York City (New York Twenty-fourth). Winning Negro candidates in these districts and others in Chicago, Detroit, and St. Louis will be sent to Congress within the next few elections as the districts, under pressure of the ghetto system, take on a progressively darker hue.

Recognizing the Negro's growing political potential, both major parties will undoubtedly intensify their efforts to win his support in 1948. Certainly any progressive third-party movement will seek to integrate the Negro into its basic structure. Which way will Negro voters turn? Who will be their favorite candidate? To whose blandishments will they respond? It does not now appear that either party will get the overwhelming support that went to President Roosevelt, who in 1944 carried Negro districts in Detroit, Pittsburgh, and New York approximately four to one. While Roosevelt won wide personal following among Negro citizens, he did not win them to the Democratic party. He could not so long as Bilbo, Rankin, and Talmadge sailed under that party's banner. He did, however, cut them loose from their traditional Republican moorings and launched them on a career of political independence. The professional Negro politicians, just as the politicians of any other race, have already taken sides, but the independent Negro leaders and the Negro masses

will have some very definite demands to make before they give support to either side. They will want to know how the candidates and
the parties stand on such vital issues as fair employment practices,
abolition of the poll tax, the protection of the right to vote, elimination of Jim Crow in all government agencies, the suppression of mob
violence, the outlawing of segregation in public life, the extension of
civil rights, particularly in the vulnerable District of Columbia. In
short, they will want to know what practical steps the candidates
and the parties will be able and willing to take to implement the
proposals submitted by the President's Committee on Civil Rights.

The universal and enthusiastic response of colored citizens to the
committee's memorable, and indeed revolutionary, report gave
early indication that this historic document would play an important
role in the 1948 campaign. While it is not generally anticipated that
adoption of the thirty-five recommendations for legislative, executive, and educational action will mean the immediate eradication of
discrimination from all phases of American life, there is wide con-
currence with the committee's conclusion that government "must
assume greater leadership" and "that the time for action is now."
The committee, appointed by President Harry S. Truman and composed of fifteen distinguished and representative Americans, called
for an end of all forms of discrimination and segregation in public
life. "The protection of civil rights," the committee report said, "is a
national problem which affects everyone. We need to guarantee the
same rights to every person regardless of who he is, where he lives, or
what his racial, religious or national origin."

Walter White, the executive secretary of the National Association
for the Advancement of Colored People, hailed the report as "the
most uncompromising and specific pronouncement by a governmental agency on the explosive issue of racial and religious bigotry.
. . . The report puts Congress, and particularly the conservative
Republican-Southern Democratic bloc, squarely on trial. But the
job is not one for Congress alone, as the report points out. State
legislatures, private organizations and each individual American
have been told by the President's committee what needs to be done."[1]
The Negro press, which has grown cynical about governmental pronouncements, joined in the chorus of praise for the work of the committee. "In a short time," the Pittsburgh *Courier* asserted, "the
United States can become a perfect democracy if there is only the
will to implement the recommendations of the President's Commit-

[1] New York *Herald Tribune*, November 9, 1947.

tee on Civil Rights *now*." To the Chicago *Defender* it was "a call to the American people to accept the challenge of ruthless racism which has so long crippled our democracy. . . . It is a call to freedom which must be heeded." The committee, the *Journal and Guide* of Norfolk, Virginia, said, "has provided the blueprint for putting democracy into practice." The Baltimore *Afro-American* valued the report as "one of the most significant documents of all time."

The ink on the report was hardly dry before it was projected into the political arena. Lem Graves, the *Courier's* Washington correspondent, exclaimed: "For Negroes of America, their 1948 political issue has been found! It will be on the basis of the committee report and recommendations that candidates will be weighed, Democratic or Republican . . . and his record through the years will be an indication of his sincerity. . . . He will be faced with the inevitable question: Will you support with your vote the legislation recommended by President Truman's Committee on Civil Rights? And on the answer may well hinge the direction of the Negro vote next year."

The report on civil rights was followed by the equally forthright report of the President's Commission on Higher Education which, with only four white Southerners dissenting, reached the conclusion "that there will be no fundamental correction of the total condition [inequalities in educational opportunities] until segregation legislation is repealed." The non-conforming Southerners expressed the belief "that pronouncements such as those of the Commission on the question of segregation . . . impede progress, and threaten tragedy to the people of the South, both white and Negro."

Certainly the reports embody all the basic long-standing issues with which the Negro minority is vitally concerned. And only as their recommendations are implemented will the race move toward its goal of equality of citizenship. The dynamic political content of the reports will become even more apparent as the 1948 campaigns get under way. Neither party, nor any candidate for the presidency, can afford to dismiss it. The extent and kind of reservations that may be expressed will depend upon many factors—the prospective closeness of the election, the extent of opposition that may be developed among prejudiced white voters, the amount of support that can be rallied among progressive whites, the stability of international relations, and the skill and intelligence of Negro leadership, political and non-political alike, in pressing for positive action on the national level. It has become increasingly evident that the country can no longer maintain the status quo in race relations. Either we must move ahead toward an inclusive and equalitarian democracy, or we must openly embrace racism as a political instrument of oppression. The trend has been in the direction of greater democracy. The need now is for acceleration of that trend.

The Negro voter in 1948 looks to political action as a means of speeding up the process of revitalizing democracy. With this in view he is prepared to scrutinize more carefully than ever before the claims and proposals of the competing parties and candidates. Action is what is demanded, and action *now*. It is not likely that either party will be able to get away with the vague and inconclusive pronouncements on the plight of the Negro which characterized the party platforms of 1944. And whatever promises are made will be suspect unless there is some clear indication during the second session of the Eightieth Congress that an honest effort is being made to clear the national board of the accumulated debris of discrimination and segregation in line with the recommendations of the President's Committee on Civil Rights. An honest effort will call for a long-overdue showdown on the filibuster. Amendment of the Senate rules to curb the filibuster by making it easier to limit debate is the necessary first step toward enactment of anti-lynching and anti-poll-tax bills and passage of fair employment practice legislation. So long as the Senate rules remain unchanged, southern reactionaries (including some who now pose as liberals on other issues) will continue to block any legislation which threatens to impair the current southern mores. It will not be enough for Republicans and northern Democrats to give lip service to this legislation. If they are honest they will move speedily to revise the archaic rule which now permits a minority to bottle up legislation which this entrenched bloc opposes.

The colored citizen is an American as well as a member of a disadvantaged minority. Because of the inclement climate of the culture in which he lives, he is compelled to divert a great portion of his time, energy, and thinking to defensive and protective measures. Nevertheless, as an American and as a citizen of the New World of the Atomic Age he is vitally concerned with the larger issues of war or peace, of scarcity or plenty, of depression or prosperity. But he rightly sees that the problem of the color line is an integral phase of these major international and domestic issues. For generations the South has maintained that the race problem is her own peculiar area to be handled in her own provincial manner. The problem has long since ceased to be regional or even national. It is, as W. E. B. Du Bois prophetically warned half a century ago, one of the major problems of the twentieth century. Neither time nor science nor humanity will permit this nation to continue in the outmoded racial practices of the nineteenth century. Both President Truman and Mrs. Franklin D. Roosevelt expressed recognition of this inescapable development in their addresses before the Lincoln Memorial at the Washington conference of the NAACP in July 1947. Mrs. Roosevelt told of the embarrassments she suffered at sessions of the United Nations when some foreign representative called her attention to newspaper accounts of discriminations against Negroes in this country. And Mr. Truman unequivocally called for national leadership in the fight against discrimination. We can no longer wait until the most backward areas catch up with the main movement of liberalism, he said.

After the NAACP had presented its petition to the United Nations, praying for relief from the discriminations suffered by the Negroes in the United States, Attorney General Tom Clark, a Texan, expressed dismay that any citizens of this country should feel compelled to go over the heads of their government in seeking redress of grievances and further stated that he intended to remedy such evils in so far as the law and the Constitution permitted. Shortly thereafter Soviet delegates to the United Nations Subcommission on Minorities and Discrimination, meeting in Geneva, proposed making a crime of the "advocacy of national, racial and religious hostility or of national exclusiveness or hatred and contempt as well as of any action establishing privilege or discrimination based on distinctions of race, nationality or religion." The hapless American delegates were again caught out on a limb. Not only in areas under Soviet domination but elsewhere throughout the world the denial of basic rights to Negro citizens in America is bringing the nation into ill repute, alienating potential allies in any future conflict.

Not only in the international field but also on the domestic front discrimination is proving costly. Certainly a more wholesome distribution of the national wealth through fair employment practices would help stave off another depression through the spreading of mass purchasing power. The low wages paid to Negro workers in the South is an important factor in depressing the standard of living for both whites and blacks in that region. Unemployment and underemployment of any considerable segment of the population reduces the market for the producers of consumer goods throughout the nation. This is a factor seldom considered by those Americans who look upon the FEPC merely as a measure to aid Negro and other minority-group workers. Fair employment practices contribute to full employment. And full employment means prosperity for the nation. Thus the Negro's urgent demands are inextricably interwoven with the basic needs of the country.

It is with these considerations in mind that the Negro faces the presidential campaign of 1948. Among the presidential candidates most prominently mentioned there is none—save Henry A. Wallace —who appears able to stir the hopes and imagination of the colored citizens of this country as did President Roosevelt. Mr. Wallace's championship of the underdog, his demand for an end to racial discrimination, his defiance of the South's segregation pattern, and his call for the Century of the Common Man have enhanced his stature among colored citizens. Nor have they been unduly disturbed by the name-calling to which he has been subjected—Communist, dreamer, dilettante, agitator. Were the impossible to happen, nomination by a major party, undoubtedly an overwhelming majority of Negro voters would cast their ballots for the man who told the poll taxers to their teeth that the "poll tax must go; equality of opportunity must come." It is impossible, however, to say how large a number of Negro voters will follow Mr. Wallace, or any other candidate, in any futile third-party effort in 1948. This would only be a gesture of protest and despair, an acknowledgment of defeat and hopelessness. The stakes are higher than those in 1948. The black minority cannot afford the luxury of futile protest.

Mr. Wallace's candidacy may, however, prove a blessing in disguise. Because of his well-known popularity among colored voters, the Wallace supporters will undoubtedly expend every effort to rally these voters for the third-party ticket. This effort may drive both the Republicans and the Democrats into a more forthright position on issues vital to Negro progress and welfare. The likelihood of both executive and legislative action on the recommendations of the President's Civil Rights Committee may be enhanced by an aggressive third-party campaign. Wallace may find unexpected strength among Negro voters in those southern states in which he may succeed in getting on the ballot and where the voters may be undeterred by fear of being read out of the Democratic party. In the North, where the black politicians are more integrated into the existing party machinery, it is less likely that Mr. Wallace will muster a really substantial Negro vote, although his support may well be proportionately greater among colored citizens than among the total population. His unqualified endorsement of the report of the President's Civil Rights Committee will have an effect but is unlikely to swing the majority of the Negro voters because they realize that he cannot be elected and, accordingly, will be in no position to implement his endorsement of the committee's recommendations.

Mr. Wallace's popularity rests more upon his pronouncements than upon his record of performance. He has captured the Roosevelt appeal without matching the performance of his mentor. On the other hand, Harry S. Truman, who lacks his predecessor's appeal, has sought to improve the record of performance.

The case of President Truman is a historical paradox. On the record, he has been more forthright in his demand for equal opportunity for Negroes than President Roosevelt ever was. As a senator he not only voted for the social-reform measures of the New Deal but also for cloture in behalf of legislation directly helpful to Negroes. As President he demanded of Congress that immediate action on the FEPC bill be taken. He went further and lent the prestige and weight of his office to the defeat of the congressman from his home state of Missouri who took pride in boasting that he had killed the bill by bottling it up in the House Rules Committee. He appointed William H. Hastie governor of the Virgin Islands and named the first Negro to a continental federal judgeship. He has risen above the provincialism of his origins. To investigate and report on the status of civil rights in the nation, he named a representative committee whose forthright and uncompromising report he hailed as "a new charter of human freedom" and as a "declaration of our renewed faith in the American goal—the integrity of the individual human being, sustained by the moral consensus of the whole Nation, protected by a government based on equal freedom under just laws."

The President's prestige among Negroes was greatly enhanced by his message to Congress on February 2, 1948. The President urged Congress to "enact legislation at this session directed toward the following specific objectives:

1. Establishing a permanent Commission of Civil Rights, a Joint Congressional Committee on Civil Rights, and a Civil Rights Division in the Department of Justice.
2. Strengthening existing civil-rights statutes.
3. Providing federal protection against lynching.
4. Protecting more adequately the right to vote.

5. Establishing a Fair Employment Practice Commission to prevent unfair discrimination in employment.
6. Prohibiting discrimination in interstate transportation facilities.
7. Providing home rule and suffrage in presidential elections for the residents of the District of Columbia.
8. Providing statehood for Hawaii and Alaska and a greater measure of self-government for our island possessions.
9. Equalizing the opportunities for residents of the United States to become naturalized citizens.
10. Settling the evacuation claims of Japanese-Americans.

To be effective in our efforts to establish human rights on the international plane, Mr. Truman asserted, "we must protect our civil rights so that by providing all our people with the maximum enjoyment of personal freedom and personal opportunity we shall be a stronger nation—stronger in our leadership, stronger in our moral position, stronger in the deeper satisfactions of a united citizenry." He promised to follow up his message with an executive order banning discrimination in the federal service.

The reaction of the Bourbon South to this simple plea for decency in human relations was as revealing as it was violent. Throughout the sub-Potomac region all the way to the Rio Grande could be heard the petulant wail of America's spoiled children—the backward-looking Southerners—threatening to quit the game unless it were played according to their rules. The President was accused of trying to undermine the southern way of life, of "stabbing his friends in the back," of wrecking the Democratic party. Secession from the Democratic party was proposed. Opposition to the nomination of Truman was assured. In Virginia, Governor William M. Tuck moved to deny the voters of that state the right to cast their ballots for a presidential candidate of their own choice. His proposal to disfranchise the Democrats of that state was finally abandoned in the face of popular demand.

Despite all these cries of anguish from professional Southerners there were indications of sanity among substantial elements in the South. A Gallup poll taken about the time the President sent his message to Congress indicated that three fourths of the southern voters would cast their ballots for Mr. Truman in November. Clark Foreman, president of the Southern Conference for Human Welfare, warned: "The party will certainly succumb if you [southern] governors insist upon the denial of civil rights to that large part of our population which is colored. Thousands of members of the Southern Conference who live in your states oppose [your attempt to get the Democratic leadership to back down on the civil-rights proposals]. You cannot speak for them." The Southern Regional Council, a middle-of-the-road interracial organization of business-men, educators, church, civic, and labor leaders, approved "the principle of federal anti-lynching legislation," called for enactment of an FEPC law, and urged the elimination of segregation in all graduate and professional schools, both public and private. In North Carolina, the leading politicians and other spokesmen stood aloof from the frantic demand of the political zombies to ditch President Truman.

Meanwhile the President gave no indication of retreating from his stand. Among Negroes, many of whom had been critical of the inadequacies of the administration, the hope grew that some of the President's proposals would be enacted into law. There was dan-ger, however, that the unbridled ravings of the Dixie demagogues would drive away from the Democratic party large numbers of northern Negro voters who had faithfully supported Franklin D. Roosevelt.

In his address to the NAACP Truman openly acknowledged the responsibility of the federal government to extend equal protection to all citizens. Altogether he has been more forthright than his predecessor. Mr. Roosevelt never challenged Congress on an issue of primary concern to Negro citizens. Nevertheless, neither the actions nor the words of Mr. Truman carry the conviction that was inherent in Roosevelt's every word and move. There are great numbers of American citizens who remain unconvinced by anything the Presi-dent says or does. This is true not only among Negroes but equally so among white citizens. There are trade unionists who question the sincerity of his veto of the Taft-Hartley labor-control act. In part, this is due to his shifting positions on such issues as labor relations, price control, and foreign affairs. Nor have the people any faith in many of his close advisors. The confidence which President Roose-velt inspired has not carried over into the Truman administration.

To most Negro citizens Senator Robert A. Taft is merely a stream-lined Herbert Hoover—cold, aloof, and indifferent to their urgent needs. Even in Ohio, Negro Republicans who have worked with him and for him cordially dislike the inflexible Taft. The stanchly Republican *Call and Post* of Cleveland terms him "a very obdurate person" who by his actions "has already alienated the labor vote from the party in Ohio. He now seems hell-bent to eliminate the Negro vote. . . . No one questions Taft's ability, but we must certainly question his judgment. Whether he knows it or not, his present action [delay and emasculation of the FEPC bill] is doing more to drive hundreds of thousands of Negro votes away from the Republican party than anything the New Deal has ever done." There is little in Senator Taft's record or personality that attracts Negro voters. His sponsorship of restrictive labor legislation, his assassination of price controls, his defense of Big Business interests, his blindness to our international obligations, as well as his satisfaction with the status quo in race relations, leave the Negro voter cold and unresponsive. His sponsorship of public housing legislation and his role in the rejection of Senator Bilbo by the Eightieth Congress are his only appeals to these voters.

Senator Taft has, of course, his Negro henchmen, but they will be unable to deliver the vote for him, unless perchance the Democrats burden their ticket with an unacceptable southern vice-presidential candidate. One of the misfortunes which the policies of the southern Bourbons have brought upon their region is the closed door to the White House for any of its sons. Governor J. M. Broughton of North Carolina lamented this cul-de-sac after the rejection of James F. Byrnes's vice-presidential aspirations by the 1944 Democratic National Convention upon the insistence of Sidney Hillman, the PAC chairman, and Walter White, executive secretary of the NAACP. Possibly such a Southerner as Ellis G. Arnall, Claude Pepper, or Hugo Black could carry some Negro votes in the North, but telling arguments could be made against the record of any one of them. They have all indicated support of the specious "white-supremacy" doctrine in one way or another. If the Democrats hope for mass Negro support in the crucial northern states, they would be well advised to forego the luxury of a southern nominee on their national ticket. The liberal Kentuckian, Wilson Wyatt, could perhaps rally stronger support among Negro voters than any other candidate south of the Mason and Dixon line.

Of all the Republican candidates, Thomas E. Dewey is regarded as having the best record of performance on racial issues. What the coldly calculating New York governor lacks in warmth of personality he has made up in large measure with recognition of Negro citizens in New York. After having scuttled a plan for a state FEPC in 1944 he returned in 1945 and pushed through the legislature the bill for the State Commission against Discrimination regarded in many quarters as a model of fair employment practice legislation. He appointed Negroes to important positions in the state government—positions never before held by colored citizens. By making an interim appointment he made possible the election of Francis E. Rivers as a $17,500-a-year judge in New York City. He carried unpredictable Harlem in 1942 but lost it in 1938, 1944, and 1946. Strictly on racial issues, Governor Dewey has achieved a good record in comparison with other candidates. Nevertheless, failures in other areas have alienated many Negro voters. The Negro trade unionists are not likely to support him, nor are the schoolteachers, who deeply resent his handling of their demands for substantial pay increases. Moreover, he has to contend with a strong Tammany organization in Harlem. Of him it has been said: One really needs to know him to dislike him. Yet not knowing him personally, a great many people of all races hold him suspect. More flexible than Taft, he is equally as cold.

In the late winter of 1947–48 Governor Dewey was confronted with a new problem the solution of which may have an important bearing upon the extent of Negro support he may be able to muster. Assemblyman William T. Andrews's bill to abolish segregation in the New York National Guard was reported out of committee. It was generally recognized that the governor's control of the Republican-dominated legislature was such that the bill would be passed if he wished it, inasmuch as it already had overwhelming Democratic support. The demand for elimination of Jim Crow in the armed services was heightened by the victory in New Jersey where, in accordance with provisions of the new state Constitution, the National Guard units are to be re-established on an integrated basis. New York Negroes renewed their demand for legislative action to end Jim Crow in the state's armed services.

The generals—Eisenhower[2] and MacArthur—are enigmas. As members of the top Army brass, they must share the blame for the Army's Jim Crow policies and for the unforgotten indignities, humiliations, and discriminations suffered by Negro servicemen during the war. Likewise, each may claim a hand in the relaxation of some of the worst discriminations during the latter part of World War II. At best, this can be only a claim to mitigation of the most flagrantly discriminatory features of Army life, leaving the basic pattern of dis-

[2]Since this was written General Eisenhower definitely refused to be considered as a candidate.

crimination and segregation unimpaired. The bitter experiences of Negro servicemen have not enhanced their regard for Army leaders. Of course, should either of the generals succeed in winning nomination, his public relations man would soon dig up some Negro sergeant who faithfully served the general through long years, and spread the story through the Negro press together with photographs of the candidate graciously receiving the warm congratulations of his long-time servitor. Such a likely stunt would make good publicity, but it it questionable as to how many votes it would win. The generals will have to offer more than their present records indicate to arouse any great enthusiasm among colored citizens.

Governor Earl Warren of California is little known by Negro citizens outside of his own state, where he has never been able to rally their support. In the gubernatorial race of 1946 in which he swept both the Democratic and Republican primaries, Governor Warren lost the Negro wards in San Francisco and Los Angeles overwhelmingly to Robert Kenny, the Democratic candidate, who, because of his record of liberalism, enjoys great popularity among colored Californians. Likewise, Governor Warren failed to carry these wards in 1942 against the Democratic incumbent, Governor Culbert L. Olson. In 1947, when the governor had twenty-five judicial appointments to make, he failed to name a Negro to any of the vacancies. Negro organizations and the Negro press of the state were loud and unrestrained in their denunciation of his failure to give to them the political recognition he gave to other elements in the state. Carl Johnson of Los Angeles, the only Negro delegate to the state Republican Party Assembly in October 1947, cast the sole vote against endorsement of Warren for the presidency. He was likewise censured by the active Women's Political Study Clubs, composed of Negro Republicans. Close to the governor is the popular University of California assistant football coach, Walter A. Gordon, chairman of the State Board of Prison and Parole, to which he was appointed by Governor Warren. Other Negro appointments by the governor include Norman O. Houston, state boxing commissioner; Floyd Covington, a member of the State Crime Commission, and a few members of Rent Control Boards.

Governor Warren has consistently paid lip service to principles of liberalism, recommending legislative action for a state FEPC, and advocating a state health insurance bill. However, he has failed to get any of the measures enacted by the Republican-dominated state legislature. As a consequence, there are many who believe that his pronouncements are primarily for the record. On the other hand, he has not sponsored reactionary legislation. While indulging in wishful thinking on the housing problem, he has failed to take a forthright position in behalf of sorely needed public housing. On the whole, the governor's record with regard to issues vital to colored people has little positive achievement; but there has also been little indication of any active opposition to the aspirations of the group.

Former Governor Harold E. Stassen of Minnesota has set forth at considerable length where he stands on labor relations and foreign policy, but as late as February 1948 had found little to say as to his stand on racial discrimination and segregation. In his book, *Where I Stand,* he notes this omission and indicates discussion of it at a later date. On his southern pre-convention tour in November of 1947 he did disavow the support of the lily-white Republicans of Mississippi. This was not particularly significant inasmuch as the lily-whites were unrecognized by the Republican National Committee and the "black-and-tan" outfit, led by Perry Howard, which Stassen also discredited, was generally considered as being pretty much in Taft's vest pocket. In his home state, Minnesota, where the potential Negro vote in 1940 was only 7150, representing less than half of 1 per cent of the total, Mr. Stassen has had only limited incentive to indicate how he stands on issues affecting the well-being of colored citizens. Queried by the NAACP, he gave "general support" to the Civil Rights report and promised "to speak on its recommendations in detail in the coming months."

The Speaker of the House, John W. Martin, Jr., of Massachusetts, comes from a district with no more than a few hundred Negro voters. Accordingly, Mr. Martin has heretofore felt no need to consider seriously the needs of so limited a constituency. His attitude has been reflected in his congressional record. He has failed to use his party leadership to line up support for passage of an FEPC bill, despite the party commitment. He has been opposed to national health legislation, to price control, to public housing, and other New Deal reforms. He has supported restrictive labor legislation and a tax program offering substantial reductions for persons with high income and very little for those in the low-income brackets. His record indicates only slight concern for the welfare of the masses of Americans, either black or white.

For Senator Arthur H. Vandenburg and the other dark-horse hopefuls there has been no indication of widespread support among Negro voters. The Michigan senator's long opposition to New Deal reforms certainly has not endeared him to Negro citizens. He does not appear to have in Michigan the close tie-in with Negro leaders that Governor Dewey has cultivated in New York. He supported the Taft-Hartley labor-control act which is a vital issue with the 1,000,000 Negro trade unionists who, together with their families, are a substantial segment of the black electorate. A great many of these members of organized labor will be influenced by labor's opposition to candidates who have voted for or endorsed restrictive labor legislation. Senator Leverett Saltonstall of Massachusetts, while voting with his Republican colleagues for restrictive labor laws, has supported FEPC, health and housing legislation.

Even before Negro voters attained their present numerical strength and strategic distribution, realistic politicians were concerned with the attitude of the race toward any prospective candidate for the presidency. One of the tests frequently applied to a presidential aspirant is—can he get the Negro vote? The late Senator Borah of Idaho failed to pass that test in 1936 and was denied the Republican nomination. Borah's consistent support of the southern Bourbons in the Senate had antagonized Negro voters in the North. In his preconvention campaign in 1935 he was picketed and heckled by colored citizens in Brooklyn whose embarrassing questions he was unable to answer satisfactorily. Likewise, the rejection of southern vice-presidential candidates on the Democratic ticket has, in part, been in response to the demands of northern Negro voters. In 1948 these considerations may well be an even greater factor in determining who will be selected to head the tickets of the two major parties. And surely no progressive third-party movement would fail to name candidates entirely acceptable to the masses of Negro voters whose potential strength in 1940 represented nearly 10 per cent of the total.

While the economic and social pressures under which the Negro lives—his restriction to the ghetto, his denial of equal opportunity, the job discrimination which he faces—all tend toward solidifying Negro opinion, there are other factors which forestall the development of solid bloc voting except in the extremity of a candidate openly opposing the extension of basic democratic rights to the race as a group. The social and economic stratification of the race which was accelerated during the war years fostered the development of conflicting interests. The Negro landlord was as eager for the removal of rent control as the white owner of rental property. The Negro businessman welcomes the organization of his workers no more than does the white employer. The Negro policy baron stands shoulder to shoulder with the white gamblers in support of local administrations which tolerate their illegal activities. All these diverse interests have political roots, and the elements which derive benefits from them are often more influenced by their economic interests than by racial considerations. Thus, while there is such an entity as the Negro vote, in that a considerable segment of the black electors may be swayed by racial considerations, it is not a unified vote. There has always been a minority vote among Negroes as among any group. Its strength may range from a few dissenters to a substantial bloc, depending upon a variety of factors.

Bloc voting, even necessary defensive bloc voting, may result in solidifying the bulk of white votes along racial lines. As Ralph Bunche points out: "The extreme nationalists, the 100 per cent Americans, the white supremacy defenders have always the potentiality of power and, in a period of crisis or confusion, can make rapid headway. Given the proper circumstances, demagogic leaders might foment movements, which could easily nullify whatever progress the Negro has been able to make since emancipation, and do to the Negro what Germany has so efficiently done to the Jews there."[3] White bloc voting was long ago developed in the South. In more recent years it has made some headway in the North, as in the Detroit municipal elections of 1943 and 1945. On the national level such voting by the white majority could, of course, completely overwhelm even an unrestricted Negro vote. While race consciousness is deeply rooted in the American tradition it has not yet become, for the nation as a whole, the dominant political consideration that it has been in the South. The fearful fact is, as Dr. Bunche indicates, that racism can be developed into a powerful national political instrument by fascist-minded demagogues.

The vote of Negro citizens in 1948 will certainly not be a bloc vote. It will probably not go overwhelmingly to either party unless one of the parties chooses completely unacceptable candidates. Nor is it likely to be captured by a third party, however progressive. Neither party is likely to receive the generous support which went to Franklin D. Roosevelt. Where the majority of this vote will go will depend primarily upon what the parties have to offer the Negro by way of meeting his demands. The efficiency of the party organization and propaganda will, of course, contribute to the direction this vote will take. The position of organized labor will be an important factor certainly upon the large trade-union membership and the increasing

[3]Op. cit.

number of political liberals within the race. The Negro vote today is in the vest pocket of no party. It is certainly as independent as the vote of any other considerable segment of the American electorate. According to Walter White, "No person and no organization can deliver the Negro vote; it is an imponderable and independent vote, and the Negro increasingly demands results for his support."[4]

[4] Walter White, "Will the Negro Elect Our Next President?", *Collier's Magazine,* November 22, 1947.

CHAPTER XII

The Ultimate Objective

WHAT THE NEGRO WANTS IN THIS POST-WAR WORLD IS simple and obvious. His hopes may be summed up in a phrase—full equality and the elimination of Jim Crow. In this, Negroes are united as never before. Indeed, the attainment of that goal is today more than a mere hope. It is now the grim determination of practically all elements within the race.

It would be a mistake to assume, as many white persons appear to do, that this demand is something artificial—something cooked up and stimulated by the Negro press and other race spokesmen for demagogic purposes. Rather it is a demand which wells up from the masses and is merely articulated by the militant Negro press and the responsible Negro leaders. Indeed, it is not uncommon to find among the masses a more insistent demand for equal rights than that voiced by the leaders. This determination to achieve equality has been reinforced by the return of nearly a million veterans disillusioned and embittered by the discriminations they have encountered in the armed services—senseless discriminations with which many of them had had no previous experience.

What does the Negro mean when he says that he hopes for equality? Simply this: that he is entitled to and must have every right, privilege, and opportunity accorded to any other citizen group. Negroes must have equal opportunity for the development of individual personality, the attainment of a fair and adequate share of the world's economic goods, and the enjoyment of life. This is little enough to hope for. This need is not alone for Negroes; America needs it to become a truly democratic nation. There are certain basic equalities without which that objective cannot be gained. They are economic, political, civil, and educational.

The Negro must have the right to work, to be upgraded, to occupy any position for which he may be individually qualified by training, experience, and skill. He must have the opportunity to demonstrate his abilities in the industrial field. Discriminations, both by employers and certain unenlightened labor unions, have restricted the opportunities of colored workers for employment and promotion to skilled jobs and responsible positions. To halt such discrimination is the Negro's first objective.

In the field of politics the Negro demands the unrestricted exercise of those political rights guaranteed to every American by the Constitution. The right to participate freely in the selection of local, state, and federal officials. The right to be elected to any office for which the candidate may obtain the necessary votes. The right to hold appointive office in accordance with individual merit, including appointments to the judiciary, to administrative positions—to the Cabinet itself. The right to vote has been restricted by the poll tax, the "white primary," complicated registration and educational requirements, and by intimidation and lynch terror. The right to hold responsible office has been limited by the selfishness, timidity, and lack of understanding of politicians. Denial of political rights imposes a status of second-class citizenship, which the Negro is no longer willing to accept. Elimination of all discriminatory restrictions is demanded.

Civil equality is basic to any democratic society. The civil rights of the citizen must be protected, irrespective of race, color, creed, national origin, economic status, or political affiliation. Every citizen has the right to expect protection of the law and even-handed justice in the courts of the nation. It is only a matter of time before we get rid of Jim Crow in transportation, hotel accommodations, restaurants, recreation and entertainment, and in all other public facilities. It has long since been demonstrated that so-called equal but separate accommodations mean inferior facilities for Negroes.

Finally, and urgently, the Negro must have equal educational opportunity. His children must have facilities and instruction equal to those offered to other children of the nation. Educational opportunities must be equalized at all levels, from the nursery school through professional and graduate training offered at the university level. Equalization will inevitably bring an end to segregation in education. The sheer cost of maintaining an adequate dual system will lead to its collapse. Meanwhile it is necessary to resort to legal tests and mobilize for political action in the drive to push back the frontiers of segregation in education as well as in all other fields.

While Negroes are insistent in the demand for equality, there is realization, among the advance guard at least, that equality in the status quo is not enough. What is it to be equal to the undernourished white sharecropper in South Carolina? What is it to be equal in the disease-infested slums of Detroit? Were the status of Negroes in Mississippi miraculously elevated overnight to that of the white population, they would still be in a sad plight. Their social, economic, and cultural levels would still be far below standard. Equality is not enough.

The struggle must be for equality with meaning. Such equality requires the raising of the social, economic, and cultural levels of the common people throughout this country. In a word, that means we must have a new society in which poverty can be abolished and racial prejudices eradicated—a society in which equality is possible.

To end job discrimination, we must first achieve full, stable employment. Then there need be no mad scramble for jobs; no need to exclude or restrict large bodies of workers because of race, sex, creed, or national origin; no fear of insecurity. With jobs for all, we can work hopefully and consistently toward economic equality—an equality with significance, a status from which stems all other equalities.

Were there decent homes enough for all the people of America, it would be impossible to crowd Negroes or other racial minorities into the back alleys and filthy slums of our great industrial cities. Our slums and blighted areas could be cleared. With planning, the ghetto and all the evil it spawns could be erased from the map of America. Likewise there must be food and clothing enough to meet the needs of the nation and at prices within reach of the masses. Only in an economy of abundance can we hope for full equality.

Equality the Negro must have. And that equality can have meaning only in terms of the level of our total society. And even after meaningful equality shall have been attained, as eventually it must be, there remains the objective of a society in which equality will be not only possible but also normal and effortless. Once this is achieved, the white "liberal" who now derives great satisfaction out of "doing good for the poor colored people" will be stripped of his cloak of self-righteousness. Such a society will free the individual Negro of any hindering sense of personal obligation for any advantages he may receive as a special favor. No longer will he need to depend upon the patronage of his "good white folks." Not, however, until the people of America are able to view racial differences in proper perspective may we expect a society in which equality is normal.

Now, whenever the Negro raises this demand, he is confronted with those who say: "Be patient—you can't go too fast—let's take this easy. Remember, you've made wonderful progress in three generations—don't upset the applecart." Those millions who have been penalized in America because of their color never like that kind of talk from white persons, whether or not they claim to be friends. They ask: "Who is to determine when progress is too fast or too slow?" To reactionaries living in a dead past, to those who reap unclean profits out of race hate, *any* progress in racial relations is too fast. Among those striving to make democracy a living reality, the present pace is all too slow. The doctrine of gradualism finds scant acceptance among the Negro people today. While it is recognized that all the barriers against the race cannot be eradicated overnight by executive fiat, court decree, or legislative action, the Negro people of America believe that it is the obligation of government, of the labor movement, and of all true progressives to take a clear, consistent, and unequivocal line against racial discrimination and segregation. They believe that the objective of national policy should be full equality for all citizens. And they have been encouraged in this conviction by the report of the President's Committee on Civil Rights.

Recognizing that the attainment of this goal depends upon the social progress of the nation as a whole, Negroes are coming to realize the necessity for co-operating with and supporting those organizations, agencies, and individuals who are committed to the task of improving the lot of the common man. It is among these that the Negro should find his natural allies in the struggle for equal rights. It is not by accident that some of our worst labor baiters also hate Negroes, Jews, Latin Americans, and other minority groups. These elements are intent upon obstructing every step in the direction of a better world of decent human relations. Not until we are able to eliminate them from positions of power can we hope to improve the conditions of the common man and create a society in which equality is possible and acceptable.

Despite the bitter opposition of entrenched reaction, President Roosevelt's program of social legislation contributed immeasurably to the advancement of the common people of this country. The New Deal not only recognized the need for raising the economic, social, and cultural levels of the masses of the American people; it was also aware of the special disabilities under which the Negro minority lives. Accordingly, the administration took certain positive steps to assist the Negro in overcoming these disadvantages. It is only through such combined efforts, improving the lot of the common man and exerting special effort to overcoming the Negro's underprivileged position, can we move forward to our goal of full equality. Many Negroes believe that the steps taken have been inadequate and far too cautious. Nevertheless, it is generally realized that a sound beginning has been made. And further, those who have studied the voting record of Congress know that much of the New Deal social-reform program was sabotaged by reactionary members of Congress, Tory-minded northern Republicans in "unholy alliance" with Negro-baiting southern Democrats. Intelligent political action on the part of Negro voters, in collaboration with other progressives, can assure and accelerate the fight for full, significant, and normal equality.

Clearly this goal can be reached only through federal action of a strong and representative central government. The states have repeatedly demonstrated their inability or unwillingness to provide a broad program to improve the status of the common man. Those states where the need is greatest are commonly the ones least able and least willing to undertake such a program. Certainly such a program cannot be implemented under the discredited and tattered banner of "States' Rights" which certain Republican elements have lately espoused. So long as any states are permitted to exclude large segments of the population from active participation in politics, the phrase "States' Rights" will remain, as it originated, an anti-democratic slogan to further the interests of the ruling oligarchy. The banishment of this doctrine should be accompanied by the abolition of the outworn electoral college in order that every citizen's vote may count directly in determining who shall be President.

The universal demand among Negroes is for full equality. In order to attain that objective and invest it with significance, we must have an economy of abundance—a society with jobs for all, decent housing available to the masses, plenty of food, and adequate educational, health, and recreational facilities. Under the New Deal, government recognized its responsibility to develop such a society. The initial steps have already been taken. The adoption of Roosevelt's eight-point Bill of Economic Rights as a national objective would give additional evidence of the government's recognition of its responsibility to create a new and healthier society.

APPENDIX I

RECOMMENDATIONS OF THE PRESIDENT'S COMMITTEE ON CIVIL RIGHTS

I. To strengthen the machinery for the protection of civil rights, the President's Committee recommends:

1. The reorganization of the Civil Rights Section of the Department of Justice to provide for:

The establishment of regional offices;

A substantial increase in its appropriation and staff to enable it to engage in more extensive research and to act more effectively to prevent civil rights violations;

An increase in investigative action in the absence of complaints;

The greater use of civil sanctions;

Its elevation to the status of a full division in the Department of Justice.

The creation of regional offices would enable the Civil Rights Section to provide more complete protection of civil rights in all sections of the country. It would lessen its present complete dependence upon United States Attorneys and local FBI agents for its work in the field. Such regional offices should be established in eight or nine key cities throughout the country, and be staffed with skilled personnel drawn from the local areas. These offices should serve as receiving points for complaints arising in the areas, and as local centers of research, investigation, and preventive action. Close cooperation should be maintained between these offices, local FBI agents, and the United States Attorneys.

The Department of Justice has suggested that heads of these regional offices should have the status of Assistant United States Attorneys, thereby preserving the centralization of federal criminal law enforcement. The President's Committee is fearful that under this plan the goal of effective, courageous, and nonpolitical civil rights protection in the field will not be reached unless satisfactory measures are taken to prevent these assistants from becoming mere political subordinates within the offices of the United States Attorneys.

Additional funds and personnel for research and preventive work would free the Civil Rights Section from its present narrow status as a prosecutive agency. Through the use of properly developed techniques and by the maintenance of continuous checks on racial and other group tensions, much could be done by the Section to reduce the number of lynchings, race riots, election irregularities, and other civil rights violations. Troublesome areas, and the activities of organizations and individuals who foment race tensions could be kept under constant scrutiny.

A larger staff and field-office facilities would also make it possible for the Section to undertake investigations of suspected civil rights violations, without waiting for the receipt of complaints. There are many problems, such as the possible infringement of civil rights resulting from practices used in committing persons to mental institutions, which might be so studied. These investigations in the absence of complaints could also be combined with educational and mediation efforts to check chronic incidents of police brutality or persistent interferences with the right to vote.

The difficulty of winning convictions in many types of criminal civil right cases is often great. The Committee believes that the Civil Rights Section should be granted increased authority, by Congress if necessary, to make appropriate use of civil sanctions, such as suits for damages or injunctive relief, suits under the Declaratory Judgment Act, and the right of intervention by means of briefs amicus curiae in private litigation where important issues of civil rights law are being determined.

Finally, the Committee urges congressional action raising the Civil Rights Section to full divisional status in the Department of Justice under the supervision of an Assistant Attorney General. We believe this step would give the federal civil rights enforcement program prestige, power, and efficiency that it now lacks. Moreover, acceptance of the above recommendations looking toward increased activity by the Civil Rights Section and the passage by Congress of additional civil rights legislation would give this change added meaning and necessity.

2. The establishment within the FBI of a special unit of investigators trained in civil rights work.

The creation of such a unit of skilled investigators would enable the FBI to render more effective service in the civil rights field than is now possible. At the present time, its investigators are concerned with enforcement of all federal criminal statutes. In some instances, its agents have seemingly lacked the special skills and knowledge necessary to effective handling of civil rights cases, or have not been readily available for work in this area.

These special agents should work in close harmony with the Civil Rights Section and its regional offices.

3. The establishment by the state governments of law enforcement agencies comparable to the federal Civil Rights Section.

There are large areas where, because of constitutional restrictions, the jurisdiction of the federal government as a protector of civil rights is either limited or denied. There are civil rights problems, unique to certain regions and localities, that can best be treated and solved by the individual states. Furthermore, our review of the work of the Civil Rights Section has persuaded us of the cardinal importance of developing specialized units for the enforcement of civil rights laws. We believe that this is true at the state level too. States which have, or will have, civil rights laws of their own, should buttress them with specially designed enforcement units. These would have the further effect of bringing the whole program closer to the people. They would also facilitate systematic local cooperation with the federal Civil Rights Section, and they would be able to act in the areas where it has no authority.

Here and elsewhere the Committee is making recommendations calling for remedial action by the states. The President's Executive Order invited us to consider civil rights problems falling within state as well as federal jurisdiction. We respectfully request the President to call these recommendations to the attention of the states and to invite their favorable consideration.

4. The establishment of a permanent Commission on Civil Rights in the Executive Office of the President, preferably by Act of Congress;

And the simultaneous creation of a Joint Standing Committee on Civil Rights in Congress.

In a democratic society, the systematic, critical review of social needs and public policy is a fundamental necessity. This is especially true of a field like civil rights, where the problems are enduring, and range widely. From our own effort, we have learned that a temporary, sporadic approach can never finally solve these problems.

Nowhere in the federal government is there an agency charged with the continuous appraisal of the status of civil rights, and the efficiency of the machinery with which we hope to improve that status. There are huge gaps in the available information about the field. A permanent Commission could perform an invaluable function by collecting data. It could also carry on technical research to improve the fact-gathering methods now in use. Ultimately, this would make possible a periodic audit of the extent to which our civil rights are secure. If it did this and served as a clearing house and focus of coordination for the many private, state, and local agencies working in the civil rights field, it would be invaluable to them and to the federal government.

A permanent Commission on Civil Rights should point all of its work towards regular reports which would include recommendations for action in the ensuing periods. It should lay plans for dealing with broad civil rights problems, such as those arising from the technological displacement and probable migration of southern Negroes to cities throughout the land. It should also investigate and make recommendations with respect to special civil rights problems, such as the status of Indians and their relationship to the federal government.

The Commission should have effective authority to call upon any agency of the executive branch for assistance. Its members should be appointed by the President with the approval of the Senate. They should hold a specified number of regular meetings. A full-time director should be provided with an adequate appropriation and staff.

Congress, too, can be aided in its difficult task of providing the legislative ground work for fuller civil rights. A standing committee, established jointly by the House and the Senate, would provide a central place for the consideration of proposed legislation. It would enable Congress to maintain continuous liaison with the permanent Commission. A group of men in each chamber would be able to give prolonged study to this complex area and would become expert in its legislative needs.

5. The establishment by the states of permanent commissions on civil rights to parallel the work of the federal Commission at the state level.

The states should create permanent civil rights commissions to make continuing studies of prejudice, group tensions, and other local civil rights problems; to publish educational material of a civil rights nature; to evaluate existing legislation; and to recommend new laws. Such commissions, with their fingers on their communities' pulses, would complement at the state level the activities of a permanent federal Commission on Civil Rights.

6. The increased professionalization of state and local police forces.

The Committee believes that there is a great need at the state and local level for the improvement of civil rights protection by more aggressive and efficient enforcement techniques. Police training programs, patterned after the FBI agents' school and the Chicago Park District Program, should be instituted. They should be oriented so as to indoctrinate officers with an awareness of civil rights problems. Proper treatment by the police of those who are arrested and incarcerated in local jails should be stressed. Supplemented by salaries that will attract and hold competent personnel, this sort of training should do much to make police forces genuinely professional.

II. To strengthen the right to safety and security of the person, the President's Committee recommends:

1. The enactment by Congress of new legislation to supplement Section 51 of Title 18 of the United States Code which would impose the same liability on one person as is now imposed by that statute on two or more conspirators.

The Committee believes that Section 51 has in the past been a useful law to protect federal rights against encroachment by both private individuals and public officers. It believes the Act has great potential usefulness today. Greater efforts should be made through court tests to extend and make more complete the list of rights safeguarded by this law.

2. The amendment of Section 51 to remove the penalty provision which disqualifies persons convicted under the Act from holding public office.

There is general agreement that this particular penalty creates an unnecessary obstacle to the obtaining of convictions under the Act and that it should be dropped.

3. The amendment of Section 52 to increase the maximum penalties that may be imposed under it from a $1,000 fine and a one-year prison term to a $5,000 fine and a ten-year prison term, thus bringing its penalty provisions into line with those in Section 51.

At the present time the Act's penalties are so light that it is technically a misdemeanor law. In view of the extremely serious offenses that have been and are being successfully prosecuted under Section 52, it seems clear that the penalties should be increased.

4. The enactment by Congress of a new statute, to supplement Section 52, specifically directed against police brutality and related crimes.

This Act should enumerate such rights as the right not to be deprived of property by a public officer except by due process of law; the right to be free from personal injury inflicted by a public officer; the right to engage in a lawful activity without interference by a public officer; and the right to be free from discriminatory law enforcement resulting from either active or passive conduct by a public officer.

This statute would meet in part the handicap in the use of Section 52 imposed by the Supreme Court in *Screws* v. *United States*. This was the case in which the Court required prosecutors to establish that defendants had willfully deprived victims of a "specific constitutional right." In later prosecutions, the Civil Rights Section has found it very difficult to prove that the accused acted in a "willful" manner. By spelling out some of the federal rights which run against public officers, the supplementary statute would relieve the Civil Rights Section of this extraordinary requirement.

The Committee considered and rejected a proposal to recommend the enactment of a supplementary statute in which an attempt would be made to include a specific enumeration of all federal rights running against public officers. Such an enumeration would inevitably prove incomplete with the passage of time and might prejudice the protection of omitted rights. However, the committee believes that a new statute, such as the one here recommended, enumerating the rights for the protection of which Section 52 is now most commonly employed, is desirable.

5. *The enactment by Congress of an antilynching act.*

The Committee believes that to be effective such a law must contain four essential elements. First, it should define lynching broadly. Second, the federal offense ought to cover participation of public officers in a lynching, or failure by them to use proper measures to protect a person accused of a crime against mob violence. The failure or refusal of public officers to make proper efforts to arrest members of lynch mobs and to bring them to justice should also be specified as an offense.

Action by private persons taking the law into their own hands to mete out summary punishment and private vengeance upon an accused person; action by either public officers or private persons meting out summary punishment and private vengeance upon a person because of his race, color, creed or religion—these too must be made crimes.

Third, the statute should authorize immediate federal investigation in lynching cases to discover whether a federal offense has been committed. Fourth, adequate and flexible penalties ranging up to a $10,000 fine and a 20-year prison term should be provided.

The constitutionality of some parts of such a statute, particularly those providing for the prosecution of private persons, has been questioned. The Committee believes that there are several constitutional bases upon which such a law might be passed and that these are sufficiently strong to justify prompt action by Congress.

6. *The enactment by Congress of a new criminal statute on involuntary servitude, supplementing Sections 443 and 444 of Title 18 of the United States Code.*

This statute should make full exercise of congressional power under the Thirteenth Amendment by defining slavery and involuntary servitude broadly. This would provide a basis for federal prosecutions in cases where individuals are deliberately deprived of their freedom by public officers without due process of law or are held in bondage by private persons. Prosecution under existing laws is limited to the narrow, technical offense of peonage or must be based upon the archaic "slave kidnaping" law, Section 443.

7. *A review of our wartime evacuation and detention experience looking toward the development of a policy which will prevent the abridgment of civil rights of any person or groups because of race or ancestry.*

We believe it is fallacious to assume that there is a correlation between loyalty and race or national origin. The military must be allowed considerable discretionary power to protect national security in time of war. But we believe it is possible to establish safeguards against the evacuation and detention of whole groups because of their descent without endangering national security. The proposed permanent Commission on Civil Rights and the Joint Congressional Committee might well study this problem.

8. Enactment by Congress of legislation establishing a procedure by which claims of evacuees for specific property and business losses resulting from the wartime evacuation can be promptly considered and settled.

The government has acknowledged that many Japanese American evacuees suffered considerable losses through its actions and through no fault of their own. We cannot erase all the scars of evacuation; we can reimburse those who present valid claims for material losses.

III. To strengthen the right to citizenship and its privileges, the President's Committee recommends:

1. Action by the states or Congress to end poll taxes as a voting prerequisite.

Considerable debate has arisen as to the constitutionality of a federal statute abolishing the poll tax. In four times passing an anti-poll tax bill, the House of Representatives has indicated its view that there is a reasonable chance that it will survive a court attack on constitutional grounds. We are convinced that the elimination of this obstacle to the right of suffrage must not be further delayed. It would be appropriate and encouraging for the remaining poll tax states voluntarily to take this step. Failing such prompt state action, we believe that the nation, either by act of Congress, or by constitutional amendment, should remove this final barrier to universal suffrage.

2. The enactment by Congress of a statute protecting the right of qualified persons to participate in federal primaries and elections against interference by public officers and private persons.

This statute would apply only to federal elections. There is no doubt that such a law can be applied to primaries which are an integral part of the federal electoral process or which affect or determine the result of a federal election. It can also protect participation in federal election campaigns and discussions of matters relating to national political issues. This statute should authorize the Department of Justice to use both civil and criminal sanctions. Civil remedies should be used wherever possible to test the legality of threatened interferences with the suffrage before voting rights have been lost.

3. The enactment by Congress of a statute protecting the right to qualify for, or participate in, federal or state primaries or elections against discriminatory action by state officers based on race or color, or depending on any other unreasonable classification of persons for voting purposes.

This statute would apply to both federal and state elections, but it would be limited to the protection of the right to vote against discriminatory interferences based on race, color, or other unreasonable classification. Its constitutionality is clearly indicated by the Fourteenth and Fifteenth Amendments. Like the legislation suggested under (2) it should authorize the use of civil and criminal sanctions by the Department of Justice.

4. *The enactment by Congress of legislation establishing local self-government for the District of Columbia; and the amendment of the Constitution to extend suffrage in presidential elections, and representation in Congress to District residents.*

The American tradition of democracy requires that the District of Columbia be given the same measure of self-government in local affairs that is possessed by other communities throughout the country. The lack of congressional representation and suffrage in local and national elections in the District deprives a substantial number of permanent Washington residents of a voice in public affairs.

5. *The granting of suffrage by the States of New Mexico and Arizona to their Indian citizens.*

These states have constitutional provisions which have been used to disfranchise Indians. In New Mexico, the constitution should be amended to remove the bar against voting by "Indians not taxed." This may not be necessary in Arizona where the constitution excludes from the ballot "persons under guardianship." Reinterpretation might hold that this clause no longer applies to Indians. If this is not possible, the Arizona constitution should be amended to remove it.

6. *The modification of the federal naturalization laws to permit the granting of citizenship without regard to the race, color, or national origin of applicants.*

It is inconsistent with our whole tradition to deny on a basis of ancestry the right to become citizens to people who qualify in every other way.

7. *The repeal by the states of laws discriminating against aliens who are ineligible for citizenship because of race, color, or national origin.*

These laws include the alien land laws and the prohibition against commercial fishing in California. The removal of race as a qualification for naturalization would remove the structure upon which this discriminatory legislation is based. But if federal action on Recommendation 6 is delayed, state action would be eminently desirable.

8. *The enactment by Congress of legislation granting citizenship to the people of Guam and American Samoa.*

This legislation should also provide these islands with organic acts containing guarantees of civil rights, and transfer them from naval administration to civilian control. Such legislation for Guam and American Samoa has been introduced in the present Congress.

9. The enactment by Congress of legislation, followed by appriate administrative action, to end immediately all discrimination and segregation based on race, color, creed, or national origin, in the organization and activities of all branches of the Armed Services.

The injustice of calling men to fight for freedom while subjecting them to humiliating discrimination within the fighting forces is at once apparent. Furthermore, by preventing entire groups from making their maximum contribution to the national defense, we weaken our defense to that extent and impose heavier burdens on the remainder of the population.

Legislation and regulations should expressly ban discrimination and segregation in the recruitment, assignment, and training of all personnel in all types of military duty. Mess halls, quarters, recreational facilities and post exchanges should be nonsegregated. Commissions and promotions should be awarded on considerations of merit only. Selection of students for the Military, Naval, and Coast Guard academies and all other service schools should be governed by standards from which considerations of race, color, creed, or national origin are conspicuously absent. The National Guard, reserve units, and any universal military training program should all be administered in accordance with these same standards.

The Committee believes that the recent unification of the armed forces provides a timely opportunity for the revision of present policy and practice. A strong enunciation of future policy should be made condemning discrimination and segregation within the armed services.

10. The enactment by Congress of legislation providing that no member of the armed forces shall be subject to discrimination of any kind by any public authority or place of public accommodation, recreation, transportation, or other service or business.

The government of a nation has an obligation to protect the dignity of the uniform of its armed services. The esteem of the government itself is impaired when affronts to its armed forces are tolerated. The government also has a responsibility for the well-being of those who surrender some of the privileges of citizenship to serve in the defense establishments.

IV. To strengthen the right to freedom of conscience and expression the President's Committee recommends:

1. The enactment by Congress and the state legislatures of legislation requiring all groups, which attempt to influence public opinion, to disclose the pertinent facts about themselves through systematic registration procedures.

Such registration should include a statement of the names of officers, sources of financial contributions, disbursements, and the purposes of the organization. There is no question about the power of the states to do this. Congress may use its taxing and postal powers to require such disclosure. The revenue laws should be changed so that tax returns of organizations claiming tax exemption show the suggested information. These returns should then be made available to the public.

The revenue laws ought also to be amended to require the same information from groups and organizations which claim to operate on a non-profit basis but which do not request tax exemption. The Committee also recommends further study by appropriate governmental agencies looking toward the application of the disclosure principle to profit-making organizations which are active in the market place of public opinion.

Congress ought also to amend the postal laws to require those who use the first-class mail for large-scale mailings to file disclosure statements similar to those now made annually by those who use the second-class mail. The same requirement should be adopted for applicants for metered mail permits. Postal regulations ought also to require that no mail be carried by the Post Office which does not bear the name and address of the sender.

2. Action by Congress and the executive branch clarifying the loyalty obligations of federal employees, and establishing standards and procedures by which the civil rights of public workers may be scrupulously maintained.

The Committee recognizes the authority and the duty of the government to dismiss disloyal workers from the government service. At the same time the Committee is equally concerned with the protection of the civil rights of federal workers. We believe that there should be a public enunciation by responsible federal officials of clear, specific standards by which to measure the loyalty of government workers.

It is also important that the procedure by which the loyalty of an accused federal worker is determined be a fair, consistently applied, stated "due process." Specific rules of evidence should be laid down. Each employee should have the right to a bill of particular accusations, representation by counsel at all examinations or hearings, the right to subpoena witnesses and documents, a stenographic report of proceedings, a written decision, and time to prepare a written brief for an appeal. Competent and judicious people should have the responsibility for administering the program.

The Attorney General has stated to the Committee in a letter, "It is my firm purpose, insofar as my office has control over this program, to require substantial observance of the safeguards recommended by the President's Committee."

V. To strengthen the right to equality of opportunity, the President's Committee recommends:

1. In general:
The elimination of segregation, based on race, color, creed, or national origin, from American life.

The separate but equal doctrine has failed in three important respects. First, it is inconsistent with the fundamental equalitarianism of the American way of life in that it marks groups with the brand of inferior status. Secondly, where it has been followed, the results have been separate and unequal facilities for minority peoples. Finally, it has kept people apart despite incontrovertible evidence that an environment favorable to civil rights is fostered whenever groups are permitted to live and work together. There is no adequate defense of segregation.

The conditioning by Congress of all federal grants-in-aid and other forms of federal assistance to public or private agencies for any purpose on the absence of discrimination and segregation based on race, color, creed, or national origin.

We believe that federal funds, supplied by taxpayers all over the nation, must not be used to support or perpetuate the pattern of segregation in education, public housing, public health services, or other public services and facilities generally. We recognize that these services are indispensable to individuals in modern society and to further social progress. It would be regrettable if federal aid, conditioned on nonsegregated services, should be rejected by sections most in need of such aid. The Committee believes that a reasonable interval of time may be allowed for adjustment to such a policy. But in the end it believes that segregation is wrong morally and practically and must not receive financial support by the whole people.

A minority of the Committee favors the elimination of segregation as an ultimate goal but opposes the imposition of a federal sanction. It believes that federal aid to the states for education, health, research and other public benefits should be granted provided that the states do not discriminate in the distribution of the funds. It dissents, however, from the majority's recommendation that the abolition of segregation be made a requirement, until the people of the states involved have themselves abolished the provisions in their state constitutions and laws which now require segregation. Some members are against the nonsegregation requirement in educational grants on the ground that it represents federal control over education. They feel, moreover, that the best way ultimately to end segregation is to raise the educational level of the people in the states affected; and to inculcate both the teachings of religion regarding human brotherhood and the ideals of our democ-

racy regarding freedom and equality as a more solid basis for genuine
and lasting acceptance by the peoples of the states.

2. For employment:

*The enactment of a federal Fair Employment Practice Act pro-
hibiting all forms of discrimination in private employment,
based on race, color, creed, or national origin.*

A federal Fair Employment Practice Act prohibiting discrimination
in private employment should provide both educational machinery and
legal sanctions for enforcement purposes. The administration of the act
should be placed in the hands of a commission with power to receive
complaints, hold hearings, issue cease-and-desist orders and seek court
aid in enforcing these orders. The Act should contain definite fines for
the violation of its procedural provisions. In order to allow time for
voluntary adjustment of employment practices to the new law, and to
permit the establishment of effective enforcement machinery, it is
recommended that the sanction provisions of the law not become opera-
tive until one year after the enactment of the law.

The federal act should apply to labor unions and trade and professional associations, as well as to employers, insofar as the policies and
practices of these organizations affect the employment status of workers.

The enactment by the states of similar laws;

A federal fair employment practice statute will not reach activities
which do not affect interstate commerce. To make fair employment
a uniform national policy, state action will be needed. The successful
experiences of some states warrant similar action by all of the others.

*The issuance by the President of a mandate against discrimi-
nation in government employment and the creation of adequate machinery to enforce this mandate.*

The Civil Service Commission and the personnel offices of all federal agencies should establish on-the-job training programs and other
necessary machinery to enforce the nondiscrimination policy in government employment. It may well be desirable to establish a government fair employment practice commission, either as a part of the
Civil Service Commission, or on an independent basis with authority to
implement and enforce the Presidential mandate.

3. For education:

*Enactment by the state legislatures of fair educational practice
laws for public and private educational institutions, prohibiting
discrimination in the admission and treatment of students based
on race, color, creed, or national origin.*

These laws should be enforced by independent administrative commissions. These commissions should consider complaints and hold hear-

ings to review them. Where they are found to be valid, direct negoti-
ation with the offending institution should be undertaken to secure
compliance with the law. Wide publicity for the commission's findings
would influence many schools and colleges sensitive to public opinion
to abandon discrimination. The final sanction for such a body would
be the cease-and-desist order enforceable by court action. The Committee believes that educational institutions supported by churches and
definitely identified as denominational should be exempted.

There is a substantial division within the Committee on this recommendation. A majority favors it.

4. For housing:

*The enactment by the states of laws outlawing restrictive
covenants;*

*Renewed court attack, with intervention by the Department of
Justice, upon restrictive covenants.*

The effectiveness of restrictive covenants depends in the last analysis
on court orders enforcing the private agreement. The power of the
state is thus utilized to bolster discriminatory practices. The Committee
believes that every effort must be made to prevent this abuse. We would
hold this belief under any circumstances; under present conditions,
when severe housing shortages are already causing hardship for many
people of the country, we are especially emphatic in recommending
measures to alleviate the situation.

5. For health services:

*The enactment by the states of fair health practice statutes for-
bidding discrimination and segregation based on race, creed,
color, or national origin, in the operation of public or private
health facilities.*

Fair health practice statutes, following the pattern of fair employment practice laws, seem desirable to the Committee. They should
cover such matters as the training of doctors and nurses, the admission
of patients to clinics, hospitals and other similar institutions, and the
right of doctors and nurses to practice in hospitals. The administration
of these statutes should be placed in the hands of commissions, with
authority to receive complaints, hold hearings, issue cease-and-desist
orders and engage in educational efforts to promote the policy of these
laws.

6. For public services:

*The enactment by Congress of a law stating that discrimina-
tion and segregation, based on race, color, creed, or national
origin, in the rendering of all public services by the national
government is contrary to public policy;*

The enactment by the states of similar laws;

The elimination of discrimination and segregation depends largely on the leadership of the federal and state governments. They can make a great contribution toward accomplishing this end by affirming in law the principle of equality for all, and declaring that public funds, which belong to the whole people, will be used for the benefit of the entire population.

> *The establishment by act of Congress or executive order of a unit in the federal Bureau of the Budget to review the execution of all government programs, and the expenditures of all government funds, for compliance with the policy of nondiscrimination;*

Continual surveillance is necessary to insure the nondiscriminatory execution of federal programs involving use of government funds. The responsibility for this task should be located in the Bureau of the Budget which has the duty of formulating the executive budget and supervising the execution of appropriation acts. The Bureau already checks the various departments and agencies for compliance with announced policy. Administratively, this additional function is consistent with its present duties and commensurate with its present powers.

> *The enactment by Congress of a law prohibiting discrimination or segregation, based on race, color, creed, or national origin, in interstate transportation and all the facilities thereof, to apply against both public officers and the employees of private transportation companies;*

Legislation is needed to implement and supplement the Supreme Court decision in *Morgan* v. *Virginia*. There is evidence that some state officers are continuing to enforce segregation laws against interstate passengers. Moreover, carriers are still free to segregate such passengers on their own initiative since the *Morgan* decision covered only segregation based on law. Congress has complete power under the Constitution to forbid all forms of segregation in interstate commerce. We believe it should make prompt use of it.

> *The enactment by the states of laws guaranteeing equal access to places of public accommodation, broadly defined, for persons of all races, colors, creeds, and national origins.*

Since the Constitution does not guarantee equal access to places of public accommodation, it is left to the states to secure that right. In the 18 states that have already enacted statutes, we hope that enforcement will make practice more compatible with theory. The civil suit for damages and the misdemeanor penalty have proved to be inadequate sanctions to secure the observance of these laws. Additional means, such as the revocation of licenses, and the issuance of cease-and-desist orders by administrative agencies are needed to bring about wider compliance. We think that all of the states should enact such

legislation, using the broadest possible definition of public accommodation.

>   7. *For the District of Columbia:*
>
>   *The enactment by Congress of legislation to accomplish the
>   following purposes in the District;*
>
>   *Prohibition of discrimination and segregation, based on race,
>   color, creed, or national origin, in all public or publicly-sup-
>   ported hospitals, parks, recreational facilities, housing projects,
>   welfare agencies, penal institutions, and concessions on public
>   property;*
>
>   *The prohibition of segregation in the public school system of
>   the District of Columbia;*
>
>   *The establishment of a fair educational practice program
>   directed against discrimination, based on race, color, creed, or
>   national origin, in the admission of students to private educa-
>   tional institutions;*
>
>   *The establishment of a fair health practice program forbid-
>   ding discrimination and segregation by public or private
>   agencies, based on race, color, creed, or national origin, with
>   respect to the training of doctors and nurses, the admission of
>   patients to hospitals, clinics, and similar institutions, and the
>   right of doctors and nurses to practice in hospitals;*
>
>   *The outlawing of restrictive covenants;*
>
>   *Guaranteeing equal access to places of public accommodation,
>   broadly defined, to persons of all races, colors, creeds, and
>   national origins.*

In accordance with the Committee's division on antidiscrimination
laws with respect to private education, the proposal for a District fair
education program was not unanimous.

Congress has complete power to enact the legislation necessary for
progress toward full freedom and equality in the District of Columbia.
The great majority of these measures has been recommended in this
report to Congress and to the states to benefit the nation at large. But
they have particular meaning and increased urgency with respect to the
District. Our nation's capital, the city of Washington, should serve as a
symbol of democracy to the entire world.

>   8. *The enactment by Congress of legislation ending the system
>   of segregation in the Panama Canal Zone.*

The federal government has complete jurisdiction over the government of the Panama Canal Zone, and therefore should take steps to
eliminate the segregation which prevails there.

VI. To rally the American people to the support of a continuing program to strengthen civil rights, the President's Committee recommends:

> *A long term campaign of public education to inform the people of the civil rights to which they are entitled and which they owe to one another.*

The most important educational task in this field is to give the public living examples of civil rights in operation. This is the purpose of our recommendations which have gone before. But there still remains the job of driving home to the public the nature of our heritage, the justification of civil rights and the need to end prejudice. This is a task which will require the cooperation of the federal, state, and local governments and of private agencies. We believe that the permanent Commission on Civil Rights should take the leadership in serving as the coordinating body. The activities of the permanent Commission in this field should be expressly authorized by Congress and funds specifically appropriated for them.

Aside from the education of the general public, the government has immediate responsibility for an internal civil rights campaign for its more than two million employees. This might well be an indispensable first step in a large campaign. Moreover, in the armed forces, an opportunity exists to educate men while in service. The armed forces should expand efforts, already under way, to develop genuinely democratic attitudes in officers and enlisted men.

TOTAL NUMBER OF POTENTIAL VOTERS AND TOTAL NUMBER OF POTENTIAL NEGRO VOTERS IN THE UNITED STATES, 1940

STATE	TOTAL NUMBER OF CITIZENS OF VOTING AGE	TOTAL NUMBER OF NEGRO CITIZENS OF VOTING AGE	PER CENT NEGRO VOTERS OF TOTAL
Alabama	1,555,369	520,981	33.5
Arizona	263,346	10,042	3.8
Arkansas	1,098,986	270,973	24.7
California	4,455,677	89,584	2.0
Colorado	688,410	8,766	1.3
Connecticut	1,011,658	19,977	2.0
Delaware	171,856	22,863	13.3
Florida	1,187,827	310,228	26.1
Georgia	1,768,969	580,687	32.8
Idaho	305,311	460	.2
Illinois	5,119,854	262,856	5.1
Indiana	2,198,935	80,360	3.7
Iowa	1,608,926	11,044	.7
Kansas	1,144,823	42,960	3.7
Kentucky	1,630,772	137,961	8.5
Louisiana	1,364,933	473,332	34.7
Maine	493,506	755	.2
Maryland	1,153,510	183,320	15.9
Massachusetts	2,575,477	30,661	1.2
Michigan	3,131,722	137,138	4.4
Minnesota	1,730,547	7,150	.4
Mississippi	1,195,079	563,715	47.2
Missouri	2,463,726	164,494	6.7
Montana	343,180	831	.2
Nebraska	817,280	9,636	1.2
Nevada	70,327	538	.8
New Hampshire	295,859	271	.9
New Jersey	2,592,978	142,156	5.5
New Mexico	275,227	3,152	1.1
New York	8,327,563	361,555	4.3

STATE	TOTAL NUMBER OF CITIZENS OF VOTING AGE	TOTAL NUMBER OF NEGRO CITIZENS OF VOTING AGE	PER CENT NEGRO VOTERS OF TOTAL
North Carolina	1,925,483	493,108	25.6
North Dakota	358,090	157	.4
Ohio	4,404,423	219,672	5.0
Oklahoma	1,362,438	97,089	7.1
Oregon	717,121	1,903	.3
Pennsylvania	6,031,192	298,756	5.0
Rhode Island	424,876	5,830	1.4
South Carolina	989,841	383,660	38.8
South Dakota	378,405	320	.8
Tennessee	1,703,391	309,400	18.2
Texas	3,710,374	540,565	14.6
Utah	298,160	904	.3
Vermont	214,248	240	.1
Virginia	1,567,517	364,224	23.2
Washington	1,123,725	5,645	.5
West Virginia	1,046,107	70,048	6.7
Wisconsin	1,914,603	8,101	.4
Wyoming	150,031	691	.5
Total[1]	79,863,451	7,375,609	9.2

[1]Exceeds total of states because it includes District of Columbia.

CITIZENS OF VOTING AGE FOR TOTAL POPULATION AND NEGROES FOR CITIES WITH 50,000 OR MORE NEGRO INHABITANTS, 1940

CITY	TOTAL POPULATION	NEGRO	PER CENT NEGRO
Total	14,689,254	1,751,148	11.9
New York, N.Y. ...	4,474,689	287,528	6.43
Chicago, Ill.	2,212,128	191,242	8.65
Philadelphia, Pa. ...	1,240,469	162,574	13.1
Washington, D.C. ..	474,793	126,850	26.7
Baltimore, Md.	560,251	106,472	19.0
Detroit, Mich.	971,301	99,212	10.7
New Orleans, La. ..	326,837	94,397	28.9
Memphis, Tenn. ...	200,352	83,070	41.5
Birmingham, Ala. ..	173,358	68,349	39.4
St. Louis, Mo.	564,257	75,085	13.3
Atlanta, Ga.	202,762	67,917	33.5
Houston, Tex.	257,238	59,352	23.1
Cleveland, O.	544,241	55,742	10.2
Los Angeles, Calif. .	1,025,708	46,835	4.57
Pittsburgh, Pa.	429,146	40,570	9.45
Jacksonville, Fla. ...	114,936	40,432	35.2
Richmond, Va.	132,359	39,467	29.8
Cincinnati, O.	317,258	37,227	11.7
Indianapolis, Ind. ..	266,347	34,387	12.9
Dallas, Tex.	200,824	34,440	17.2

APPENDIX IV

POPULAR VOTES FOR PRESIDENT BY STATE AND PERCENTAGE SHIFT NEEDED TO CHANGE VOTE, 1944

STATE	ACTUAL VOTE FOR PRES. '44 (by party)		NUMERICAL MARGIN	TOTAL VOTE FOR PRESIDENT	ELECTORAL VOTES		% SHIFT NEEDED TO CHANGE VOTE
					Roosevelt (Democrat)	Dewey (Republican)	
Alabama	D	198,918	77,190	244,743	11	....	31.5
	R	44,540					
Arizona	D	80,926	12,319	137,634	4	....	9.0
	R	56,287					
Arkansas	D	148,965	42,708	212,954	9	....	20.0
	R	63,551					
California	D	1,988,564	237,800	3,520,875	25	....	6.8
	R	1,512,965					
Colorado	R	268,731	17,201	505,039	....	6	3.4
	D	234,331					
Connecticut	D	435,146	22,310	831,990	8	....	2.7
	R	390,527					

State	Party	Votes	Plurality	Total			%
Delaware	D	68,166	5,710	125,361	3	....	4.6
	R	56,747					
Florida	D	339,377	98,082	482,592	8	....	20.3
	R	143,215					
Georgia	D	268,187	105,841	328,111	12	....	32.3
	R	56,506					
Idaho	D	107,399	3,632	208,321	4	....	1.7
	R	100,137					
Illinois	D	2,079,479	70,083-	4,036,061	28	....	1.7
	R	1,939,314					
Indiana	R	875,891	47,245	1,672,091	....	13	2.8
	D	781,403					
Iowa	R	547,267	23,696	1,052,599	....	10	2.3
	D	499,876					
Kansas	R	442,096	77,320	733,776	....	8	10.5
	D	287,458					
Kentucky	D	472,589	40,071	867,921	11	....	4.6
	R	392,448					
Louisiana	D	281,564	106,908	349,383	10	....	30.6
	R	67,750					
Maine	R	155,434	7,402	296,400	....	5	2.5
	D	140,631					
Maryland	D	315,490	11,271	608,439	8	....	1.9
	R	292,949					
Massachusetts	D	1,035,296	56,974	2,009,993	16	....	2.8
	R	921,350					

STATE	ACTUAL VOTE FOR PRES. '44 (by party)		NUMERICAL MARGIN	TOTAL VOTE FOR PRESIDENT	ELECTORAL VOTES Roosevelt (Democrat)	ELECTORAL VOTES Dewey (Republican)	% SHIFT NEEDED TO CHANGE VOTE
Michigan	D	1,106,899	11,239	2,205,217	19	....	.5
	R	1,084,423					
Minnesota	D	589,864	31,225	1,125,529	11	....	2.8
	R	527,416					
Mississippi	D	158,515	77,387	180,080	9	....	43.0
	R	3,742					
Missouri	D	807,357	23,092	1,571,678	15	....	1.5
	R	761,175					
Montana	D	112,556	9,697	207,355	4	....	4.7
	R	93,163					
Nebraska	R	329,880	48,318	563,126	....	6	8.6
	D	233,246					
Nevada	D	29,623	2,507	54,234	3	....	4.6
	R	24,611					
New Hampshire	D	119,663	4,874	229,625	4	....	2.1
	R	109,916					
New Jersey	D	987,874	13,270	1,963,761	16	....	.7
	R	961,335					
New Mexico	D	81,389	5,351	152,225	4	....	3.5
	R	70,688					

State							
New York	*D R	3,304,238 2,987,647	158,296	6,316,790	47	....	2.5
North Carolina	D R	527,399 263,155	132,123	790,554	14	....	16.7
North Dakota	R D	118,535 100,144	9,196	220,171	....	4	4.2
Ohio	R D	1,582,293 1,570,763	5,766	3,153,056	25		.2
Oklahoma	D R	401,549 319,424	41,063	722,636	10	....	5.7
Oregon	D R	248,635 225,365	11,636	480,147	6	....	2.4
Pennsylvania	D R	1,940,479 1,835,048	52,716	3,794,787	35	....	1.4
Rhode Island	D R	175,356 123,487	25,935	299,276	4	....	8.7
South Carolina	D R	90,601 4,547	43,028	103,375	8	....	41.6
South Dakota	R D	135,365 96,711	19,328	232,076	....	4	8.3
Tennessee	D R	308,707 200,311	54,199	510,792	12	....	10.6
Texas	D R	821,605 191,425	315,091	1,150,330	23	....	27.4
Utah	D R	150,088 97,891	26,099	248,319	4	....	10.5

*Includes American Labor and Liberal parties vote.

STATE	ACTUAL VOTE FOR PRES. '44 (by party)		NUMERICAL MARGIN	TOTAL VOTE FOR PRESIDENT	ELECTORAL VOTES		% SHIFT NEEDED TO CHANGE VOTE
					Roosevelt (Democrat)	Dewey (Republican)	
Vermont	R	71,527	8,854	125,361	....	3	7.1
	D	53,820					
Virginia	D	242,276	48,517	388,485	11	....	12.5
	R	145,243					
Washington	D	486,774	62,543	856,328	8	....	7.3
	R	361,689					
West Virginia	D	392,777	34,980	715,596	8	....	4.9
	R	322,819					
Wisconsin	R	674,532	12,060	1,339,152	....	12	.9
	D	650,413					
Wyoming	R	51,921	1,252	101,340	....	3	1.2
	D	49,419					
Total[1]	D	25,602,505	1,798,114	48,025,684	432	99	3.7
	R	22,006,278					

[1]Exceeds state totals because it includes the District of Columbia.

APPENDIX V

ESSENTIAL REGISTRATION AND VOTING REQUIREMENTS IN THE SOUTHERN STATES

1946*

STATE	RESIDENT REQUIREMENTS	LITERACY, EDUCATION, AND CHARACTER TESTS	PROPERTY QUALIFICATIONS	POLL TAX REQUIREMENTS	FEATURES RELATING TO THE PRIMARY
ALA. ...	Two yrs. in the state, 1 yr. in the county, and 3 mos. in the precinct. Qualified electors having changed residence after Jan. 1, 1903, must not be disqualified by literacy and character requirements. (See Boswell Amendment, 1946.)	Read, write, understand, and explain any section of the U.S. Constitution, to satisfaction of county board of registrars. Be of good character and "understand the duties and obligations of good citizenship under a republican form of government." Have lawful employment for greater part of 12 mos. before registration.	None (Repealed in 1946 by the Boswell Amendment.)	$1.50 annual cumulative poll tax. Period of liability, 21 to 45 yrs. of age. Veterans granted exemption.	State Executive Committee of political party concerned permitted to "fix and prescribe . . . political or other qualifications . . . and declare and determine who shall be entitled to vote in primary elections or to be candidate."
ARK. ...	One yr. in the state, 6 mos. in the county, and 1 mo. in the precinct.	None	None	$1.00 annual non-cumulative poll tax. Veterans granted permanent exemption.	Political parties granted right to prescribe qualifications for membership and for voting in primaries. Separate primaries for election of federal and of state officials.

*Reprinted from *The Negro Year Book, 1947*, Tuskegee Institute, Alabama, by permission of Jessie P. Guzman, Editor.

STATE	RESIDENT REQUIREMENTS	LITERACY, EDUCATION, AND CHARACTER TESTS	PROPERTY QUALIFICATIONS	POLL TAX REQUIREMENTS	FEATURES RELATING TO THE PRIMARY
FLA.	One yr. in the state, 6 mos. in the county.	None	None	None (Repealed in 1937.)	Democratic primary rule permits white persons only to participate. Separate registration for primaries.
GA.	One yr. in the state, 6 mos. in the county.	Applicant must be "of good character and understand the duties and obligations of citizenship under a republican form of government," or correctly read and write (or if physically unable, give a "reasonable interpretation") any paragraph of the Constitutions of the U. S. or Georgia when read by one of the registrars.	None	None (Repealed in 1945.)	(1945 Constitution omits reference to the primary.)
KY.	One yr. in the state, 6 mos. in the county, and 60 days in the precinct.	None	None	None	
LA.	Two yrs. in the state, 1 yr. in the parish, and 3 mos. in the precinct.	Read and write any clause of the Constitution of U.S. or state; or be a person of good character and reputation who can give a reasonable interpretation of either Constitution when read.	None	None (Repealed in 1934.)	Must be registered voter with additional qualifications imposed by party. Democratic party prescribes only white persons may vote. "May not be associated with or an adherent to any organization, association, or

State	Residence requirements	Be of good character and understand duties of citizenship.		Poll tax	
MISS.	Two yrs. in the state and 1 yr. in the district or city or town.	Read any section of the Constitution or give a reasonable interpretation when it is read.	None	$2.00 annual poll tax, to be paid for 2 yrs. preceding election yr. Veterans exempt during period of service.	party opposed to the Democratic party, or which teaches any doctrine inconsistent with those of the party or to Constitution of state or the U. S." Must not be excluded by any regulation of party expressed through State Executive Committee or other authorized party agency.
N.CAR.	One yr. in the state and 4 mos. in the precinct.	Read and write any section of the Constitution to the satisfaction of the registrar.	None	None (Repealed in 1921.)	
OKLA.	One yr. in the state, 6 mos. in the county, and 30 days in the precinct.	Read, write, and understand any section of the Constitution of Oklahoma.	None	None	
S.CAR.	Two yrs. in the state, 1 yr. in the county, and 4 mos. in the precinct for general elections.	Read and write any section of the state constitution. (Alternative for property test.)	Payment of taxes on property assessed at $300 or more, during preceding year. (Alternative for literacy test.)	$1.00 annual non-cumulative poll tax for general elections. Veterans exempt during period of service.	(Primary removed from state control, by special legislative action 1944.) (Three separate ballots —one for federal officers, one for state officers, and one for constitutional amendments and special elections.)

STATE	RESIDENT REQUIREMENTS	LITERACY, EDUCATION, AND CHARACTER TESTS	PROPERTY QUALIFICATIONS	POLL TAX REQUIREMENTS	FEATURES RELATING TO THE PRIMARY
TENN.	One yr. in the state and 6 mos. in the county.	None	None	$1.00 annual non-cumulative poll tax. Counties may levy an additional poll tax up to $1.00. Veterans' tax for 1 yr. paid by 3 mos. service, for 2 yrs. by 6 mos. service.	Primaries mandatory for U.S. senator, governor, and state offices, not for county offices, not for county legislators, or representatives, utility commissioners. Must be qualified elector and member of party.
TEX.	One yr. in the state and 6 mos. in the county or district.	None	None. (In municipal elections concerning expenditures of money or assumption of debt, only city property taxpayers may vote.)	$1.50 annual non-cumulative poll tax. Counties may levy additional $.25. City poll tax may be made prerequisite to voting in city elections only. Veterans not exempt.	Party given power to "in its own way determine who shall be qualified to vote."
VA.	One yr. in the state, 6 mos. in county, and 30 days in the precinct.	Registration blank must be filled out by person in presence of registration official, unless applicant is physically unable to do so.	None. (General Assembly may prescribe property qualifications not exceeding $250 for county and municipal elections.)	$1.50 per yr, cumulative for 3 yrs. General Assembly may authorize cities and counties to levy additional $1.00.	Elector must be member of party. Democratic party rule under ¶227 prescribes that voter must be white.

249

Index

Adams, Julius J., *quoted,* 170
Alabama: Boswell Amendment, 182–83, 185; disfranchisement of poor whites, 74; disfranchising convention (1901), 41; Hoover election, 108; Negro suffrage, 179; Negro voters in majority (1860s), 60; opposition to Negro voting, 116; poll tax, 74; primary (1944), 23; registration tests, 177–78; Republican candidates, 75; Scottsboro case, 123–25; white supremacy, 19
Allen, James E., 171
Alsop, Stewart, *quoted,* 180
Anderson, Hank, 88
Andrews, William T., 166, 209
Arizona: Smith, Alfred E., Negro support, 106
Arkansas: Hoover election, 108; poor-white migration to Detroit, 149; primaries, dual system, 182; Smith, Alfred E., Negro support, 106; white primary, 176; white voters in majority (1860s), 60
Armstrong, General Samuel C., 69
Arnall, Ellis G., 189, 194, 208; *quoted,* 180
Arthur, Chester Alan, 76
Atlanta, Ga.: corruption, 44; labor-Negro unity, 144; Negro group action, 192–93; Negro suffrage, 176, 179; Negroes' part in southern politics, 187; Negroes, serious voters, 186; school expansion program, 176
Augusta, Ga.: Negro suffrage, 179; vote buying (1878), 41
Avery, Mrs. Daisy Lester, *quoted,* 162

Baldwin, William H., *quoted,* 148
Baltimore, Md.: Hoover election, 18; Negro population, 198; Roosevelt, Negro support, 35
Barnett, Claude, 107
Barnett, Ida Wells, 100
Bernstein, Victor, *quoted,* 187
Bethune, Albert, 193
Bethune, Mary McLeod, 28, 35, 107
Bilbo, Theodore G., 19, 20, 26, 62, 187, 195, 199, 208
Birmingham, Ala., Negro suffrage, 176
Black, Hugo, 208

Blaine, James G., 42
Blair, Montgomery, 42
Blease, Coleman L., 95
Borah, William E., 212
Boston, Mass.: campaign for Negro support, Democrats, 88, 89; Negro office holders (1890s), 86; Niagara Movement meeting, 100
Brooks, Paul C., 89
Broughton, J. M., 208
Broun, Heywood, *quoted,* 111–12
Brown, Earl, *quoted,* 171
Brown, Edgar G., 29; *quoted,* 37–38
Brown, John, 99
Brownell, Herbert, 35
Bruce, B. K., 64
Bruce, Herbert L., 166, 167, 168
Bryan, William Jennings, 92, 93
Buck, Paul H., *quoted,* 66
Buffalo, N.Y.: labor-Negro unity, 144; Negro population, 198; Niagara Movement meeting, 99, 100; Roosevelt votes (1944), 36
Bunche, Ralph J., *quoted,* 10, 45, 52–53, 73, 177, 189, 213
Buxton, Judge, *quoted,* 55
Byrd, Daniel E., 193
Byrd, Harry F., 20, 189
Byrnes, James F., 9, 12, 208

Caffey, Francis G., *quoted,* 74
Campbell, Tunis, 64
Capehart, Homer E., *quoted,* 24
Cardoza, Francis L., 64
Cardozo, Benjamin N., *quoted,* 114–15
Carey, Bishop Archibald E., 49
Carey, James B., 134
Carleton, William G., *quoted,* 22, 72, 189
Carter, Elmer A., *quoted,* 45
Carter, Richard, 137
Cayton, Horace R., *quoted,* 50, 89
Chalmers, Allan Knight, 125
Chattanooga, Tenn.: Kefauver, congressman, 189; Negro suffrage, 176; political machines, 52; Robinson, Walter, 193–94
Chavez, Dennis, *quoted,* 24–26
Chicago: city control (1890s), 85; Democratic campaign for Negro support, 89; Democratic Conven-

tion (1940), 31; Hoover election, 18; Memorial Day Massacre (1937), 134; National Negro Congress, 126–27; Negro congressional candidates, 199; Negro office holders, 86; Negro population, 48–49, 83, 198; Negro recognition, 48, 49; Negro vote shift, 27; Negro voters (1890), 84; patronage, 52; race riot (1919), 50; Roosevelt votes (1936), 18–19, (1944), 36

Church, Robert R., 108, 176

Cincinnati, Ohio: conventions (1860s), 98; Hoover supporters, 18; Negro population, 83, 198

Clark, Amos, 158

Clark, Tom, 203

Cleveland, Grover, 78, 90, 91, 96

Cleveland, Ohio: Hoover supporters, 18; Negro political advance, 46; Negro population, 83, 198; patronage, 52; Roosevelt supporters (1936), 19

Cohen, Walter L., 108

Cohn, Mrs. Jacob, quoted, 162

Colorado: job discrimination, 132; Smith, Alfred E., Negro support, 106

Columbus, Ohio: Hoover supporters, 18

Connally, Tom, 25

Connecticut: job discrimination legislation, 135; Smith, Alfred E., Negro support, 106; suffrage restrictions, 55, 56

Coolidge, Calvin, 104

Costello, John M., 140

Covington, Floyd, 210

Cox, E. E., 20

Croker, Richard, 89

Crosswaith, Frank R., 122, 125

Crump, Edward, 52, 156

Cuney, Norris Wright, 64, 72, 79, 84; quoted, 76, 80

Dabney, Wendell P., quoted, 84

Dakotas, Non-Partisan League, 139

Dallas, Tex., Negro suffrage, 176

Daniels, John, quoted, 86–87, 88, 89, 93

Daniels, Josephus, 17

Davis, Ben (Ga.), 108

Davis, Benjamin J. (N.Y.), 121, 167, 169, 170–72, 173

Davis, John P., 127

Dawson, William L., 199

Dayton, Ohio, labor-Negro unity, 144

Delaware: electoral college votes, 198; Roosevelt votes (1944), 36; suffrage restrictions, 55

De Priest, Oscar, 49, 113

Detroit, Mich.: bloc voting (1943, 1945), 213; housing, 149, 154–55; labor-Negro unity, 144, 149–50; mayoralty campaign (1945), 149–56; Negro community contrasts, 149; Negro congressional candidates, 199; Negro participation in local campaigns, 146, 147; Negro population, 83, 148; poor-white in-migration from southern states, 149; race issue in election campaign, 160; race riot (1943), 36, 148, 155, 168; racial and national minorities, 148; Roosevelt votes (1932), 18; (1944), 199; slums, 217; Detroit-Willow Run area, Negro population, 198

Dewey, John, 100

Dewey, Thomas E., 34, 35, 167, 208–09, 212

Dies, Martin, 20, 140

District of Columbia: Negro party affiliations, 200; Republican National Committee, Negro delegates, 91. See also Washington

Dobbs, John Wesley, quoted, 190–91

Doll, Tracy M., 151

Domingo, W. A., 122

Douglass, Frederick, 78, 84, 87, 98, 118; autobiography, 69; Cleveland, Grover, opinion of, 91; death, 76; Federal Civil Rights Law (1866), 80; Grant, U. S., state's ballot cast for, 86; Johnson, Andrew, clash with, 57–58, 97; Mass. Anti-Slavery Society, 68; Negro migrations, 83; quoted, 45, 89–90

Drake, St. Clair, quoted, 50, 89

Du Bois, W. E. B., "Appeal to America," 107; Communism, 120; Crisis, editor of, 101; Niagara Movement, 99–100; Parker, Judge, defeat of, 112; Philadelphia Negro, study of, 47, 84–85; race problem, 202–03; Reconstruction, 66, 67; Wilson election, 95–96; quoted, 35, 46, 57, 60, 61, 65, 69–70, 77–78

Dunn, Oscar J., 64

Dunning, William A., quoted, 65, 71

Durham, N.C.: "Capital of Black Bourgeoisie," 195; Negro group unity, 195; Negro-labor unity, 196; Negro office holders, 177, 188; Negro suffrage, 176; non-partisan elections, 47

Dyer, L. C., 116

Edwards, George, 151

Eisenhower, Dwight, 209

Elliott, Robert Brown, 64

Elmore, George, 183, 184

Ethiopia, Italian rape of, 125–26
Ethridge, Mark, 191

Farley, James A., 17
Feidelson, Charles N., *quoted*, 181
Fields, William H., *quoted*, 181
Fish, Hamilton, 140; *quoted*, 53
Florida: Hoover election, 107; Negro group action, 193; Negro political power (1890s), 69; Negro voters in majority (1860s), 60; Negro voters' increase, 179; primary (1944), 23; Republican National Committee, Negro delegates, 91; restrictive legislation, 183; Smith, Alfred E., Negro support, 106; suffrage restrictions, 55; white primary, 176
Folsom, James E., 183, 185
Foraker, Joseph B., 84
Foreman, Clark, 28; *quoted*, 206–07
Fort Worth, Tex.: Negro suffrage, 176; non-partisan elections, 47
Forte-Whiteman, Lovett, 122
Frankensteen, Richard T., 149–56; *quoted*, 153
Frankfurter, Felix, *quoted*, 103
Franklin, John Hope, 55

Galveston, Tex.: Negro suffrage, 176; non-partisan elections, 47
Garfield, James A., 42
Garner, John Nance, 17
Garnett, Henry Highland, 98
Garrison, William Lloyd, 68, 94
Garvey, Marcus, 122
George, Walter F., 20; *quoted*, 27
Georgia: corruption, 44; Hoover election, 108; lynchings (1946), 186; Negro suffrage, 176, 179; Negro voting strength, 186–87; new Negro vote, 45; opposition to Negro voting, 116, 160; poll tax, 73; primary election laws, removal of, 182; reform movement, 46; segregation in voting, 189; Smith, Alfred E., Negro support, 106; suffrage restrictions, 54, 101; white primary bill, 183; white voters in majority (1860s), 60
Gibbs, Jonathan, 64
Gibson, Truman K., 29
Glass, Carter, 20, 41, 42, 157, 159
Goldstein, Jonah J., 169
Gompers, Samuel, 137–38
Gordon, Walter A., 210
Gosnell, Cullen B., 27, 43
Gosnell, Harold F., *quoted*, 48, 49, 50–51, 85
Grady, Henry W., 40, 42; *quoted*, 41
Granger, Lester B., 125
Grant, Mrs. Edmonia White, 193

Grant, Ulysses S., 48, 69, 86
Graves, John Temple, 191; *quoted*, 22
Graves, Lem, *quoted*, 201
Greeley, Horace, 69
Green, John P., 86
Greener, Richard T., 83
Greensboro, N.C., Negro suffrage, 176
Grimke, Francis J., 100
Groner, D. Lawrence, 156
Grovey, R. R., 115
Guffey, Joe, 30
Gunther, John, 117

Haiti, revolution (1801), 54
Hampton, Wade, 42, 46, 59
Hancock, Gordon, 35
Hanna, Mark, 80
Harding, Warren G., 104
Hare, Maud Cuney, 84, 87
Harlem, N.Y.C.: Communism, 121; district leadership, 166; mayoralty campaign (1945), 169–73; Negro capital, 147; proportional representation, 169; race riots, 167–68. *See also* New York City
Harpers Ferry, W. Va., 99
Harris, James H., 64
Harris, Roy V., 194
Harris, S. Henry, *quoted*, 181
Harrison, Carter Henry, 89
Hart, Albert Bushnell, *quoted*, 55, 63, 75
Hastie, William H., 28, 35, 205
Hayes, Rutherford B., 65, 66, 68, 76
Hendricks, Thomas A., 42; *quoted*, 46
Herndon, Angelo, 120
Hill, Charles, 151, 152
Hill, Lister, 23, 189
Hill, Oliver W., 157, 159–65
Hill, T. Arnold, 29
Hillman, Sidney, 34, 140, 142, 208; *quoted*, 143
Holmes, Oliver Wendell, *quoted*, 114
Holsey, Albon L., 105
Hood, James Walker, 64
Hoover, Herbert, 17, 207; campaign (1928), 105, 107–08; (1932), 18, 113; Parker nomination to Supreme Court, 109–12, 185
Horne, Frank S., 28
Houston, Charles, *quoted*, 160
Houston, Norman O., 210
Houston, Tex.: Negro suffrage, 176; white primary, 115
Howard, Perry, 108, 109, 211
Hughes, Langston, 120
Humphrey, Norman D., *quoted*, 148

Ickes, Harold L., 28
Illinois: electoral college votes, 198; job discrimination legislation, 132;

Negro office holders (1876), 86; Negro population (1900), 83; Negro vote balance-of-power factor, 84; Negro vote strength, 10; Republican campaign for Negro support (1890s),87; Roosevelt votes (1944), 36; Smith, Alfred E., Negro support, 106. *See also* Chicago

Indiana: electoral college votes, 198; job discrimination, 132, 135; Negro population (1900), 83; Negro vote balance-of-power factor, 84; Negro vote strength, 10; Republican campaign for Negro support (1890s), 87; Smith, Alfred E., Negro support, 106

Indianapolis, Ind.: Negro Democrats' National Convention (1911), 93; Negro population, 198

Jackson, Emory O., 177
Jackson, Dr. Luther P., *quoted,* 157, 163
Jackson, Miss.: all-white primary, 175
Jacksonville, Fla.: Negro group action, 193; Negro office holders, 188; Negro suffrage, 176, 179
Jeffries, Edward J., 148, 149–56
Johnson, Andrew, 57, 59, 97; *quoted,* 58
Johnson, Colonel Campbell C., 28
Johnson, Carl, 210
Johnson, Charles S., 35
Johnson, Clarence R., 28
Johnson, James Weldon, 104, 107
Johnson, Sol, 193
Johnson, Tom L., 46
Johnston, Olin D., 182, 194
Jones, Eugene Kinckle, 107
Jones, J. Raymond, 166–67, 170, 171, 173
Jones, John, 86

Kansas: Negro population (1900), 83; Republican campaign for Negro support (1890s), 87; Smith, Alfred E., Negro support, 106
Kansas City, Mo.: Negro vote, 51; Pendergast machine, 18, 51; Roosevelt votes (1944), 36
Kefauver, Estes, 189
Kelly, Ed (mayor of Chicago), 48, 199
Kenny, Robert, 210
Kentucky: electoral college votes, 198; Hoover election, 107; poor-white migration to Detroit, 149; Republican campaign for Negro support (1890s),87; Roosevelt votes (1944), 36; segregation in public services and facilities, 191; Smith, Alfred E.,

Negro support, 106; suffrage restrictions, 55
Knoxville, Tenn., Negro suffrage, 176
Koelman, Elbert D., 193
Kroll, Jack, 143

La Follette, Robert M., Sr., 138
La Guardia, Fiorello, 46, 150, 167–68, 169, 170, 172, 173
Lamar, L. Q. C., 42; *quoted,* 43
Lanier, R. O'Hara, 28
Lautier, Louis, *quoted,* 29
Lawrence, William, 188
Lee, Alfred McCluny, *quoted,* 148
Lee, Edward F., 89
Lee, Robert E., *quoted,* 56–57
Lehman, Herbert L., 167
Leibowitz, Samuel, 124
Lewinson, Paul, 58, 175, 176–77; *quoted,* 59, 73–74, 102, 109
Lewis, Edward S., 171
Lewis, John L., 139
Lewis, William Henry, 93
Lincoln, Abraham, 24, 56, 58, 68; Emancipation Proclamation, 57
Link, Arthur S., *quoted,* 94, 95, 96
Litvinoff, Maxim, 125–26
Lochard, Metz T. P., 35
Long, Huey, 62
Longstreet, Mrs. James, 183
Los Angeles, Cal.: Negro congressional candidates, 199; Negro population, 83
Louisiana: corruption, 44; dual governments (1876), 65; grandfather clause, 102; Hoover election, 108; Negro political power (1890s), 69; Negro suffrage, 179; Negro voters, elimination of, 71, 73–74; Negro voters in majority (1860s), 60; reform movement, 46; suffrage restrictions, 55; U.S. *v.* Classic case, 115
Lynch, John R., 90, 91

MacArthur, Douglas, 209
Maine, Negro suffrage, 85
Marshall, Thurgood, 183
Martin, John W., Jr., 211
Martin, Louis, *quoted,* 22
Maryland: electoral college votes, 198; Roosevelt votes, 35; Smith, Alfred E., Negro support, 106; suffrage restrictions, 55
Massachusetts: job discrimination legislation, 135; Negro office holders (1866), 86; Negro suffrage, 85; Smith, Alfred E., Negro support, 106
Maverick, Maury, 52
McCorvey, Gessner T., 185–86
McCray, John H., 194

McDonald, "Goose-neck Bill," 106
McGill, Ralph, *quoted*, 45–46
McGlockten, John W., 193
McGrath, J. Howard, *quoted*, 196
McGraw, Booker T., 29
McKaine, Osceola, *quoted*, 194
McKay, Claude, 120
McKellar, Kenneth D., 20
McKinley, William, 80
Memphis, Tenn.: Crump, 52, 156; Negro suffrage, 117, 176; patronage, 52
Meyers, Gustavus, 88
Miami, Fla., Ku-Klux Klan, 186
Michigan: electoral college votes, 198; Negro population, 198; Negro vote strength, 10; Roosevelt votes (1944), 36; suffrage restrictions, 56
Miller, Kelly, 97; *quoted*, 80–81, 93
Mills, Ogden, 132
Minnesota: Farm-Labor party, 139; Smith, Alfred E., Negro support, 106; Stassen and colored citizens, 211; suffrage restrictions, 56
Mississippi: Bilboism, 44; flood (1927), 105; grandfather clause, 102; Hoover election, 108; lily-white Republicanism, 80; Negro suffrage, 179; Negro voters in majority (1860s), 60; Negro voters, reduction of, 71; Negro voting, opposition to, 116, 160; Negro witnesses at Bilbo investigation, 187; primary voters, restrictions, 183; Republican National Committee, Negro delegates, 91; Stassen, support of, 211; substandards of white population, 217
Missouri: electoral college votes, 198; Negro vote strength, 10; Republican campaign for Negro support (1890s), 87; Roosevelt votes (1944), 36; segregation in public services and facilities, 191; Smith, Alfred E., Negro support, 106
Mitchell, Arthur R., 18; *quoted*, 53
Mitchell, Charles L., 86
Mitchell, J. E., 35
Montgomery, Ala., registration of Negro voters, 178
Moon, Henry Lee, *quoted*, 28
Moore, Harry T., 193
Moore, Richard B., 122
Morris, Newbold, 169–70, 171
Morton, Ferdinand Q., 106, 165, 167
Moskowitz, Dr. Henry, 100
Moton, Robert R., 104, 107, 111; *quoted*, 105
Murphy, Carl, 107
Murray, Philip, 137, 138, 139, 143
Murray, W. H. C., 159–64

Myrdal, Gunnar, *quoted*, 10, 19, 47, 64, 66

Nansemond County, Va., Negro office holders, 188
Nashville, Tenn.: Negro office holders, 188; Negro suffrage, 176; non-partisan elections, 47
Nearing, Scott, *quoted*, 141
Nebraska: Smith, Alfred E., Negro support, 106; suffrage restrictions, 56
Nelson, Bernard, *quoted*, 92
New Hampshire, Negro suffrage, 85
New Jersey: electoral college votes, 198; job discrimination legislation, 132, 135; National Guard on integrated basis, 209; Negro population (1900), 83; Negro vote strength, 10; Roosevelt votes (1944), 36; Smith, Alfred E., Negro support, 106; suffrage restrictions, 55
New Orleans, La.: conventions (1860s), 98; Negro group action, 193
New York City: Democratic campaign for Negro support (1870s), 88–89; Democratic Negro voters, 165; labor-Negro unity, 144; Negro congressional candidates, 199; Negro participation in local campaigns, 147; Negro political advance, 46; Negro population, 83, 198; patronage, 52; proportional representation, 169; Roosevelt votes (1944), 36, 199; Tammany Hall, 18, 39, 85, 88, 89, 165, 166, 167, 168, 169, 171, 209; Tweed, Boss, 62, 63, 85, 88
New York State: American Labor party, 139; electoral college votes, 198; job discrimination, 132, 135; Negro population (1900), 83; Negro presidential elector (1872), 86; Negro suffrage restrictions, 55, 85; Negro vote balance-of-power factor, 84; Negro vote, strength of, 10; Republican campaign for Negro support (1890s), 87; segregation in armed services, 209; Smith, Alfred E., Negro support, 106
Newport News, Va., Negro suffrage, 176
Nixon, Dr. L. A., 114
Norfolk, Va.: Negro office holders, 188; Negro suffrage, 176
North Carolina: group factions, 195; Hoover election, 107; Negro disfranchisement, 17; Negro political power (1890s), 69; Negro suffrage, 176, 177; Parker nomination to Supreme Court, 111; Populist-Re-

publican fusion, 72; reform movements, 46; Republican candidates, 75; Smith, Alfred E., Negro support, 106; suffrage restrictions, 55; Truman nomination, aloof to opposition to, 207; white primary, 156; white voters in majority (1860s), 60
Nowlin, William F., quoted, 64, 93
Nye, Gerald P., 140

Oates, William C., quoted, 74
Oberlin, Ohio, Niagara Movement meeting, 100
O'Dwyer, William, 167, 169, 171, 172, 173; quoted, 170
Ohio: electoral college votes, 198; job discrimination legislation, 132; Negro office holders (1881), 86; Negro population (1900), 83; Negro vote balance-of-power factor, 84; Negro vote strength, 10; Republican campaign for Negro support (1890s), 87; Smith, Alfred E., Negro support, 106; suffrage restrictions, 55, 56; Taft, dislike of, 207–08
Oklahoma: grandfather clause, 102–03; poor white migration to Detroit, 149; Smith, Alfred E., Negro support, 106
Oliver, William, 137
Olson, Culbert L., 210
Oregon, job discrimination, 135
Ottley, Roi, quoted, 86, 89
Overton, John H., quoted, 23–25
Ovington, Mary White, 101; quoted, 100
Owen, Chandler, 122
Oxley, Lawrence A., 28

Parker, John Johnson, 110–12; quoted, 109, 185; senators voting for his confirmation defeated by Negro vote, 113
Pegler, Westbrook, 120–21
Pennsylvania: electoral college votes, 198; job discrimination legislation, 132; Negro disfranchisement, 86; Negro population (1900), 83; Negro vote strength, 10; Republican campaign for Negro support (1890s), 87; Roosevelt votes (1944), 36; Smith, Alfred E., Negro support, 106; suffrage restrictions, 55
Pepper, Claude, 23, 189, 208
Philadelphia, Pa.: Democratic National Convention (1936), 23; Hoover supporters (1932), 18; Negro congressional candidates, 199; Negro office holders (1890s), 86; Negro population, 83, 198; Negro

voters (1897), 84–85; patronage, 52; political clubs (1890s), 85; Roosevelt votes (1936), 19; (1944), 36; transit workers' strike, 33
Phillips, Charles H., quoted, 163
Phillips, Wendell, 68; quoted, 42
Pinchback, P. B. S., 64
Pittsburgh, Pa.: CIO convention (1938), 134; Negro population, 83; Roosevelt votes (1932), 18; (1944), 36, 199
Portland-Vancouver area, Negro population, 198
Portsmouth, Va., Negro suffrage, 176
Poston, Ted, 28
Powell, Adam Clayton, 168, 170, 199

Rainey, Dr. Homer P., 189; quoted, 180–81
Raleigh, N.C.: Negro office holders, 177, 188; Negro suffrage, 176; nonpartisan elections, 47
Randolph, A. Philip, 30, 116, 122, 123, 125, 127, 135, 171; quoted, 128
Rankin, John E., 19, 26, 120, 199
Ransom, Bishop Reverdy C., 107
Ransome, Rev. W. L., 158
Rapier, J. T., 64
Redmond, Charles L., 98
Reed, Stanley F., quoted, 115
Reid, Ira De A., 28; quoted, 45
Revels, Hiram, 64
Reynolds, Grant, 168
Rhode Island, Negro suffrage, 85
Richmond, Va.: campaign for Negro candidate for state legislature (1947), 158–65; labor-Negro unity, 144, 159–61; Negro office holders, 188; Negro participation in local campaigns, 146–47; Negro suffrage, 176; nomination in primaries tantamount to election, 161; poll tax, 157, 160; segregation, 164, 191; white primary abolished, 156
Riddick, Vernon C., 170, 173; quoted, 172
Rivers, Francis E., 167, 209
Roanoke, Va., Negro suffrage, 176
Robeson, Paul, 35, 120
Robinson, Edgar Eugene, quoted, 31
Robinson, Walter, 194
Rooks, Milton, 193
Roosevelt, Mrs. Eleanor, 28, 182; equal-rights championship, 21–22, 203; Negro admiration for, 36, 38; O'Dwyer campaign, 172
Roosevelt, Franklin D., 12, 47, 168, 197; Atlantic Charter, 53; Economic Bill of Rights, 142, 219; election (1944), 10, 140–41, 199;

electoral college votes (1944), 198; FEPC (Executive Order 8802), 30, 33, 133; fourth term, 34–35; Harlem voters' support (1932), 167; Negroes: admiration of, 36, 204; attitude toward, 17; criticism by, 36, 37; vote, 23, 27, 30, 31, 35, 139, 207, 213; (1932), 18; (1936), 19; New Deal, 18, 19, 20, 21, 22, 28, 29, 30, 46, 132, 141, 176, 177, 181–82, 197, 218–19; PAC campaign (1944), 140; purge of reactionary congressmen, 27; race relations reforms, 21, 28–30; southern support, efforts to develop, 176; third term, 32; *quoted,* 136

Roosevelt, Theodore, 17, 92, 93, 94, 95

Ruggles, David, 98

Russell, Charles Edward, 100

St. Louis, Mo.: Negro congressional candidates, 199; Negro population, 198; Roosevelt votes (1944), 36

Saltonstall, Leverett, 212

San Antonio, Tex.: Negro suffrage, 117, 176; Negro support of candidates, 192; patronage, 52

San Francisco, Cal.: AFL convention (1947), 138; Negro population, 198

Savannah, Ga.: Negro group action, 193; Negro suffrage, 176, 179; nonpartisan elections, 47; political machine, 43, 44

Schurz, Carl, 69

Schuyler, George S., 122; *quoted,* 37

Scott, Dred, 42

Scott, Emmett J., 97

Sengestacke, John, 35

Simmons, Roscoe Conkling, *quoted,* 113

Slaughter, Roger C., *quoted,* 51

Smith, Alfred, 28

Smith, Alfred E., 18, 106

Smith, Ellison D. (Cotton Ed), 20, 23, 27, 34, 140

Smith, Gerald L. K., 152

Smith, Hoke, 95

Smith, Dr. Lonnie E., 115

Snipes, Macio, 186

Solomon, Sam, 186

South Carolina: dual governments (1876), 65; eight-ballot-box trick, 71; fear of good Negro government, 65; Hoover election, 108; Negro political power (1890s), 69; Negro suffrage, 179; Negro voters in majority (1860s), 60; Negro voting, opposition to, 116; primary election laws, removal of, 182, 183; Progressive Democratic party, 194; re-

form movement, 46; registration tests, 177; sharecroppers, condition of, 217; Smith, Cotton Ed, 23; suffrage restrictions, 54

Spain, civil war, 126

Sparks, Chauncey, *quoted,* 181

Spaulding, C. C., 107

Starnes, Joe, 29, 34, 140

Stassen, Harold E., 211

Stephens, Alexander H., 42; *quoted,* 41

Stephens, James E., 166

Stevens, Thaddeus, 57, 59, 61, 68

Stewart, Tom, *quoted,* 25, 26

Stone, Alfred, 183

Stoney, George C., *quoted,* 20, 43

Sumner, Charles, 57, 59, 61, 68, 69

Taft, Robert A., 189, 207–08, 209

Taft, William Howard, 78, 92, 94, 109; *quoted,* 93

Talmadge, Eugene, 19, 186, 195, 199

Tappan, Arthur, 68

Tappan, Lewis, 68

Taylor, Alrutheus A., *quoted,* 63

Taylor, Robert R., 28

Tennessee: admittance to Union, 59; anti-lynching legislation, 177; group factions, 195; Hoover election, 107; Negro political power (1890s), 69; Negro suffrage, 176, 177; Negro voters and Crump machine, 189; poor-white migration to Detroit, 149; Republican candidates, 75; Smith, Alfred E., Negro support, 106; suffrage restrictions, 55; TVA, 53; white primary, 156

Texas: Hoover election, 107; lily-white Republicanism, 79–80; Negro political power (1890s), 69; Negro suffrage, 75, 179; primary case, Supreme Court decision (1944), 188; Republican National Committee, Negro delegates, 91; restrictive legislation, 183; segregated polling places, 189; Smith, Alfred E., Negro support, 106; Texas Regulars (anti-Roosevelt organization), 22, 190; white primary, 114, 115, 156, 176; "White Republican Clubs," 79; white voters in majority (1860s), 60

Thomas, John W. E., 86

Thomas, Norman, 17

Thomas, R. J., 140

Thomas, William Hannibal, *quoted,* 62–63

Thompson, Big Bill, 48–50

Thompson, Dorothy, 45; *quoted,* 40

Thompson, M. E., 182, 189

Tilden, Samuel J., 65, 66

Tillman, Benjamin R., 95
Tillman, Ray, 193
Tinkham, George H., 92
Tinsley, Dr. J. M., 158; *quoted*, 162
Tobias, Channing H., 107, 170, 171; *quoted*, 35
Toney, Charles E., 166
Townsend, Willard S., 35, 137
Trent, William, 28
Trotter, James M., 90
Trotter, William Monroe, 92, 95, 97, 100; *quoted*, 96
Truman, Harry S.: citizens' lack of confidence in, 207; Civil Rights Committee, 196, 200, 202, 204, 205, 218; FEPC bill, 36, 51; labor-management conference (1945), 137; message to Congress (Feb. 2, 1948), 205–06; prestige among Negroes, 205; race problem, recognition, 203
Truth, Sojourner, 98
Tubman, Harriet, 98
Tuck, William M., 206
Turner, Henry, 64
Turner, Nat, 55
Tweed, William Marcy, 62, 63, 85, 88

United Nations, NAACP petition, 203

Vandenburg, Arthur H., 211–12
Vann, Robert L., 18
Vardaman, James K., 41, 42, 95; *quoted*, 40
Vermont, Negro suffrage, 85
Villard, Oswald Garrison, 94
Virginia: Byrd, Negro opposition to, 189; civil rights organization, 191; disfranchisement, 74; group factions, 195; Hoover election, 107; Negro political power (1890s), 69; Negro suffrage, 75, 176–77; poll tax, 157; Reconstruction, 63; Republican candidates, 75; segregation, 191; suffrage restrictions, 54; Truman nomination, opposition to, 206; white primary, 156, 176; white voters in majority (1860s), 60
Voorhees, D. W., 83

Wagner, Robert F., *quoted*, 111
Walden, A. T., 193
Waldron, Rev. J. Milton, 94, 95
Walker, Edward G., 86, 88, 89
Walker, W. O., *quoted*, 37
Wallace, Henry A., 34, 139, 172, 204; *quoted*, 33
Walling, William English, 100–01

Walter, Noah C. A., 137
Walters, Bishop Alexander, 95, 100
Wardlaw, Ralph W., 41; *quoted*, 43
Waring, Judge J. Waties, 183–85
Warren, Earl, 210–11
Washington, Booker T., 8, 40, 69, 97, 118; Atlanta Compromise, 77, 104; leadership, 76–78; *quoted*, 61, 82, 91
Washington, D.C.: conventions (1860s), 98; National Negro Congress, 127
Watson, James S., 166
Watson, Tom, 95; *quoted*, 72
Weaver, George L-P., 134
Weaver, Robert C., 28, 35; *quoted*, 132
Webber, Charles C., 159, 160
Weightman, Philip, 137
Wesley, Carter, 35, 189; *quoted*, 191
West Virginia: electoral college votes, 198; Hoover election, 107–08; Roosevelt votes (1944), 36; segregation in public services and facilities, 191
White, Edward D., *quoted*, 102
White, George W., 64, 72
White, Walter, 27, 107, 125; Byrnes, opposition to, 208; Civil Rights Committee report, 200; NAACP, 117, 118, 123; Parker nomination to Supreme Court, 112; racial plank in Democratic platform, 33; *quoted*, 200, 214
Williams, Rev. Kenneth R., 188
Williams, Rev. L. K., 107
Williams, Oliver D., 170
Willkie, Wendell, 31; *quoted*, 32
Wilson, Woodrow; anti-Negro bias, 17, 103; election (1912), 93, 95; segregation in government departments, 96–97, 104; *quoted*, 94
Wilson, Mrs. Woodrow, 96
Winston-Salem, N.C.: labor-Negro unity, 143–44; Negro office holders, 188
Wisconsin: job discrimination legislation, 135; Progressive party, 139; suffrage restrictions, 56
Wood, Robert N., 95
Woodson, Carter G., 83
Wright, Edward H., 48, 49, 85
Wright, Ernest, 193
Wright, Bishop R. R., 35
Wright, Richard, 120, 130
Wyatt, Wilson, 208

Young, P. B., 35